Falkland Palace

For John & Jean & Co.
with love, from
Michael & Barbara
Nina & Ann
Mariette & Frances
Thomas & Elspeth.

STATELY GARDENS OF BRITAIN

by Thomas Hinde

Photographs by Dmitri Kasterine

EBURY PRESS
London

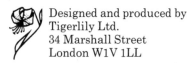 Designed and produced by
Tigerlily Ltd.
34 Marshall Street
London W1V 1LL

Published by Ebury Press
National Magazine House
72, Broadwick Street London W1V 2BP

First impression 1983
Copyright © Thomas Hinde 1983

ISBN 0 85223 263 2

Illustrations by Biddy O'Grady

Filmset in Great Britain by
Advanced Filmsetters (Glasgow) Ltd.
Printed and bound by
Arti Grafiche Amilcare Pizzi s.p.a.

*Page one: steps by the orangery at
Sezincote. Page two: terrace border at
Powis Castle. Below: campanulas in the
blue garden at Great Dixter.*

CONTENTS

A BRIEF HISTORY

The British are often said to be the passionate gardeners they are because they enjoy a mild, moist climate in which a wide variety of plants flourish. Despite these advantages they were not early gardeners and the art when it developed was not native born. Though castles in Britain as elsewhere had small pleasure gardens, there was little gardening in today's sense of the word during mediaeval times.

What there was consisted of the growing of herbs or simples for their medicinal properties, and of fruit and vegetables for the table. Cottagers and monks exercised these skills, but the aristocracy took little interest in gardening, practical or ornamental, till the Renaissance. Then those who began to make gardens for pleasure rather than their produce – Cardinal Wolsey at Hampton Court, the Duke of Buckingham at Thornbury, Sir Thomas More in Chelsea – did so in imitation of gardens they had seen or heard about on the continent, mainly in Italy and France.

The gardens they made were at first similar to monastery gardens, taking the form of walled or hedged enclosures. Fruit was grown against the walls. For decoration they introduced raised beds, or knots: groups of small box- or thrift-hedged beds filled with such plants as lavender, rue and thyme, sometimes alternating with patches of coloured earth and gravel, and arranged in patterns which at their most elaborate made them seem to twist over and under each other like rope.

'Mounts' complemented the knots by providing the overhead view needed to see their patterns. Some were of timber, some of earth, and they might take the form of circular mounds or of raised walks. Mazes, statues, fountains and topiary also became fashionable. So did scented flowers. During the reigns of Elizabeth, James I and Charles I, new plants were gradually introduced as they were brought home by collectors like the John Tradescants, father and son (both were gardeners to Charles I). Imported too were Mediterranean fruit trees like oranges and lemons. In winter these needed shelter and such shelters developed into orangeries, and ultimately into today's greenhouses. But throughout the period gardens in the main continued to be formal and to have the character of outdoor rooms. Though Francis Bacon in his essay on gardens (1625) suggested that a garden should be partly wild, his advice was not taken for almost 100 years.

A few fragments of early gardens can still be seen. At Melford Hall, Suffolk, there are some old walls. Earth 'mounts' survive here and there, for example at Cranborne Manor, Dorset; Rockingham Castle, Northamptonshire and Packwood, Warwickshire. They have lasted better perhaps because they are less easily erased. And knot gardens have been created or revived in a number of gardens: Hatfield House and Cranborne Manor in England; Edzell Castle and Tyninghame in Scotland, some exclusively using plants which were available in the sixteenth century. But no complete garden of those times has survived unchanged throughout the intervening centuries.

Meanwhile on the continent grander formal gardens were being laid out. Already before the Civil War in Britain, French gardeners had come to England to work on similar projects, at Hatfield House, Hertfordshire, and at Wilton House, Wiltshire, for example, but British imitation of the new fashion did not become general till after the Restoration of 1660. By this time the French garden designer of Versailles, André le Nôtre, was the accepted authority. Royalists returning from abroad knew his work and sent their gardeners to learn to copy him. The gardens they made were still formal but the small knot gardens of earlier times were replaced by vastly bigger areas of patterned beds, known as parterres. The larger of the two parterres at Chatsworth, Derbyshire, measured 473 feet by 227 feet. The parterre at Drummond Castle, Tayside, (a 19th-century creation) and the modern parterre at Blenheim Palace, Oxfordshire, show what they were like.

The gardens of which such parterres formed a part were conceived as wholes rather than as collections of separate enclosures, all parts related to each other and to the house. More statues and more topiary work were introduced. So were waterworks – for example the great cascade at Chatsworth (1696) with its accompanying fountains. Formal avenues radiated from the parterres, these sometimes known from the shape of their plans as 'pattes d'oie' (goose feet).

During this period, through the reigns of Charles II, James II, William III and Anne, two gardeners dominated British garden design: George London and Henry Wise. They established a nursery of 100 acres at Brompton Park, Kensington, and worked together on many gardens, including Chatsworth. Both became royal gardeners, and Wise, the younger man, created the original parterre at Blenheim Palace.

At Chatsworth, at Blickling, Norfolk, in the terraces at Powis Castle, Powys, and elsewhere, features from gardens of this period can be seen. At Melbourne Hall, Derbyshire, a much overgrown but significant part of the late seventeenth century garden survives, but once again most of these gardens were swept away by the fashion which succeeded them.

This, the great landscape movement, was the first to be developed by native gardeners, but poets and philosophers rather than gardeners provided the original inspiration. Nature was what they admired, and the gardens they called for would enhance rather than regiment nature. In Italy and France, Joseph Addison had little to say in favour of the Villa d'Este and Versailles, but admired mountains, streams and volcanoes. In Twickenham, Pope created his own garden, now mostly lost, considered highly informal by the standards of the time. Their ideal garden would imitate on the ground the landscapes painted by Salvator Rosa, Claude Lorraine and the Poussins. Typically these had woody foregrounds, some classical incident or ruin in the middle distance, then mountains and space beyond.

The year 1719 is sometimes considered to date the start of the movement, when William Kent, a young architect and painter, returned from Italy with his patron, the Duke of Burlington. From villas like Chiswick House, London, in the Palladian manner, Kent turned to gardens, which closely conformed to those the poets were demanding. At Rousham, Oxfordshire, a William Kent garden survives almost intact, complete with classical arcade and theatre, temples, groves and a mock ruin or 'eye-catcher' in the middle distance. Flower beds were swept away, lawns surrounded the house, the park came close, cattle being excluded by the newly devised ha-ha – a sunken wall invisible from above.

It was Lancelot 'Capability' Brown, however, best known of all British gardeners, who developed the style into something still more peculiarly English. By 1751 Brown had risen from north country garden boy, via

A BRIEF HISTORY

Auratum lily at Howick.

apprenticeship to William Kent at Stowe, Buckinghamshire, to set himself up in London. Here he was soon recognized as the country's leading garden designer. His name, 'Capability', came from his habit of telling his clients that their gardens had 'great capability for improvement'. In the next 32 years he designed well over 100 gardens, creating *le jardin anglais,* as it came to be called, destroying in the process both the Tudor gardens of little enclosures and knots, and the later seventeenth-century continental-style garden of parterres, allées, water works and topiary. The typical Brown garden substituted for these, clumps of trees, undulating lawns and lakes. It was designed to make more picturesque the natural landscape and though his critics would say that Brown tamed, rather than enhanced nature by eliminating its wilder features, his achievements were immense, in many cases splendid – and, unlike those of his predecessors, long lasting.

Of those who followed him, Humphry Repton is best remembered. He would incorporate his plans for a new garden in a 'Red Book' (he claimed to have prepared 400 of these), which would include paintings of the garden as it existed with flaps to show how his proposals would transform it. Though Repton worked in the Brown tradition, he was willing to re-introduce some formality near the house.

Repton died in 1818, and during the following 50 years a number of garden styles become fashionable, including neo-Italian, of which Drummond Castle is such a fine example. It is easiest, however, to get a general view of the gardens of the period from the opinions of those who, from about 1870 onwards, reacted against them. Of these, William Robinson was the most vociferous. He could justly claim to be the founder of modern gardening in Britain. Design of all sorts was Robinson's principal dislike; with it he included botanical gardens, conservatories, topiary work and above all bedding-out.

By contrast he favoured wild gardens, and the sort of mixed beds of shrubs and hardy perennials which are commonly, but not always correctly, called herbaceous borders. Gertrude Jekyll, the other great influence of the period, worked with architects, especially with Sir Edwin Lutyens, and her gardens were carefully 'designed' but she was Robinson's ally in favouring a return to natural gardening. Her flower gardens were necessarily less permanent than those of the landscapers, but her direct influence can be seen, for example, at Barrington Court, Somerset, and her indirect influence in almost any garden you care to name.

Alongside such general trends, a number of gardens of special kinds have grown up over the last 150 years, of which two should be mentioned because so many of the country's best-known gardens today fall into one or other category. First of these is the woodland garden. Typically it consists of an area of well-grown native trees thinned to allow the planting below them of hybrid rhododendrons, azaleas, magnolias and camellias for spring and early summer; hydrangeas, eucryphias and other late-flowering species for July and August; and small trees such as maples and sorbuses for their coloured foliage or berries in autumn. Commonly, but not essentially, the native trees of the woodland itself were supplemented by exotic conifers, in particular those which began to come from North America in the 1830s.

Some of these gardens were created where there had been only woodland before – Leonardslee, Sussex, in the 1880s; Howick, Northumberland, in the 1930s and Knightshayes, Devon, in the 1950s for example. Others were superimposed on earlier landscape gardens: on Henry Hoare's at Stourhead, Wiltshire, by various of his descendants, and on an original Brown garden at Sheffield Park, Sussex, by A. G. Soames. In two of the finest Welsh gardens, Powis Castle and Bodnant, woodland gardens have been created alongside Italianate terrace gardens.

Shrub rose at Arley Hall.

The other type of garden which has been increasingly favoured over the last 80 years represents a return to the earliest of all styles: a garden of separate rooms, each enclosed by walls or clipped hedges, each with its own character and planting. Here Hidcote, Gloucestershire, set the fashion, though Great Dixter, Sussex, was begun at almost the same time. Rodmarton, Gloucestershire, and others, followed soon afterwards and Sissinghurst, Sussex, has become even better known.

If this, in sketchy outline, suggests some of the ways in which British garden designers have worked over the last 500 years, there has also been, at least since Tudor times, another kind of gardener. Today he would be called a plantsman. Even at the end of the eighteenth century, when the landscape movement had carried all before it for 50 years, Humphry Repton claimed that British horticulturalists led the world. Since the plants themselves were the interest of such gardeners, the gardens they created were designed primarily to provide suitable plant environments rather than for their overall effect.

In practice, the distinction was often an academic one. Bodnant's terraces, for example, and Hidcote's hedges were intended to protect plants as well as to be garden features in themselves. So were the glades of many woodland gardens, since the newly arriving species of the time needed forest conditions. And although 'plantsmen' manage most of the gardens here described, their gardens are, with one exception, fully as distinguished for their design as for their plants. The exception is East Lambrook Manor, Somerset, created by Margery Fish since the Second World War. This has been included, not only because she became the leading lady of her craft in Britain during those years, and can stand for garden makers of this other type, but because her densely planted, cottage-style garden set a trend which not only influenced many small gardens, but invaded statelier ones.

Whatever the history of British gardens, by whatever accidents of ownership or management they have emerged, the first thing to say about them is that today they are abundant, magnificent and of remarkable variety. To choose a representative historical sequence of two dozen has been difficult. The next thing to say is less reassuring. This great national asset is not one we should feel confident that we have for ever. Two thirds of those described are in some form of private ownership. It is these above all, created by private inspiration and as time has passed re-created by new inspiration, which have the personality that distinguishes a garden from a public park and it is these which exist precariously.

If the future is uncertain and an autumn may lie ahead for British gardens, this is emphatically their summer, a time of full flowering, a time to wonder at their remarkable variety and luxuriate in their magnificence. Long may it last.

Overleaf: the red borders at Hidcote.

CRANBORNE MANOR

The figure emerging from the herb garden pushing a rubber-wheeled garden trolley is the Marchioness of Salisbury. She wears an ancient felt sun hat, tweed skirt, green hessian apron, rubber gloves and brown woollen stockings. She has been to Cranborne's garden shop because our walk round her garden has shown some distressing gaps. In the trolley are tricolor pansies, gold-lace polyanthus, black-leafed clover, jack-in-the-green primroses, plumed and double hyacinths and many other curiosities; for these are to be planted in her knot garden where she grows only plants which were available in the 17th century – the time when Cranborne first came into her husband's family.

Half an hour later, planting completed, she sits elegantly in Cranborne's panelled garden room and pours tea from a silver pot brought by the butler. She seems perfectly at home in both roles, though marginally happier with the garden trolley. Meanwhile her husband lies back in one of those enormously deep and slightly shabby English country-house armchairs, chain smokes cigars and reminisces about Cranborne's curious history.

The Cecils (the Salisburys' family name) acquired it in 1603, and laid out the gardens with the help, he believes, of the well-known gardener, John Tradescant the elder. Apart from formal courts around the house, Tradescant's plan, which they still have, shows long avenues of beeches or limes reaching towards the surrounding hills. Surviving trees prove that such avenues were indeed planted.

But soon after Robert Cecil bought Cranborne he also acquired Hatfield House, and most of his garden-making energy was expended there. Cranborne was neglected. During the Civil War both sides attacked it in turn – Prince Rupert was one defender – and the masonry still shows bullet marks. Worse was to follow: in the 18th century it became two farms, and the courts to west and east – one now a yew-hedged lawn known as the bowling green, the other laid out with apple hedges and beds of massed polyanthus – were used as farm-yards.

It was only in 1863 that the second Marquess of Salisbury began to take more interest in Cranborne, saving the surviving yew hedges and planting more, creating a typical labour-intensive Victorian garden with herbaceous borders and large areas for bedding out. Lord Salisbury's grandmother – at a time when you could still do such things – had the road diverted so that it no longer runs past the gate house but several hundred yards away to the south. The following generation kept up the gardens in similar style, employing eight gardeners.

Above: the Marchioness of Salisbury. Right: Cranborne's knot garden, a new creation in which she restricts her plants to those available to Tudor and Jacobean gardeners.

1 Garden Shop
and Car Park
2 Old Kitchen
Garden
3 Pergola Walk
4 Church Walk
5 North Court
6 River Garden
7 Mount
8 West Court
9 Knot Garden
10 South Court
11 Chalk Wall
Garden
12 Herb Garden
13 Church
14 Wild Garden
15 Gate Houses
16 Beech Avenue
17 Apple and
Pear Avenue
18 River Crane
19 House

CRANBORNE MANOR

The result was that when the present Salisburys came to live at Cranborne in 1954 they found an already well-established garden. It was also a much bigger garden than Lady Salisbury had ever managed before – 11½ acres – and one which was being run on lines far too extravagant for today. No wonder she was apprehensive. She was excited too. It was a garden she had known as a child, first seeing it at the age of 14, and it had stayed in her memory as 'a place of mysterious enchantment and romance.'

Some decisions had to be taken at once. Should she much simplify it, putting down large areas to grass? She has never ceased to be grateful that she decided against drastic change, and is still appalled to think of the ancient yew hedges she might have rooted out. Far from rooting them out, she has added to them, and today the most impressive of all runs parallel to one of the garden's big walls in the chalk-wall garden. Some 10 feet thick and 15 feet high, with windows looking out on the meadows beyond, it seems as old as the house itself, though it was planted a mere 18 years ago.

Simplification there had to be however, and gradually the eight gardeners have been reduced to three. 'A man and two boys,' says Lord Salisbury, 'at least they were boys when they came here 20 years ago, straight from school.'

'They are all wonderful,' Lady Salisbury says. 'They alone make our garden possible.'

John Dyer, the man in charge, was recruited from an advertisement, but when, subsequently, offered promotion to the position of 'head gardener' he refused it. He would only accept the responsibility when the title was dropped. 'He is a machine,' Lord Salisbury says. 'He never stops – except when the hour sounds for the end of his day. Then he puts down his hoe even if he's in the middle of a stroke.'

The changes at Cranborne over the last 28 years have in large part resulted from the reduction in its staff. The marvellous and restful softness which it has – every lawn is a temptation to roll – is part design, more the natural consequence of not having too many gardeners working at it. 'Overmedicated,' is the term Lord Salisbury uses for other gardens which can afford more help. Everywhere there is a sense that just enough but not too much has been done, by gardeners who work with, not against nature.

Though in another sense the whole creation of this soft and luxuriant garden is against nature, for it lies on hard, inhospitable chalk. 'We were in despair,' Lady Salisbury says, 'until we got advice from Sir Frederick Stern,' whose garden at Goring-by-Sea was made in a chalk pit. It was not the chalk itself which the plants disliked, he explained, but the fact that they could not get their roots down into it. The secret was to break up the chalk as deep as three feet. Manure, on the other hand, could be applied near the surface. This policy of deep cultivation before planting, then regular heavy manuring, was what she followed; and it transformed her results. Every three years each part of the garden is manured, and every year dressed with compost, leaf-mould or peat. It fits perfectly with another of her beliefs: that to nourish healthy plants is better than to spray diseased ones.

Almost all spraying has been abandoned. Nowhere is there the horrible smell of death left by chemical sprays. Not only has this produced a great saving in labour, but there has been no increase in disease. Roses, for example, which were full of blackspot when they used to be sprayed, now that they are nourished instead, have little.

Exceptions there are, of course, for Lady Salisbury is pragmatic. Treatment for bindweed was one of them. When it was still a problem at Cranborne she would put on old woollen gloves over rubber ones and dip them in a bucket of weak MCPA, then smear the bindweed trailers. Today, if she could find something equally effective against ground elder, she would make another exception.

The place to start a tour of Cranborne is the mount. So-called mounts were a feature of Elizabethan and Stuart gardens, intended to give a pleasant view of the countryside beyond. Sometimes they consisted of raised walks round the periphery, but Cranborne's is a low circular mound, perhaps flattened out for cultivation during its time as a farm. It has been made impressive in itself by its many drum-shaped yews which suggest stately and ominous human presences. More important, it provides just the needed elevation to show how the Cranborne estate lies in a shallow bowl, surrounded by tree-fringed hills which in other counties would be called hangers. At the bowl's centre is the house itself with its formal courts, but closely interwoven are a rivulet with a series of little cascades, tall trees with a rookery and cawing rooks, and many acres of wild garden. At once you realize how important to the atmosphere of Cranborne are these wild gardens, where below ancient beeches or new orchards of crabs, narcissuses flower in spring in their thousands.

Not just narcissuses, but a great abundance of wild flowers, including at least six varieties of orchis. 'You know how keen gardeners are to get at long grass and mow it,' Lady Salisbury says. 'We had to make an absolute rule

Lady Salisbury, a working gardener is as at home with a watering can as she is with a silver tea pot.

The lavender cotton-edged beds of Cranborne's herb garden, enclosed by tall yew hedges.

that there should be no mowing before the last week of July. The result was astonishing. Not only do the existing wild flowers now seed themselves and multiply, but all sorts of new ones have appeared. Cowslips and primroses, of course, and grape hyacinths and anemones and cyclamen; but the orchis, they were a real surprise. We now have early purple, bee, white helleborine, pyramidal, butterfly and twayblade. They move about from place to place, here one year, somewhere else the next. Purple and white fritillaries came too. They all arrived as if from nowhere. Yes, we helped, with oxslips for instance, which we brought as seed from Normandy, and with other primulas. The primulas hybridize with the primroses so now we find pink and blue primroses.'

South from the mount, one stretch of yew hedge which used to surround the first of these wild gardens *has* been rooted out. It ran beside a paddock, just close enough for one of Lady Salisbury's yearling colts to reach his head across and graze it. The colt was dead in 90 minutes. The gap is now replanted with holm oak.

From here the old roadway (which Lord Salisbury's grandmother closed to the public) leads in front of the gatehouse and below beeches which look 300 years old (though beech trees rarely live to this age). The view into the front court shows the first of many signs that Lady Salisbury, like all gardeners, is continually reshaping her garden. At the centre of patterns of brown and grey cobble which she laid long ago, there is to be a fountain. On the cobbles, as if it has come to help with the cementing, stands Lord Salisbury's Range Rover. Lady Salisbury would prefer not to have cars in her front court. 'Alas,' she says sadly, 'my husband is the worst offender.'

Up more banks of narcissuses, the way leads into a series of ever more secret gardens, the second edged with that massive yew hedge with its square windows. Here in spring you pass through one of many scent pools of a heady sensuality, created by a tall *Viburnum* x *burkwoodii*. Scented plants are another of Lady Salisbury's enthusiasms, and another return to an earlier gardening tradition, in which the visual was not all important but rubbed shoulders with the sweet smelling and the edible.

Finally comes the herb garden. Here, as elsewhere, the emphasis is on the stranger herbs from the past. With golden marjoram, many different sages and thymes, dill and rosemary, there is wormwood, pennyroyal, sweet Cecily ('It spreads everywhere'), the strange moss-covered *Artemesia abrotanum*, and Russian comfrey. Lady Salisbury belongs to the Henry Doubleday Institute which devotes itself to the promotion of this herb for use as compost. She also admires the Institute's work in preserving old vegetable species. 'How appalling that some bureaucrat in Brussels should forbid us to grow "King Edward" potatoes.'

Though the herb garden is mainly for herbs, here she is no purist. Tulips grow next to thyme, double primroses beside chives and the walls are spread with roses. Other small roses like *centifolia* 'Blanchefleur' can be found alongside rue or bergamot. The beds are edged with lavender cotton which in summer adds a spicy aromatic scent to this whole secret square.

The herb garden leads to the garden shop, which, though relatively close to the house, is entirely hidden by further huge chalk walls. 'Too huge,' Lord Salisbury says, noting a sinister new crack. It is run by Ken Haskell, once head gardener to the house, a local like all the Cranborne staff. 'If a hundred villagers are going up hill to Cranborne's pub, the Fleur-de-Lis,' says Lord Salisbury, 'and you shout "Haskell", ninety of them turn round.' 'Our Haskell is a true plantsman,' says Lady Salisbury, 'but he became more interested in vegetables.'

Back in the east court, the character of the garden changes so completely that it might belong to a different house. Partly this is because Cranborne church tower forms a perfect background, partly because of its walls of mellow brick, but the true reason is that here fruit, flowers and even vegetables have been most successfully combined. The effect is far more cottagey. There are ancient apples – 'Ribston Pippin' for example – and also new apple hedges (though the species are again traditional), kept a mere two feet high. There is an apple tunnel. There are beds of tulip, double button daisies, primulas and pinks backed by lines of soft fruit bushes, all intermingled here and there with rhubarb, strawberries or purple-sprouting broccoli.

The most ancient apples and pears of all stand behind the house – so ancient and much pruned that their gnarled trunks suggest those of Mediterranean olives. A big growth of mistletoe decorates one, as it has since Lady Salisbury first remembers them. Their names are long forgotten. They stand in an avenue which once continued up the opposing hillside as Cornish elms, but a few years ago these became victims of Dutch elm disease. 'So now we have all this horrid wire,' Lady Salisbury says. The wire protects new trees – not elms, though she was advised that this could be risked after seven years, but London planes. 'That's not so strange as it sounds. They grow quickly, and they were often used by Tradescant.'

Between the apple and pear avenue, and what will become the avenue of London planes, there used to run a little winter bourn with grassy banks, but it was dry for most of the summer. It is in fact the River Crane, which gives Cranborne its name. Six or seven years ago – another example of Lady Salisbury's perennial energy for improvement – she decided to try to keep water in the bourn by enclosing it in a stone channel and breaking its flow with a series of pools and small cascades. 'Perhaps it was prettier before,' she says, 'but at least we have water till August.' Certainly it seems pretty enough today, the water as wonderfully clear as in all chalk streams (water cress is a village industry), its embanked sides carpeted with the flowers of the new beds which the stone channel has made possible.

At its far end it arrives below a little stone bridge. Across this lies the crab apple orchard, where the narcissuses are as dense as a field of corn, a brilliant yellow and white blanket, and where for later in the year Lady Salisbury has planted quantities of autumn crocuses to remind her of French meadows. A gate leads back to the west court where the garden reverts to its most formal: just a fine square of lawn surrounded by stern yew hedges. It is here, however, in an angle between the house and the wall of the front court where it could easily be missed, that Lady Salisbury has made her knot garden.

When she came to Cranborne she read all the gardening books of the Elizabethan and Stuart gardeners and became an expert on the subject. 'They were great collectors even then,' she says, 'before what is generally thought of as the collecting times, in the 18th and 19th century. Tradescant the elder went to Russia and Morocco, and his son collected the species which is named after him in Virginia in 1629.' Were there any Tradescantia in her knot garden? No, it was another thing which she must put right. Though some would be large for a format which best suits small plants.

Minute box hedges, six inches high, enclose little rectangular beds, many of them only a yard square. Here grow all those curiosities she was bringing on her trolley and many others: the old perennial double wall-flower, the small spiky crimson and white candlestick or lady tulips (correctly *clusiana*, so named after the emperor Maximilian's gardener), muscari in plenty, ancient pinks, double sweet rocket, Gerard's double primrose as well as the elegant gold-lace polyanthus with its dark velvet petals edged in yellow.

Here too is Pheasant's Eye, which Lady Salisbury collected herself this spring on a patch of sandy waste outside Casablanca airport. She simply wrapped it in polythene and carried it home, no questions asked.

Along the half-enclosing wall of the knot garden, bumble bees buzz in

the Snake's Head fritillaries, and at its far end St Rocco looks down on this delightful little rectangle, staff in hand, wallet at his waist, scallop shells on his cape to prove he has made his pilgrimage to Santiago. He looks charmingly weary, and has to be wrapped in bracken and hessian to protect him from the frost. Though he forms the garden's focus, in spring he dominates it less completely than its Crown Imperials. Out of scale with the rest but somehow entirely appropriate, these astonishing fritillaries, both the orange and the primrose yellow, are surely the most wonderful survival from those earlier gardening times.

To help such plants to survive and to recreate at Cranborne something of those times has been Lady Salisbury's passion. But her gardening enthusiasm began before she had even seen Cranborne. At ten she was given a box of seeds as a present and a patch of ground of her own. Candytuft, eschschollzia, larkspur, she still remembers their names. Cranborne's $11\frac{1}{2}$ acres are a long way from that small girl's patch, but the secret of its charm is that it has been created by a gardener who has kept a child's delight in making things grow.

The River Crane, which gives Cranborne its name, has been encased in a stone channel and is today a series of pools and cascades.

19

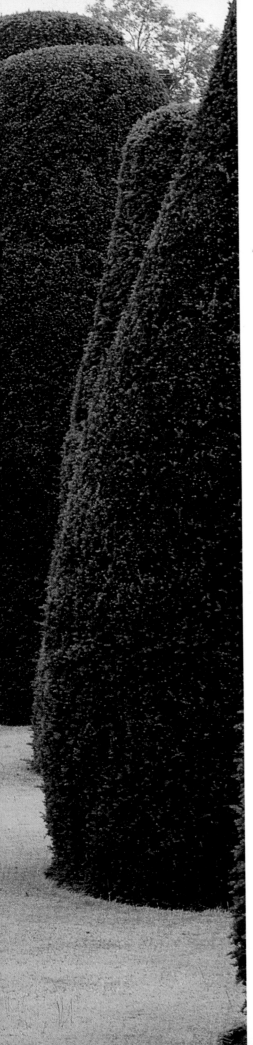

PACKWOOD HOUSE

John Ellis, still in his twenties, with curly bronze hair and bronze beard, has charge of one of England's oldest and most celebrated topiary gardens. His job is to care for the yew trees – almost 100 of them, many over 20 feet high – which stand in the South Garden at Packwood House, Warwickshire. 'You might think a child could keep them clipped,' he says. 'I'm only just learning the problems.'

It is true that few of them are subtly shaped. Their size and their multitude are what impress. For 80 years, indeed, they have been described as the Multitude attending the Sermon on the Mount.

This is precisely what they suggest. High above the rest on a circular mount at the most southerly point of the garden stands a single yew, called the Master. Ranged below him on a terrace are 16 giants known as the 12 Apostles and the four Evangelists (the legend permits duplication). Below again, on a gently sloping lawn stands the Multitude itself. Fat and thin, tall and short, they are just like the men, women and children of any political demonstration or municipal soup canteen queue. 'But we don't vary them for effect,' John Ellis says. 'It's to keep them healthy.

'That's the big problem here on clay, where they wouldn't occur naturally.' He points to a modest sized member of the crowd which seems to be copper tinted with the new foliage of early summer. 'That one's not right,' he says, and shows that many of the small leaves are semi-desiccated. 'So we've started a plan to cut each of them right back once every 50 years.' Despite their 50-year cutbacks, some of the Multitude still occasionally need replacing and Packwood grows replacements in its old kitchen garden. They can be moved into their final positions even when eight feet tall and 15 years old, but only if they have been given one or two previous moves to keep their root systems compact.

For at least 80 years it was assumed that the yews at Packwood dated back to Charles II's time, when John Fetherston – one of many Fetherstons to own Packwood – laid out the garden, and that they had always been meant to represent the biblical episode they appear to. But when Graham Thomas, recently retired Garden Consultant to the National Trust, investigated the story he could find no reference to the name before 1901, and even then it was only reported as a gardener's tale. The Apostles, the Evangelists and the Master may have been planted in the 17th century, but the gently sloping lawn where the Multitude now stands and listens was apparently an orchard

Giant topiary, said to represent the Multitude attending the Sermon on the Mount.

till it was uprooted around the middle of the 19th century.

In 1904 the Ash family bought Packwood and it was Graham Baron Ash who so carefully and lovingly restored the house and garden between the wars and then in 1941 gave Packwood to the National Trust in memory of his parents. The National Trust aims both to preserve the garden's 17th-century character, and to perpetuate some of Ash's original additions as historical examples of gardening practices of the 1930s.

'Our problem isn't just the soil,' John Ellis says. 'It's the visitors who consolidate it. The trees that suffer worst are those at the centre, where most people walk on their way to the mount. So what we're really trying to do is change the whole nature of the soil. We dig holes in it and fill them with gravel or other porous material. And we slice it mechanically then fill the slices with gungey manure. In winter it gets too wet, so we've given each tree its own drainage system. And in summer it gets too dry.'

As if all this was not enough, the yews have been suffering from scale. For this John Ellis has tried most things, including a mixture of methylated spirits and cow dung. Now he uses malathion, and has controlled the infestation on the yews, though not entirely elsewhere.

'As for the clipping,' he says, 'we have to get outside help with that. I've only got one full-time assistant, and he doesn't like heights. Anyway, moving the heavy ladders would be too much for us.' But he is not happy about the care with which the contractors do the job. He aims to make all his trees, big or small, conform in shape. 'And that's not just a matter of clipping, you've got to tie the branches internally, otherwise when they get long and heavy they flop and leave gaps.'

Although John Ellis's assistant doesn't like climbing tall ladders, he is continually anxious about the yews. ('I tell him they only take us on average two month's work a year, so why not forget them for the other ten?') He is invaluable too because he has worked at Packwood for 30 years and is a link with the past. Links with the past are important at Packwood – not just the past of mellow brick walls and gazebos from the 17th century or of Graham Baron Ash's roses and herbaceous borders from the 1930s, but of the gardening habits of Dennis Lindup, John Ellis's predecessor at Packwood. Like many a head gardener, he left a mark at least as distinctive as his better-remembered employer.

Part of Dennis Lindup's authority derived from the fact that he had briefly overlapped with Graham Baron Ash. He arrived here in 1946, a year before Ash finally left. Thirty-six years later when he retired, it had become hard to disentangle Dennis Lindup's personal notions of how a garden should be run from those of his one-time master.

Wherever they came from they are original. 'In this garden you might as well throw away the text book,' John Ellis says, standing on the terrace which crosses the South Garden immediately below the Multitude. A paved path runs the length of this terrace, ending at east and west in a gazebo, and the herbaceous beds to either side flow across the stones with cornucopial abundance, so that at no place can the edges of the paving be seen. 'Technically almost all the plants here are too tall for such narrow borders. What's more, they're planted so thickly they're just about on top of each other. But that's the way Dennis Lindup did it, because that's the way he

John Ellis, Packwood's head gardener. Trimming the Multitude takes two months a year.

said Mr Ash did it. And it seems to work.'

Below the terrace, on the opposite side from the Multitude and separating it from the house, is a large square brick-walled court, with two further and older gazebos at the inner corners. Today it is largely grass, but at one side is Graham Baron Ash's most important introduction: the Sunk Garden. Here, around a narrow lily pond, there is the same profuse planting. Roses, lavender, delphiniums, peonies, campanula, anchusa, stokesia, bergenia, irises, huge bunches of catmint, tiny pockets of pinks and pansies, at least three colour variations of hybrid aquilegia – the list could be made much longer and would be different in each summer month. 'We never use big blocks of a particular plant,' John Ellis says. 'A week ago there were poppies everywhere, but now they've gone you don't miss them.'

To balance the Sunk Garden, on the empty lawn to its west, the National Trust plans to re-introduce a group of small box-edged knots, similar to those established here by Graham Baron Ash in the thirties but grassed over to save labour during the war, and thus bring back a typical 17th-century feature.

Against the south facing wall of this walled garden, and again in the East Court there are two deeper herbaceous borders. In these another Ash/Lindup method is retained. Early in summer you can see that the whole bed has been staked with pea sticks. These are set in the ground near the front and slope backwards towards the wall. By mid June they are barely visible, thickly covered by the plants they support.

'We don't stake the individual plants,' John Ellis says. 'There are too many – the bed would look like a porcupine. Instead we stake the border. Perhaps it only works because the planting is so dense.' These luxuriantly flowering borders planted with such jungle-like density rival any designed with more careful artistry by Gertrude Jekyll.

Here and there space has been made to bed out geraniums and dahlias. 'We're still using the stock Mr Ash used,' John Ellis says. 'At 30 years old it should by rights be full of virus, but it doesn't seem to be.' Near the back are several tall leafy plants he can't identify. 'We're not a plantsman's garden in the modern sense,' he says, 'but we've got a lot of old-fashioned plants which you don't often find. Dennis Lindup would see a plant he fancied in another garden and bring it back. Even *he* might not know its name.' Certainly there are few plant labels at Packwood, though John Ellis hopes eventually to have every plant labelled. 'People are thirsting to know, and I think we should tell them.'

Like other houses with fine gardens, Packwood has been turned back to front, perhaps more than once. In the last century it was approached from the west by an avenue running past a lake which here lies picturesquely among parkland trees. The National Trust preserve this lake as a picture to be viewed, rather than a walk to be more fully experienced. Today, roads arrive on the opposite side of the house both from north and south. But the best approach for those with energy and a large-scale map, is on foot along the public right of way known as Packwood Avenue. This avenue so obviously leads to the house that it must once have been the main approach.

Now it is a delightful grassy walk, below oak, Spanish chestnut, lime, then finally horse chestnut, which arrives at the centre of Packwood's com-

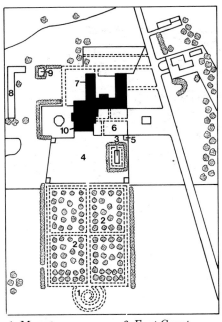

1 Mount	*6 East Court*
2 The Multitude	*7 Barn*
3 Sunk Garden	*8 Fish Curve*
4 South Garden	*9 Roman Bath*
5 North-east	*10 House*
Gazebo	

plex of lawns, walls and stabling. In spring you descend brick steps directly opposite the house into a sea of daffodils.

The brick buildings (even Graham Baron Ash's mock baronial hall which he made from a tithe barn) add to the garden's charm. Much of the orange-red brick is set with purple headers, and several gable ends are decorated with quaint sundials, painted in white and sky blue.

At the centre of all this brickwork comes Packwood House itself, which sadly is another matter. Structurally it is a timber-framed building, as early drawings show, but today it is coated in a dingy grey rendering. Though Graham Baron Ash restored many early features, he left the rendering.

Packwood's gardeners however seem to have seen it as a challenge: something like three quarters of the house's surface area must be clothed in plants. There are vast magnolias and wisterias to the west and south. To the east, now the front, are *Chaenomeles*, honeysuckle of an unknown species, *Jasminum speciosa stephanense* and *Solanum crispum* (Chilean potato tree) whose deep blue flowers have large yellow centres and grow in four-inch clusters. Most spectacular is a black Hamburg vine, said to have come from Hampton Court, which rises almost to gutter level near the south west

Packwood's sunk garden, a Thirties feature, was introduced by its owner at the time, Graham Baron Ash.

corner, travels horizontally across the whole south face and is now making progress across the east.

There are other interesting things to see in Packwood's gardens. Near the lake is the newly dredged 'fish curve', and close by the curious Roman Bath, a small deep pool at present empty. 'Some would like it filled,' says John Ellis, 'but the National Trust is afraid of losing children in it.'

In the terrace wall which faces the Multitude, between its supporting buttresses, are 15 pairs of so-called bee-boles – little brick niches in romanesque style which look as if they could equally well house a small saint each. Below the north east gazebo is a furnace once used for heating the adjoining wall to warm the peach trees which grew on it. An internal flue at about head height still runs for much of its length.

Finally there is the mount itself, which you climb by a spiral path between thick box hedges, made more impenetrable to burrowing children by an underplanting of prickly butcher's broom. From the top, where you stand as it were below the Master's skirts, the whole 113-acre Packwood estate can be seen, protected on all sides by the National Trust's own woods. It is hard to believe that you are just 11 miles from the centre of Birmingham.

The terrace border, densely planted in Graham Baron Ash style, the plants almost on top of each other.

POWIS CASTLE

The gardens at Powis Castle could hardly have more advantages. Not only are they crowned at their summit by a fairy-tale red stone castle, but the steep hillside below provides the ideal conditions for a terraced garden in the Italian style. Furthermore it would be difficult to improve on the view from the terraces, across the valley of the Severn and 2000 acres of parkland, to the Long Mountain and the Breidden Hills. 'And the beauty of Powis,' says Jim Hancock, the National Trust's head gardener here for the last twelve years, 'is that we have to be a *summer* garden.' He means that the lime content of the soil at Powis prevents the growing of rhododendrons, azaleas and other such lime-hating species.

'There are too many spring gardens,' he says, 'where everything is over by the first week of June. With a pH value of 7.0 for our soil on the terraces we couldn't be that sort of place. Instead, our season goes from early May right through to the end of September.'

About the soil on the terraces he is right, but Powis's good fortune does not end here. From the terraces a ridge of hill reaches round in a half circle to run parallel to them, some hundred yards away. Together, this ridge and the terraces suggest a used horseshoe, the terraces forming the taller, un-worn side, the ridge of hill the lower worn side. And the soil of the hill is different, the pH only 5.6. Here, below giant oaks and chestnuts, rhododendrons flourish.

The terraces at Powis not only resist the rhododendron treatment but also, according to legend, escaped the landscaping of Capability Brown. He is said to have wanted to sweep them away and return the dramatic drop below the castle to natural rock. Jim Hancock doubts the story. 'He was such a figure, every garden has to claim a connection with him.' But he admits that the history of the gardens at Powis is obscure.

Certainly the Powis family, who were Catholics, fled the country in 1688 in loyalty to James II, and William III gave the castle to his cousin, the Earl of Rochford. This earl's descendants ransacked it when they left in 1722, and as a result no records of the garden up to this time survive. Some authorities believe it was made by the Rochfords, some that it was the work of the Powises before their exile, some that they made it when they returned.

A print of 1742 proves that by this time the garden existed at least as someone's conception. The terraces appear as now, though their neat little yews are today gigantic. But the water garden shown at their foot in the flat area at the horseshoe's centre is now a huge lawn. Perhaps it was never made. Jim Hancock suggests that it may have been abandoned because the

Jim Hancock, head gardener at Powis Castle for the last 12 years. Opposite: the orangery terrace. Here, as elsewhere at Powis, fuchsias in earthenware containers are a feature.

ponds in the valley above provided insufficient water for its fountains.

By the 1850s there was definitely no water garden because a print of this time shows deer roaming up to the foot of the terraces, proving that whatever there may have been had by this time returned to parkland. It was during the next 40 years that the third Earl of Powis planted the ridge of hill with rhododendrons and other exotic trees and shrubs. He is said to have planted a total of four million trees during his life, though most of these of course were in the 5500 acres of forest which the family also owns.

The additions made by the fourth earl and his wife are better documented. He lived at Powis for 60 years, and finally gave it to the National Trust in 1952. In the early 1900s his wife developed a garden which today makes Powis's third important feature. Looking down and left from the terraces, beyond the open end of the horseshoe, there had previously been what Jim Hancock describes as a menagerie of sheds, glass houses and kitchen gardens. All these she cleared away and created three large hedged gardens of formal elegance. Here in 1908 she built the timbered bothy, which at first housed ten or twelve journeymen gardeners and is now Jim Hancock's house. In a lodge nearby lives the fifth earl's widow, aged 93. On warm summer afternoons she emerges to play a powerful game of croquet, looking no more than seventy. 'Oh yes, she's still keen to win,' Jim Hancock says.

Three glass houses tucked away beyond the hill complete Jim Hancock's responsibilities. Here, in early June, he is still potting a few leftovers, though the year's main work has been done. 'The National Trust is a bit anti-glass house,' he explains, 'but ours are essential for what we do here.' They were also built in 1908, when Lady Powis swept away the others to make her new gardens, and were heated by coal. 'Now we use electric blowers in the spring and autumn and wood in winter. The wood costs us nothing because it comes from the Powis estates. Even in the winter of 1981–82, when the temperature in the coldest house went to −4°C we lost nothing. People who write about frost oversimplify for amateurs. The degree of frost isn't all that matters but the length of time it stays freezing.

'We're mostly herbaceous perennials on the terraces,' he explains, 'but we do quite a lot of planting out of half tender species. It makes work but it has advantages. If you lose perennials there's a gap you can't fill, but we've always got some in reserve.' He favours those which can go out in April or early May – fuchsias and dahlias for example – and be in flower by early June.

'The sea is sixty miles away. Our climate is more like Shrewsbury's, 20 miles in the other direction. There may be good cold-air drainage on the terraces but frost collects in the new gardens. That's where we lost 90 percent of our rue and lavender cotton in 1981–82. It happened before in 1979–80. It's no good persisting with a thing which doesn't suit the garden. So now I'm trying golden marjoram.'

There are several routes round the Powis gardens, but the best save the terraces till last. One leads first to the opposing ridge of hill, known as the Wilderness. To reach this the path crosses the dam which holds up the lowest pool. When the National Trust took over Powis, cottagers down the valley

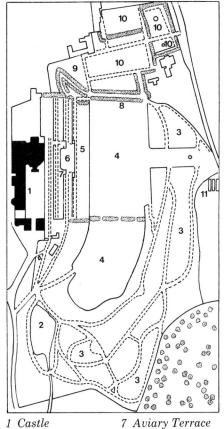

1 Castle
2 Pool
3 Wilderness
4 Great Lawn
5 Apple Slope
6 Orangery
7 Aviary Terrace
8 Yew Walk
9 Box Hedges
10 Old Kitchen Gardens
11 Greenhouses

were still using its water for their baths. Out of sight, higher up the valley, are three other pools, and higher still, against the skyline, the Douglas fir which was said to be the tallest tree in the British Isles – 181 feet – till it lost its top in a gale in 1975. Overhanging the dam, its branches dipping into the pool among yellow irises, is a double horse chestnut.

The hill itself, far from suggesting a wilderness in the modern sense, is openly planted with grassy rides below beech, chestnut and vast oaks. Powis oaks have been famous for generations and were specified by Admiral Rodney for his warships. Here and there among them are the third earl's exotic trees – a blue cedar and an eastern hemlock are especially well-grown. Together the trees provide just the sort of dappled shade needed by rhododendrons and azaleas. White and red hybrids are mingled with older mauve ponticums, an arrangement which Jim Hancock suggests was an intentional precaution. Ponticums were left because at the time the hybrids were new and their hardiness untested.

To the south east the hill gives the same parkland prospect that you get from the terraces. Below the trees here, helping to date their planting, are the graves of family dogs – Butcher 1862, Nero 1864 – complete with their own churchyard yew. From here, looking back towards the castle you have a complete view of the terraces, as it were full frontal. The Great Lawn, the size of a football pitch, which may or may not have once been the Water Garden, lies at your feet. This is the view which the print of 1742 took, but because you are aware of the hill you stand on, all seems more snugly enclosed. There are four terraces, if you include the lowest which has a grassy bank for support rather than a wall. Now for the first time it is possible to see those yews which the print shows so small and neatly clipped, but today are massive. They line the foot of the castle like a row of huge green umbrellas. Even more gigantic ones have combined to climb the right hand side of the rock face, like some great humped tree monster.

Oddly, the trees of the new gardens, to which a path descends from the tip of the Wilderness, have the controlled formality which those on the terrace have lost. The lowest of the three hedged enclosures is largely lawn, ornamented with cone-shaped yews a mere six feet high. Above, in the biggest of the three, the one overlooked by Jim Hancock's bothy, are lines of apples and pears, pruned to a similar shape, underplanted with silver foliage substitutes for the rue and lavender cotton which was frosted. A hooped vine pergola crosses between them, the vines rising from circles of that experimental golden marjoram. On one side are hybrid roses which Jim Hancock moved from the terraces when they were 18 years old. 'Up there in full sun it was too dry for them. They've done well down here.' Lady Powis's croquet hoops and a delphinium border in the third garden may properly seem Victorian, but the overall simplicity of this part-walled enclosure suggests an earlier gardening tradition.

One path climbs from here to the terraces beside a box hedge which must be unequalled in the country, 19 feet high, smoothly vertical from bottom to top, all the more astonishing since it is the same plant which elsewhere at Powis makes little foot-high edging for the herbaceous borders. This path emerges below (inside would be a better word) one of those massive yews, on to the second from bottom terrace. Here are what Jim Hancock calls his lush herbaceous borders. As well as the usual peonies and delphiniums of herbaceous borders there are big bush roses (*Rosa* x *highdownensis*), and such tall big-leafed plants as the yellow flowering *Ligularia przewalskii* and the orange flowering *Ligularia dentata* 'Desdemona'. 'On rich soil it wasn't any good putting in plants which suited the sandy conditions of a place like Surrey,' he explains. 'They grew enormous, then with the sun on them from seven in the morning they couldn't get the moisture they needed.'

The Orangery, at the centre of these borders, is deeply excavated into the hillside. Here the terraces are at their most Italian. Lead statues top the balustrade above, somewhat garish in white preservative, but probably as prominent now as they were originally. The Orangery itself has just the feeling of a Tuscan orangery, where huge pottery urns with orange trees are wintered. Jim Hancock however thinks it unlikely that oranges were ever grown at Powis. Today abutilons, 'Ashford Red' and the deeper red 'Nabob', flower here throughout the summer.

On the terrace below, the one supported by the grass bank known as the Apple Slope, one border is for May and June, the other for autumn, with a large variety of hostas in between. The wall behind is the only one which still needs rebuilding. Here, in crevices, grow pretty sprays of blue linaria. 'I was told to plant that in the border,' Jim Hancock says, 'but it's ended up on the walls, where it belongs.'

The Apple Slope has fewer apples than ornamental maples: bootlace (honey) fungus is a problem. Early in Jim Hancock's time here the National Trust garden consultant guessed that in four years' time there wouldn't be any trees on this bank. Though some of the maples seem to be suffering, the bank is still thickly tree covered. 'They're like us,' Jim Hancock says. 'When they're old an infection kills them but when they're young they throw it off.'

On the terrace above the Orangery are his dry borders. Low red and yellow flowering plants predominate here. Along the back wall are the purple and black flowering *Rhodochiton atrosanguineum* and the red and orange-trumpeted *Manettia inflata*. This is the Aviary Terrace; at its centre the Aviary itself is a shallower excavation than the Orangery. Here, in manger-like beds, a few fragrant rhododendrons fight for life. Their soil has been imported, but lime drips into it from the whitewashed walls.

The highest terrace is dominated by the ancient yews. They line the bottom of the castle, reaching out above a 30-foot wall. To one side, another makes a gnome's house over a garden bench. Close up they seem even larger than when seen from the Wilderness hill.

Here, on the steps of the castle itself, are Powis's much-photographed geraniums, in the sort of red clay pots which, all over the rest of the garden, are filled with varieties of fuchsia. To either side are two Irish yews, their upright form and dark green foliage contrasting with the lighter green, rounded shapes of the others. 'I admit they don't really belong,' Jim Hancock says, 'but they're fine trees.'

'That's *Artemesia* ''Powis Castle'',' Jim Hancock adds, pointing to big silvery clumps which hang down beside the older yews. 'The National Trust wanted *Artemesia* ''Lambrook Silver'', but I said, we have some here that's better, why not use that? A couple of years later they got all excited about it and sent samples to London to be classified. They named it *Artemesia* ''Powis

Castle". Well why not? It's nice to give Powis a bit of credit. The fact is, I'd found it in a little garden near Wakefield and brought it from there, but I didn't tell them.'

Turn away from the castle with its skirt of umbrella yews and the view is spread below in its full magnificence: the terraces, the formal gardens where Lady Powis cleared away the menagerie of greenhouses, the Great Lawn and the Wilderness; and then beyond, the many acres of parkland where black Welsh cattle graze beside the Severn, and beyond that the steep slopes of Long Mountain and the Breidden Hills.

If Powis has more natural advantages than almost any other British garden, it also has a sturdy defender in Jim Hancock with his seven assistant gardeners, as almost 60,000 visitors a year discover. Returning to his bothy in the evening he listens to promenade concerts or Mozart operas. The white goats which continually appear around the gardens, led on strings by children, are his wife's department, though in winter he allows them a nibble at the castle lawns.

The 18th-century Italianate terraces, with 250-year old yews. Below them, the aviary and orangery are set back into the terrace walls, their balustrades topped with urns and statuary.

ROUSHAM PARK

Rousham Park, situated in the Cherwell valley 12 miles north of Oxford, has been the home of the Dormer family since 1635, but comparatively little was known about the making of its gardens till the 1920s. Then Thomas Cottrell-Dormer discovered (wrapped in some old bills) a number of letters dating from the first half of the 18th century, most of them written to his ancestor Lieutenant General James Dormer by the general's agent at Rousham. They gave detailed descriptions of the creation of the gardens by the head gardener, John MacClary, to the design of William Kent. Since Rousham is the only William Kent garden to have survived unaltered, and Kent is probably the most important of early English landscape gardeners, today's interest in Rousham is not surprising.

Thomas Cottrell-Dormer still lives in Rousham house. Now aged 88, frail but alert and keenly interested in Rousham's history, he shows framed plans of early lay-outs for the gardens, while his daughter-in-law, Angela Cottrell-Dormer, opens and closes shutters to keep the damaging light from 18th-century miniatures, 19th-century costumes and other family treasures, of which Rousham has such an abundance.

The earliest plan dates from 1725 and is believed to be by Charles Bridgeman. It represents an interesting transition between the geometric garden designs of the previous century and the informality which was to follow. Already the extensive parterre behind the house has become a lawn, today called the Bowling Green, but the descending succession of woodland pools which Kent later rounded into ovals and octagons are shown square. The river Cherwell, allowed by Kent to flow below the garden with all its natural curves, has been given straight sides and precisely angled bends.

In the library, Thomas Cottrell-Dormer shows William Kent's letters preserved in a white leather volume. Mostly they date from the years between 1738 (by which time Kent was in charge) and 1741 when the General died. As well as designing the gardens, Kent redesigned the house and refurnished and decorated it – supplying many paintings himself. One letter mentions casually that he has sent down a Rubens by wagon. Thomas Cottrell-Dormer and his daughter-in-law speculate about where in the house the Rubens might be now. More typically, the agent reports to the General that 70 hands are working on clearing the river and the same number on turfing the slope below the Bowling Green. He hopes that by the time the General comes the terrace will be 'crooked as a Ram's horn . . . and all things

Venus's vale, where giant orfe swim in William Kent's octagonal pond.

33

there about Magnifique.'

The letters show that although Kent was constantly consulted and called for he probably only came to Rousham once a year, and many decisions about detail were taken by John MacClary, always called Clary. A letter of 1750 from Clary himself gives a fascinating account of the whole garden at that time.

'I am afraid,' Clary writes, 'my master and all of you will have forgot what sort of a place Rousham is, so I have sent you a description of it that it may not quite creep out of your memory.' Many head gardeners must have felt the same about their absentee employers. For six generations the Cottrell-Dormers were Masters of Ceremony at court and lived mostly in London.

General James Cottrell-Dormer left Rousham to his cousin, Sir Clement Cottrell, who was required by the General's will to add Dormer to his name. Thomas Cottrell-Dormer is the seventh, and his son Charles will be the eighth generation of direct descendants to live at Rousham. 'My father asked me whether he should leave it to the National Trust,' Charles says. 'But when we discovered what they wanted as an endowment we said no thanks. It would have left me penniless. So we carry on as best we can.' Carrying on means that, as well as supervising the house and garden, Charles runs a 1500-acre farm which includes a herd of 30 to 40 pedigree Long Horn cattle. 'The farm supports the whole shooting match,' says his wife.

Since this occupies Charles full time, house and garden are delegated to Angela. Her latest enthusiasm – no part of Kent's plan, but a 19th century curiosity – is a grotto-like fernery. This is squeezed into a narrow gap

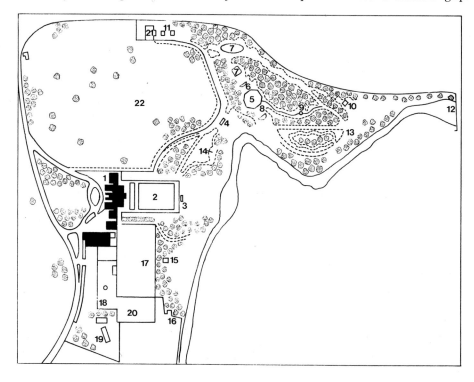

1 House
2 Bowling Green
3 Lion and Horse Sculpture
4 Praeneste Arcade
5 Octagon Pond
6 Venus's Vale
7 Site of Upper Ponds
8 Serpentine Rill
9 Cold Bath
10 Temple of Echo
11 Gothic Seat
12 Heyford Bridge
13 Statue of Apollo
14 Theatre
15 Pyramid
16 Poets Seat
17 Walled Gardens
18 Pigeon House
19 Church
20 Vegetable Garden
21 Warren Stable
22 Paddock

between the original house and one of the wing pavilions which Kent added. This gap has been roofed with glass and lined with contorted blocks of Italian volcanic tufa. It was done at the same time that the Victorian back was added to the house by 'that awful old vandal William St Aubyn', Angela Cottrell-Dormer says, referring to the architect responsible. But she has taken advantage of the grotto he made and decked the tufa with ferns – 25 varieties according to her father-in-law. Among them, succulents and long-tailed pink flowering cacti emerge from crannies while exotic lilies and small abutilons stand on sills and ledges. In the green rock pools below, tiny red fish swim.

The fernery is well placed, shaded in the morning, and getting the afternoon sun, but it has problems. Ferns need damp, and the tufa either

Above: border geraniums. Below: hybrid tea roses in Rousham's walled gardens.

dries out quickly or, if kept too wet, damages the books in the library on the far side of the wall. Today, to make things more difficult, a mole has arrived. It burrowed 20 feet alongside the mosaic of an abandoned conservatory, under the fernery wall, to throw up a molehill among the maidenhair. Angela Cottrell-Dormer, small and active, in headscarf against a cold June wind, suggests a vivacious milkmaid rather than the potential mistress of an ancient estate, and is preoccupied, like many gardeners, with the disasters of gardening, leaving the visitor to delight in all that flourishes.

The past few years could justify her attitude. For a start, directly outside the fernery the frost of 1981–82 killed three fine fountain palms – as it did all the geraniums she was wintering *inside* the fernery. Everywhere about Kent's Pleasure Garden the laurels which he planted below limes and beeches died too. 'For several nights we were the coldest place in the world,' she says. Fortunately the laurel sprouted again from the roots, but the work of clearing several acres of dead laurel, much of it five feet high, filled the following summer and was beyond Rousham's two gardeners.

The Bowling Green at the back of the house gives the best general idea of Rousham's layout and shows at once the opportunity which the site gave to Kent. Set high above the winding river Cherwell it looks across green fields which reach into the distance then rise gently to the Cotswold hills. Just below the skyline Kent set his 'eyecatcher', a line of stone arches which make no pretence to a practical purpose. Lower and slightly to the right comes Cuttle Mill which he remodeled in Gothic style and renamed the Temple of the Mill. In the foreground at the far end of the Bowling Green, is Sheemakers' sculpture of a lion killing a horse, its marble plinth designed by its size to distance the mill and eyecatcher.

To the right of the Bowling Green, beyond a yew hedge so vast that you could walk down its centre, lie the kitchen gardens. These were already here in Kent's time, probably made around 1635 by the first Dormer to live at Rousham. Below and to the left of the Bowling Green are Kent's Pleasure Gardens.

The path to these runs beside the park-like meadow known as the Paddock. At the far side of the Paddock in the estate wall is Kent's doorway, set there to give visitors a view of the house. Curious visitors were expected even then, though they were expected to gaze respectfully from a distance. Beside the gate stands Kent's castellated Warren Stable. 'We just call it Cow Castle,' says Angela Cottrell-Dormer. Her husband's Long Horns stand around it, providing just the rustic background which Kent would have wanted, or roam to within a few yards of the house, only restrained by a ha-ha which is one of the earliest in the country and also one of the longest. Kent's Gothic seat beside Warren Stable at one time gave a view over the Cherwell to the eyecatcher on the far hills, but this has long been obscured by the trees he planted.

Urns and statues edge the descending path but the first important feature it reaches is Venus's Vale. Here are the pools which Bridgeman drew square and Kent modified. Only the largest has water today. It is known as the Octagonal Pond but the name fails to give an impression of its naturalness. Below spreading white lilies, shoals of enormous golden orfe swim lazily. Few can weigh less than three pounds and they make normal goldfish look like tiddlers.

Pan, a nymph, a pair of swans and Venus herself look down on the pool, set around an arched cascade. The arch is inscribed:

In front of this stone lie the Remains of

RINGWOOD

an otter-hound of Extraordinary Sagacity.
Tyrant of the Cherwell's Flood
Come not near this sacred gloom,
Nor, with thy insulting brood,
Dare pollute my RINGWOOD'S tomb' . . .

The upper ponds once fed the cascade which fell into the Octagonal Pond, as well as many 'jets' set about the woods. Now the pool is fed by a narrow rill in a stone channel (also Kent's) which follows a dark glade of yew and beech. Half way is the Cold Bath – a small stone pool which looks chilly even on a warm day in summer. The glade leads to the northern and most peaceful end of the garden where the Temple of Echo stands below a tall Lebanon cedar. Through the chipped top of its little sarcophagus great-tits come and go to feed a cheeping family. From the Temple the view over the Cherwell – which is never lost at any point in the Pleasure Gardens – includes the stone Heyford Bridge, built by the monks of Eynsham. Echo's temple functions too. Make a loud cry here on a still summer evening and it comes echoing back from the distant hills.

A few yards down the grassy slope below the temple you get a first view of the central classical feature of Kent's design: the seven-arched Praeneste. All has been so cunningly compressed that the lime avenue you look down in fact runs only a few yards below the serpentine rill, and your eye passes across the lower end of Venus's Vale without seeing it. The ground below the trees of these avenues is carpeted with newly sprouted laurel. The 18th century gardener, Thomas Cottrell-Dormer explains, interplanted his laurels with honeysuckle, roses, syringas and lilac to give the impression that the laurels themselves were flowering.

From the Praeneste the way descends to the Theatre, where Mercury, Ceres and Bacchus stand below the surrounding trees. This small amphi-theatre seems to wait for its evening masque, even if the audience would need to watch from the river.

Beyond the Cherwell's sharpest bend comes the long green slope which 70 hands once laboured to turf – in spring it is a glorious sweep of daffodils and narcissuses – and then Kent's last structure known as the Pyramid, a misleading name for this oddly-shaped little building. Finally the riverside path reaches the Poet's Seat. It was here that such friends of the Dormers as Gay and Pope would sit and look back along the river towards a wooden bridge. Clary, the gardener, described it as 'a large bench that makes a very handsome Garden Seat where you set down, and view the River and Garden from one end to the other.'

There is a dramatic contrast between so much calculated informality, with its woodland paths and apparently casual scattering of temples, ruins and statues, and the walled kitchen gardens which at this point lie directly above. They consist of three interlocking and very different enclosures. Where they meet, an archway leads directly into the churchyard, and the tower of the 12th-century village church looks down picturesquely.

The smallest enclosure was always an orchard. Fruit trees are still trained on its stone walls, but there are now ornamental trees too, and at one end 36 little box-edged beds with hybrid roses. At the opposite end stands one of the largest pigeon houses in the country. You enter this round building to find that it is lined from floor to conical roof with nesting holes in the form of gaps in the brickwork. How many holes? Thomas Cottrell-Dormer has the answer: 744. A ladder revolving round a central post and known as a potence is still in working order, and enabled the gardener to reach any nest he chose to remove the squabs for eating. At present only a few Norfolk Croppers live here.

The second in size remains what it has always been, a productive kitchen garden. At one time the largest also produced vegetables. Enormous quantities were needed by the Cottrell-Dormers in London where their court duties required them to entertain at their own expense. Clary's letter of 1750 notes that 'on June 9th cabbages, coolworts, cauliflowers, cucumbers, lettuce, carrots, onions, parsley, horseradish, eight pounds of butter and 18 eggs' were despatched from Rousham.

Today the greater part of this huge enclosure with its mellow brick walls is lawn. If that had been the original design it could hardly have been a more pleasing one. Down one side runs an immaculately kept herbaceous border, 120 yards in length, and in the centre is a pool surrounded by a tall ring of roses. These and the border are connected by a frail rose pergola.

It was Angela Cottrell-Dormer's mother-in-law, the late Mrs Thomas Cottrell-Dormer, who was the gardener of the family and who, from 1947 onwards, recreated these two walled gardens. For the 20 previous years Rousham had been let. The first tenant not only drank but used his shot gun on the garden statues. By the end of the war the gardens had become a wilderness. While Mrs Thomas Cottrell-Dormer rescued the flower garden, two Polish ex-prisoners of war cleared the paths of the Pleasure Gardens, hacking out the temples and statues from bracken and brambles.

Though now in good order, and recovering fast from more recent natural catastrophes, Rousham remains essentially informal, not merely because Kent designed it that way, but because that is how Charles and Angela Cottrell-Dormer want it. The tone is set by the unmanned ticket machine, and the low price of the tickets, less than half the usual. Here 10,000 people a year put in their money. 'Not just in summer,' says Angela Cottrell-Dormer, 'but on Christmas Day. Or they come out from Oxford to read their Sunday papers here. They just like Rousham to be theirs for a day.'

You won't find a single plant label at Rousham but you will find a unique landscape garden. You will also find peacocks in the walled garden, Angela Cottrell-Dormer's Mille Fleur booted bantams scratching round the back door and, if you are lucky, one of Charles Cottrell-Dormer's tank-like Long Horn bulls glaring at you across the ha-ha.

Opposite: Temple of Echo, most outlying of William Kent's classical features at Rousham, where a loud cry will echo back from the hills across the Cherwell.

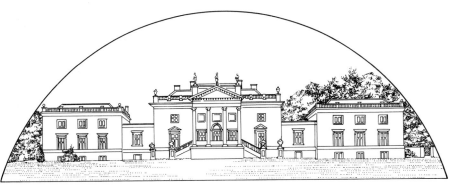

STOURHEAD

The profusion of glorious rhododendrons which decorate the lake sides and woodland walks of Stourhead – often described as the supreme achievement of British landscape gardening – are a problem. In his National Trust office in the nearby village of Stourton, Tom Burr, the Trust's regional information officer, explains why. 'Because it's a landscape garden they don't really belong. They weren't part of the original plan and they distract attention from the subtler effects of the foliage and the shapes of the valley and its skylines. So we try to hide them a bit. We're moving the old mauve ponticums away from the lake sides, then at least they aren't doubled by their reflections. But a few years ago the locals realised what we were doing and made a terrible row. It's the rhododendrons which bring the crowds, and crowds make trade.'

Successive generations of Hoares, the banking family which created Stourhead and ultimately gave it to the National Trust, also took different attitudes to exotic trees and shrubs. Henry Hoare, the original garden maker, known as 'the Magnificent' to distinguish him from other Henry Hoares, used native trees, gaining his effects by contrasting the different greens of oak, beech and conifer. His achievement can be best recognised by comparing today's densely forested valley at Stourhead with the bare chalk downs to the east. He and the architect Henry Flitcroft, with whom he worked, began to transform this Wiltshire valley in the 1740s, when there was no established tradition to follow. Lancelot (Capability) Brown, for example, did not start his London practice till 1751.

In essence what Henry Hoare did was to dam the river Stour, creating one major lake and a number of smaller ones. Around these he built classical and mediaeval monuments, carefully siting them to produce pictorial effects. Like all 18th-century landscape gardeners, it was these which he aimed for, imitating in real life the paintings of such artists as Claude Lorraine and the Poussins.

His son and both his daughters died before him and the estate passed to his grandson (who was also his great nephew). Richard Colt Hoare, Stourhead's owner from 1785 to 1838, was a purist. He removed a Turkish tent, a Chinese temple and a Gothic greenhouse. But he also planted many exotic trees, and introduced rhododendrons – both mauve ponticum and red arboreum.

The next influential owner was Hugh Richard Hoare. In his time here,

Stourhead's Pantheon, with turfed bridge leading from 'nowhere to nowhere'.

STOURHEAD

The map legend:

1 House
2 Spread Eagle Inn
3 St Peter's Church
4 Bristol Cross
5 Tunnel
6 Temple of Apollo
7 Site of Hermitage
8 Rock Arch
9 Cascade
10 Turner's Paddock Lake
11 Iron Bridge
12 Pantheon
13 Watch Cottage
14 Grotto
15 Diana's Basin
16 Lily Pond
17 Obelisk
18 The Shades
19 Temple of Flora
20 Turf Bridge

Henry Hoare, called 'the Magnificent', to distinguish him from other Henry Hoares, was a prosperous banker and the creator of Stourhead's garden. Work started in the 1740s, at a time when there was no well-established tradition of English landscape gardening.

1841 to 1857, he also planted exotic trees, in particular the Douglas firs and western hemlock which are now so well-grown. He believed that evergreens enriched the winter landscape.

Stourhead was shut up for seven years before Henry Hugh Arthur Hoare succeeded to it in 1894. He was there longer than any other Hoare, and it was he who finally in 1946 left it to the National Trust. His occupation was the one which, apart from Henry the Magnificent's, has left the strongest impression on the garden, for it was he who, in the 1920s and 1930s, replaced many ponticum rhododendrons with the Himalayan hybrids which today pain classicists but give other visitors so much pleasure; for however indiscriminate Henry Hugh Arthur's planting, the fact remains that in early summer the hybrid rhododendrons at Stourhead provide a highly popular spectacle, bringing 3000 visitors on a typical Sunday in May or June.

'Not that numbers are our main concern,' Tom Burr says. 'Next to St. Michael's Mount, Stourhead is the most visited of any National Trust property. But there's a limit to the number of visitors a garden can take without harming it and we're close to the limit. And there's another reason why numbers aren't important to us: more than half our visitors come in free because they're National Trust members, so we get no direct cash from them.'

Not that Stourhead doesn't need money; restoring the Bristol Cross a few years ago cost £90,000. And the Pantheon, now being restored, will be another £150,000. (The iron supports had rusted and were bringing down its plaster.) No private garden could begin to spend that sort of money. But it does have one financial advantage too. Besides the house and garden, Henry Hugh Arthur left the National Trust six farms totalling 2000 acres and these contribute substantially to the upkeep of the gardens.

Though Tom Burr is a knowledgeable and enthusiastic supporter of Stourhead and of the National Trust's work here, he is no practical gardener. In direct charge of the six gardeners who have the task of maintaining its 90 acres of garden is the head gardener, Fred Hunt. His enthusiasm for Stourhead might seem indiscriminate if it wasn't so professional and infectious. Continually he stops to point across lake or headland to a variegated maple, a Macedonian pine. 'I'm really fond of that tree,' he says. Or he shows how a giant sequoia, browned by the winter's frosts, is making fresh green growth from ground to tip. He is no landscape purist, as pleased by a bank of brilliant rhododendrons as by a stand of ancient beech or chestnut. Even the mauve ponticums he considers appropriate at Stourhead, and underrated. 'Look at that lot. They're not just mauve. There's purple ones and there's some so pale they're more white than pink.' Henry Hugh Arthur's copper beeches he admires too, in particular the astonishing specimen which stands near the Stone Bridge, its spread of branches brushing the ground on one side, dipping into the lake on the other.

The proper way to visit Stourhead, Fred Hunt explains, is from top to bottom, starting at the house and arriving at its different features in the order in which Henry Hoare intended. The National Trust encourages this route, though many visitors enter at the bottom from the village of Stourton, so starting with the magnificent view up the lake which should come as a climax, the reward for no short stroll.

The lawns near the house set the tone for much – though by no means all – that is to follow. Massed banks of rhododendrons stand around. In the distance, between the trunks of oak, beech, lime and chestnut, cows graze in meadowland, the garden shading into countryside as landscape gardens should.

Quickly the path dips and the house is left behind, not to be seen again. This too was Henry Hoare's intention; he never meant the garden to be a picture window prospect from the house but a complete and separate experience in itself. All around now are his original beech, oak and lime trees, here and there mingled with the conifers of later Hoares. At once, too, the scale of Stourhead becomes clear. This is a garden in which you walk rather than saunter.

Suddenly – the word is unavoidable because the garden was designed to provide a succession of such surprises – the Temple of Apollo appears across the valley, set high up among trees. Below and between lies the lake but so far it has hardly been visible.

Presently glimpses of it become more frequent, and one path descends to reach the Temple of Flora on its banks, but another continues higher up the valley side through a plantation known as the Shades. Here Henry Hoare's 200-year-old beeches are at their finest, huge at base but because they have been close planted of immense height. Even on a busy day in summer the Shades seems like a country wood. There are damp woodland smells, wood pigeons coo and jackdaws clack.

Fred Hunt, the National Trust's head gardener at Stourhead. Six gardeners manage the ninety-acre woodland garden.

Autumnal maple in one of Stourhead's woodland glades, typical of the exotic introductions of the late Henry Hugh Arthur Hoare, who finally gave the garden to the National Trust.

Finally the path descends, past those dazzling and supposedly hidden 'Britannia' rhododendrons, to reach a causeway which holds up a smaller reservoir called the Lily Lake. Moorhen, coot and mallard swim in an expanse of yellow waterlilies. Two higher pools are out of sight from this causeway, but a path which climbs beside them leads through even less tamed woodland. Here in summer you may find a hen pheasant playing wounded to protect her young, who scurry about among nettles and bracken. Where the wood ends there is only the wood-fringed top of the valley ahead. High up there a small cross known as St Peter's Pump marks the source of the River Stour.

All the way back down the west side of the main lake the views across it grow in extent and splendour. Half way, the path dips below dark yews and leads to the grotto. A mild sense of alarm grows as you pass under a dark arch and become unsure of your footing on the wet stone. Then – another dramatic moment – the white God of the River appears directly ahead, sitting on an upturned amphora, one hand raised in welcome – or warning. The nymph is only discovered later, in a recess to the right, where water flows continuously over her stone slab.

From here the way climbs to the Pantheon, a scaled-down replica of the Pantheon in Rome, perched above the water on a grassy hill so steep that it is almost impossible to mow. Fred Hunt is planting it with *Prunus laurocerasus* 'Zabeliana', which requires little attention, so that he need no longer risk losing mowers and their men in the lake. Presently the path reaches another causeway, the one which holds up the main lake, arriving as it were from below so that the huge expanse of water is first seen on eye-level. The causeway is densely hedged with berberis, rose and other spiky shrubs, intended to be child-proof. 'It's just about gardener-proof too,' Fred Hunt says. But he believes that this sort of funny old mixture, with laurel and honeysuckle too, is typically 18th century.

Now on the left is the Stone Bridge, placed here to suggest that a river is arriving below it to feed the lake and leading from nowhere to nowhere. Soon afterwards a road comes close to the garden but it is so well hidden that, passing below it by a tunnel, you hardly notice it. On the other side a steep path leads up to the Temple of Apollo. The climb is worth making, and provides the best of all Stourhead's panoramas. Now classical temples, mediaeval crosses and mock Gothic cottages seem to stand everywhere about the lake and valley sides. On the far skyline is the tip of the obelisk which Henry Hoare erected to commemorate his father who built Stourhead house.

This circle of the gardens ends below the Bristol Cross, looking oddly delicate on its swell of green turf. Henry Hoare found it in ruins in a Bristol scrap yard. Beyond is the picturesque village of Stourton, with its stone cottages and mediaeval church.

At Stourhead, as elsewhere, a worthy conscientiousness is the quality which, above others, the National Trust brings to the managing of its gardens. No doubt the uniqueness of what it has to manage here makes it doubly conscientious. Back in his village office Tom Burr shows the report prepared by five learned authorities on the management of Stourhead for the next 100 years. 'I can't think of anywhere else which is looking that far ahead,' he says.

Opposite: lakeside planting of gunnera, with reflected autumnal foliage, one of the areas which has been cleared of its overabundant ponticum rhododendrons.

SHEFFIELD PARK

Short and strongly built, Archie Skinner looks what he is, a Devon man; he has the build of many west country seamen. Two of his uncles were gardeners and so was his grandfather, but his father hated gardening – he was a timberman who survived the whole of the First World War as a Gordon Highlander. Archie returned to the family's gardening tradition, and a gardener is what he has been all his life. At 43, he became head gardener of Sheffield Park, the National Trust's finest woodland garden in southern England. 'But Sheffield Park isn't just trees,' Archie Skinner says. 'True, we've got nearly 200 varieties of conifer, but we've also got more than 200 different rhododendrons, and 1700 species in all.'

Standing on the bridge between Sheffield Park's two upper lakes, above the 25-foot waterfall where one overflows into the other, he corrects the idea that the job of a National Trust head gardener is merely to sustain what earlier generations have created. 'Over there,' he says, pointing across the two lower lakes to sunlit glades of bluebells below clumps of Scots pine and birch, 'that whole area was closed till 1977. A wilderness of bramble and bracken. Now we've got the Queen's Walk by the lake side, and up above, all that open space for wild daffodils and orchis in spring, then the bluebells. We had a problem getting rid of the bracken without harming the wild flowers. We did it by rotary mowing at a height of 12 inches.'

The two lakes he points across were the first to be made at Sheffield Park. They were the central feature of the landscape garden which Lancelot Brown created here for John Baker Holroyd, later the first Earl of Sheffield. Holroyd employed Brown from 1775, when Brown's reputation was at its height. Here he made a typical Brown landscape by damming a tributary of the River Ouse to form his two lakes and connecting them with a rocky cascade. He shaped long lawns to sweep down from the house to the lake shores and enclosed the view with carefully-sited clumps and belts of native oaks, beeches and pines. Edward Gibbon, the first Earl of Sheffield's close friend, wrote parts of 'The Decline and Fall of the Roman Empire' in the library at Sheffield Park, and must have watched Brown's work in progress.

The second period of garden making at Sheffield Park occurred a hundred years later when the third Earl, grandson of the first, employed Pulham and Sons of Chelsea, radically to alter Brown's landscape by creating two further lakes. These lie nearer the house and for this reason are confusingly known as the first and second lakes, though they were made third and fourth. They are sited in a side valley at right angles to the earlier two and at some height above them. It is these which are connected by the garden's 25-foot

Archie Skinner, head gardener, among the hostas of his new stream garden. Opposite: the highest of Sheffield Park's lakes was added in the 19th century.

waterfall. 'That's a masterpiece,' Archie Skinner says. 'All made with Sussex sandstone and Sussex clay. No cement.' Pulham's lower lake flows into one of Brown's lakes by a smaller waterfall. As a whole, the lakes now make a huge 'T', Pulham's forming the stem, Brown's the crosspiece.

Around the lakes and all about the rest of the garden, the third Earl established new plantations. In contrast to Brown's native trees, he used mainly exotic species: swamp cypresses, incense cedars, Brewer's spruce and Japanese maples, to name just a few. It was the third Earl who made Sheffield Park's cricket field. Cricket was an interest which he pursued with equal, if not greater, passion than garden making. The first Test Match between England and Australia was played at Sheffield Park. For 20 years (1876–96) the Australian tour of England always opened with a match there against Lord Sheffield's eleven, and in the long cold winter of 1890–91 he organized several matches between teams of well-known Sussex cricketers which were played on the ice of the largest lake. How the players kept their feet is not recorded.

The third period of garden making began with the sale of Sheffield Park in 1909 to Mr Arthur G. Soames. If the third Earl gave Sheffield Park most of the trees which make its autumn foliage so colourful, Arthur Soames contributed its spring and summer colours: first the dogwoods of April and early May, then the rhododendrons of May and June. Many of these flower late and were developed by Soames for this purpose. His hybrids, known as 'Angelo', have large white and pink blooms and resemble those previously created by Sir Edmund Loder at another Sussex Garden, Leonardslee (page 86), but Soames's Angelos bloom a fortnight later. Kalmias follow, both the familiar calico bush (*Kalmia latifolia*) and the less common, deeper pink, sheep laurel (*K. angustifolia*).

During the Second World War Sheffield Park, like many British gardens, was neglected. Canadian soldiers built Nissen huts and camped among its trees. Finally in 1954 the present era in its life began when the National Trust bought the gardens, though not the house, which remains

1 House
2 First Lake
3 Jubilee Walk
4 Himalaya Walk
5 Palm Avenue
6 Coronation Walk
7 Big Tree Walk
8 Queen's Walk
9 Third Lake
10 Cricket Field Plantation
11 Fourth Lake
12 Cascade Bridge
13 Lower Waterfall
14 Top Bridge and Waterfall
15 Storage or Fish Pond
16 Kalmia Walk
17 Second Lake
18 Gentian Walk leading to Stream Garden

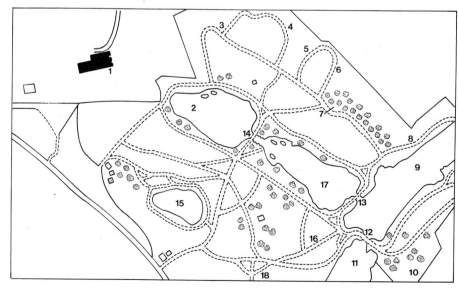

privately occupied. 'It's still an essential part of the garden,' Archie Skinner says. 'Wherever you go, it keeps turning up as the focal point of a view.' From the bridge over the waterfall it stands centrally above the highest lake, an imposing castellated gothic building designed by James Wyatt for the first Earl. Here as elsewhere it is half hidden by trees, and although it is sad that it is thus excluded, there may be merit in the effect this creates of an always-present, but never-attainable, fairy castle on a nearby hill.

The bridge above the upper waterfall is the obvious place to start a tour of Sheffield Park's 100 acres (the estate has as much woodland again, still undeveloped), because from here a general sense of the layout can best be had. Already the path from the entrance has led past two fine cider gums (*Eucalyptus gunnii*), one about 100 feet high. Now, as it continues north east, high conifers tower on all sides. Below stand rarer ones: Brewer's weeping spruce (*Picea breweriana*) with its many dark tassles, and the coffin juniper (*Juniperus recurva coxii*) which looks always as if suffering from drought. Among them rhododendrons form huge banks, some 25 feet high and 100 yards long, immense and dark in winter, brilliant red, white and pink in early summer. It was in this area, at the centre of such splendour, that Archie Skinner was asked by a lady visitor, 'Where are the gardens?'

From here two grassy loops reach out towards the boundary fence, the first – known as the Jubilee and Himalaya walk – passing the tree which attracts more specialist interest than any other: a magnificent Mexican pine (*Pinus montezumae*). In a breeze its blue-green clusters of needles (which suggest a mass of chimney sweep's brushes) shimmer like watered silk. The blue-green colour is curious: smaller Mexican pines which have been planted at Sheffield Park are a darker and greyer shade. Archie Skinner

Overleaf: beyond the second of Sheffield Park's lakes stand the exotic conifers planted by the third Earl of Sheffield.

Massed azaleas, introduced like the rhododendrons by Arthur Soames in the 20th century.

believes that its seeds came from an untypical blue-green specimen.

The second grassy loop includes a notable anomaly in a garden which strives all the time to make its contrived views and plantings seem natural: a formal avenue of palms (*Trachycarpus fortunei*). As at Leonardslee 12 miles to the west, these flourish, one on a lake island creating an especially tropical effect.

South east from here, the Big Tree Walk leads among the garden's most imposing trees of all, a well-spaced planting of redwoods, *Sequoiadendron giganteum*. With them is an equally tall but more conical Nootka cypress, the tree which Red Indians used for their canoes more commonly than the birch, Archie Skinner believes. Intermingled with these American exotics are fine oaks and sweet chestnuts. For centuries the oaks at Sheffield Park were valued for shipbuilding, especially for the strong elbow branches they produced. In 1777, as part of Brown's garden making, two enormous oak trees were felled, each of which needed a team of 24 horses to drag it at the rate of four miles a day to Lewes. The oaks, chestnuts and beeches at Sheffield Park provide the dappled shade in which rhododendrons and azaleas flourish.

At the head of Brown's upper lake, the Queen's Walk begins. It leads over wooden bridges and across a swamp by a path, built in the way the Romans built their roads. Trunks of alder were laid for the sides, their branches piled between, then mud packed on top. The whole was surfaced with a sandy pebble mixture known as hoggen.

To the left of this path all has been left undisturbed. Wetland plants flourish (water forget-me-not, sedges, yellow flags, red mace), and tufted duck and kingfisher nest below tangled willows. If a tree falls, that's the way it's left. 'Partly we do it for conservation,' Archie Skinner says. 'Now so many farm ponds are being drained, the sort of plants we get here don't have many habitats left. It's educational too. You get London children who've never seen what the bottom of a fallen tree looks like.' The Queen's Walk is some 200 yards long, and making it was one winter's heavy work for Sheffield Park's five gardeners (four full-time including Archie Skinner himself, and one part time). They had only some week-end help from Sandhurst cadets.

The swamp area at the lake's head has another function. It acts as a filter for the sediment which the stream that feeds the lakes continuously washes down from the Ashdown Forest. How often the lakes have been dredged since the 18th century isn't known, but the lower of Brown's certainly was after the First World War, when Soames paid the village unemployed to do the work. By 1970 both lower lakes were again so badly silted that their average depth was only 18 inches. The job was far beyond the garden staff and for 12 months contractors worked to drain the lakes and clear an average depth of six feet of silt from them.

Above the lakes on the old cricket field there are signs of unwelcome wild life: rabbit scrapings and mole hills. 'We shoot the rabbits and trap the moles,' Archie Skinner says. When four roe deer appear among the pines he runs at them, making a cry surprisingly like a rutting buck. They are the worst pests of all. Despite the five-foot fence which encircles the whole garden, some got inside during the hard winter of 1981–82 and now they are difficult to get out.

Back across Brown's cascade, the right hand path leads over Pulham's lower waterfall, where there is a fine Monterey pine, its big branches spread like a many pointed star. The cones of this species sometimes stay on the tree for 40 years. To the left the Kalmia Walk leads to the garden's second anomalous feature: two parallel beds of autumn flowering Chinese gentians. No attempt has been made to naturalize them and the beds run between close-mown lawns.

Beyond, the ground dips to a new stream garden – as Archie Skinner calls it, rather than a water garden. Here by contrast, extensive plantations of different hostas, primulas, primroses, irises and Solomon's Seal will presently naturalize and provide weed-supressing groundcover. Here too is the Himalayan lily, *Cardiocrinum giganteum*, which could grow to ten feet if it survives the slugs; and *Gunnera manicata*, huge leafed in summer, appearing in May in the form of lizard-like, spiked shoots. At Sheffield Park these can suffer frost damage because the high ground on all sides of the lakes creates a frost pocket.

The new stream garden, like much else at Sheffield Park, is part of a plan to provide colour and interest throughout the year, not just in May and October. So are new plantations of hydrangeas and the many varieties of water lily which are being encouraged. On any day in summer these will show 500 blooms. 'It's the same in my own garden. I like to say there's no day of the year when I can't pick some interesting flower for a buttonhole.' Gardening is Archie Skinner's hobby as well as his profession. At home he grows anything small which would be lost in Sheffield Park's acres, for example dwarf azaleas and rhododendrons.

His special interest at Sheffield Park is Ghent azaleas. These crosses between *Rhododendron luteum*, the common scented yellow azalea from the Caucusus, and such North American species as *Rhododendron viscosum* were made by a Belgian baker, hence their name. Archie Skinner has 23 hybrids, a lot more than any one else in the country. Once there were as many as a hundred, and he believes the way that many have disappeared shows the need to conserve garden as well as wild species.

These late flowering and colourful azaleas are well labelled, but many of the other trees and plants are not. In part this is policy, to emphasize that Sheffield Park is a landscape garden rather than a collection of specimen plants, but it is also because acquisitive visitors tend to remove the labels.

Successful as he has been in extending the season at Sheffield Park, its autumn colours remain its most impressive feature and October its most colourful time. Deep red Japanese maples, scarlet tupelos (there are over a hundred of these) sweet gums, medlars, swamp cypresses, rowan and birch combine to provide a display which, for variety and brilliance, rivals the woods of New England in the fall.

As head gardener for a large National Trust garden, how free is Archie Skinner to do what he pleases? Totally free to make suggestions, but he would always discuss major changes or extensions with the National Trust's experts. If, after taking advice, Archie Skinner finally decides on some major undertaking, he makes himself wait a year, then consider it again. For a man who observes such cautious principles, the amount he has achieved at Sheffield Park is remarkable.

SEZINCOTE

To anyone not expecting it, there can be few more surprising experiences than the discovery of Sezincote, deep in the Cotswold countryside. A glimpse or two of an improbable green onion dome through the tree tops of the mile-long drive may give a hint of what is to come. But the house itself when it finally appears is still incredible. This golden-stone palace with its peacock windows, Hindu pillars and Muslim minarets belongs in Kashmir not Gloucestershire. Since 1965 it has been given such a perfectly appropriate formal garden that it is hard to believe the two were not planned together.

It was her mother's design, says Mrs Peake who, with her husband David Peake, has lived at Sezincote for the last seven years. 'But my father did the water works. No, he wasn't an engineer, he was a banker. About things like building he was just incredibly competent.' Her father and mother were Sir Cyril and Lady Kleinwort, who bought Sezincote in 1944, at a time when the gardens were in a poor state. Though Mrs Dugdale, the previous owner, had gardened conscientiously, she had lacked the money Sezincote requires. The Kleinworts put all that right. Seldom can banking money have been better spent, for today there can be few more entrancing English gardens, and very few privately-owned ones which are so well maintained.

The history of Sezincote and its gardens goes back 150 years before the Kleinworts bought it from Mrs Dugdale, to the three brothers Cockerell, who had all made money with the East India Company. John Cockerell bought the estate in 1795. In 1798 he left it to his brother, Charles, who employed his other brother, Samuel Pepys Cockerell, as his architect (Samuel Pepys, the diarist, was an ancestor). Two other architects were involved: Thomas Daniell, who designed a number of the garden's Indian features and ornaments, and the better-known Humphry Repton, the leading English landscape gardener to succeed Capability Brown.

How much part Repton played is uncertain. One of his famous overlays (in which he would show a garden as it was, compared to the garden he planned to make) exists for the South Garden, but this garden did not resemble Repton's plan even before Lady Kleinwort transformed it into an Indian garden. And Repton apparently never made one of his 'Red Books' (in which he commonly incorporated his proposals) for Sezincote, nor are there any references to it in his accounts, which he kept meticulously.

Just the same, the siting of the house, backed against a wooded hillside with splendid outlook down a long sloping meadow to a brown lake set among trees at the valley bottom, is Reptonian, and he did indeed plan the

Above: Mrs David Peake, daughter of Sir Cyril Kleinwort, who resurrected Sezincote's gardens. Opposite: Lady Kleinwort's Indian garden, created in 1967 to match the oriental architecture of the 18th century house.

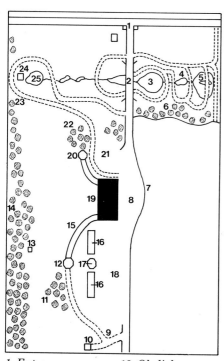

1 Entrance
2 Indian Bridge
3 Snake Pool
4 Rock Pool
5 Island Pool
6 Cedars of
Lebanon
7 Ha-ha
8 Drive
9 Grotto
10 Tennis
Pavilion
11 Copper Beech
12 Pavilion
13 Obelisk
14 Woods
15 Orangery
16 Canal
17 Fountain
18 Indian Garden
19 House
20 Tent Room
21 North Lawn
22 Copper Beech
23 Thornery
24 Temple of
Surya
25 Upper Pool

lake. It was to suggest a river winding among the trees, and this it still does. Beyond the lake the view leads on to Moreton-in-Marsh, a small settlement in the middle distance, then rises to a horizon of Cotswold hills topped at one point by the clump on Bredon. Alongside the drive, the ha-ha seems Reptonian too. It allows large gatherings of the Peakes' cattle to roam to within ten yards of the house. In fact it was created by Sir Cyril Kleinwort to replace an ugly fence.

Here on the drive you are at once aware of another of Sezincote's most fortunate features: its quietness. Some of the finest British gardens are today contaminated by noise. At Sezincote motorways seem a hundred miles away, no flight path passes overhead and agricultural machinery might not have been invented.

Here, too, you get the best overall impression of the various parts of Sezincote's gardens. Stretching down the hillside to the left, in the direction of the lake but not quite reaching it, is the old garden, known as the Thornery. Seen from this point it appears as a long belt of trees with four fine flat-topped cedars (planted 180 years ago when the house was built) as its central feature. Back and to the right is Lady Kleinwort's Indian Garden, enclosed on one side by the house's south facade, on another by a long curving orangery and on a third by a sloping bank on which grow yews and one of Sezincote's several tall copper beeches.

Above the Orangery, an obelisk – which was once its furnace chimney – commemorates Wellington's victories. Through the trees on the bank, more oriental outlines can be glimpsed. These are the farm buildings and date like the house from the early 1800s – the stable yard's wall was intended to suggest the wall of the emperor's harem. As the bank peters out there is a little Indian pavilion, built by Sir Cyril to service a grass tennis court discretely hidden beyond.

The first thing you notice in the Indian Garden itself, which lies at the dell-like centre of so much that is tall and formidable, is its slim Irish yews. In India these would have been cypresses, but yews were suggested as more reliably hardy by the National Trust's garden consultant, Graham Thomas. He was a close friend of the Kleinworts and deserves credit for much that is to be seen here today. Yews require regular attention to maintain their delicacy, Mrs Peake says, tying back a straying branch, but they repay the effort. At their centre a fountain plays, with narrow lily ponds on either side. Cordyline australis stand in containers, and the whole area is divided into four parts, representing symbolically the four rivers of life. The open end of the garden is enclosed by two low holly hedges, one lower than the other. Recently, while Mrs Peake was in London, rabbits began to nibble the holly's stems and reached half way before she returned and had them netted.

Simply as a background for the Indian Garden, the Orangery would deserve its place at Sezincote. In 1965 Sir Cyril had its crumbling stone facade replaced with a Coade stone replica. 'Then a couple of years ago we found it sagging away again,' Mrs Peake says, 'so we had to do the job a second time.' Now it is in good repair, both externally and throughout its long bright curving interior.

Against the back wall are many tender species (it has no regular heating but only a frost excluder operating at 34°F). Several varieties of abutilon are

Sezincote's gardeners: one from the left is Ted Carss, the head gardener, a Geordie trained in the Scilly Isles, who has worked here for 20 years.

particularly fine: *A.* x *suntense* 'Jermyns', *A.* x *milleri*. So is the white passion flower, *Passiflora caerulea* 'Constance Elliott', and a scented white and pale pink *Jasminum polyanthum*. In the small beds flanking its 15 ornamental doorways grow dark red fuchsias.

The North Lawn, which lies on the opposite side of the house, on the way to the Thornery, is smaller and less specifically oriental, but given an Indian flavour by Sir Charles Cockerell's Tent Room which dominates it. Just as the Orangery reaches round and encloses the Indian Garden, so the North Lawn was enclosed by a covered passageway leading to the Tent. Later the passage was enlarged to make a servants' wing, and a large iron bell set on top. When the Kleinworts were told that this was unsafe they moved the bell to its present position on the North Lawn where it could be rung to call Lady Kleinwort from her gardening at the bottom of the Thornery.

Trees and shrubs surround the North Lawn: a large group of cream-variegated dogwood, a purple nut tree, a hybrid thorn, several kinds of variegated holly and another fine copper beech. At Sezincote there are no conventional flower beds, but here as in all its different gardens a sense of being enclosed in the luxuriant growth of large trees. '"If you're buying a property, look at the trees" – that was my father's advice,' Mrs Peake says. 'You can make grass look good with a dressing of nitrogen, but you can't deceive trees.' At the same time you remain aware of the views over great stretches of countryside which are only a few paces away.

At the far end of the North Lawn rare and interesting trees stand on all sides, and the Thornery lies close ahead. Here, at its top, is the highest of a series of pools which descend the hillside, each connected to the one below by a narrow stream or small cascade, so forming the valley's watery core. Water is a recurring feature in the garden, in imitation of the way Indian gardeners value it in that dry subcontinent. Above the top pool it emerges in a natural spring, which also supplies twenty cottages on the estate. 'The water board tell us we should all be dead,' says Mrs Peake. 'They want to give us their chlorinated stuff.'

But the water doesn't naturally stay above ground. To keep it there is a

Below: Luxuriant planting along the stream bed of the Thornery, created with the house around 1800. Right: The Orangery, built at the same time, which encircles Lady Kleinwort's Indian garden to its south.

In the Thornery, left: water-loving plants around the Rock Pool. Right: the temple of Surya above the upper pool. Below: the Snake Pool with primulas, St John's wort and metal snake which refused to spout for the Prince Regent.

continual struggle. The upper pool has been concreted. The lake gives trouble too, because in places it is above the level of the surrounding land. 'We tried sheet polythene sandwiched between two layers of brick blocks,' Mrs Peake says, 'but it's creeping under that too.'

The pools in the Thornery show no sign of the hydraulic problem they present. Above the clear grey water of the highest, the Indian god Surya stands in a little stone temple. By its edge huge shells lie at the mouths of a number of small grottoes and yellow helianthemum grow on the rocks above. Behind stand more fine trees, one of which, in July, makes the garden's most spectacular feature. It appears to be a 40-foot-high pink and white rose tree, but is in fact a yew, totally enveloped in the roses 'Kiftsgate' and 'Paul's Himalayan Musk'. Here too is the Persian ironwood, *Parrotia persica*, a well-grown hardy palm, and one of the weeping beeches, now nearly 40 years old, which were the first trees the Kleinworts planted at Sezincote.

The planting round the pools and connecting stream increases in lushness as it descends. Big clumps of bamboo, tied at the waist like giant corn stooks, add to the tropical effect. Another clump is of the less common Chilean bamboo, *Chusquea couleou*, with its curious leaf-tufted stems. Below the second pool there are fine Chinese hydrangeas (*Hydrangea sargentiana*), over seven feet tall.

Here the stream with stepping stones passes under the bridge which carries the main drive to the house. Immediately below, it reaches the Snake Pool. From a central island a three-headed metal snake rises eight feet up a dead yew trunk. The snake can spout water, and is said to have been hurriedly positioned and set spouting for the visit of the Prince Regent to Sezincote in 1806, but to have stopped when it saw him because it disapproved of his private life. A less improbable tradition suggests that Sezincote confirmed him in his plans for the Brighton Pavilion, which he began to build eight years later. Today the snake can still spout, but usually doesn't because it requires all the water which would otherwise create the stream.

By the Snake Pool yellow St John's wort grows to the waterside, and the snake's tail on the island climbs from a yellow sea of *Primula florindae*, the summer flowering Chinese cowslip. Below the pool a weeping cherry is underplanted with *Primula* 'Garryarde Guinevere', the blue-pink primrose with a golden eye.

Next comes the Rock Pool, the planting still increasing in luxuriance. Here are massed *Hosta sieboldiana* and five-foot clumps of *Peltiphyllum peltatum*. Sezincote's four Lebanon cedars stand close to one side. They have lost limbs, but survived the 1981 snows better than many cedars in Gloucestershire because tree surgeons had recently thinned out their foliage to allow snow to pass through. The time will come when they must be replaced, and after about a dozen failures Mrs Peake has at last managed to propagate several young cedars which grow nearby. Here too is a fine dawn redwood (*Metasequoia glyptostroboides*), the tree which was only known about from fossils till 1941 when one was found in China and its seeds distributed around the world.

Opposite and a little below is a weeping hornbeam, believed to be the largest in the country. Its ancient branches are supported with props, but it seems in good health. Just the same, Mrs Peake has successfully propagated successors. 'If it's the largest in the country, it stands to reason that it must be near the end of its life.'

The valley opens a little at last and ends with the Island Pool. The island itself is covered with prostrate junipers, and trees surround the pool. Close to the water is a little contorted willow and further back a many-stemmed cedar, and a Noble Fir (*Abies procera*). There are also some improbable clumps of rhododendron in a small area said to be lime-free, unlike the rest of the garden. Ted Carss, the Geordie from the Scilly Isles who has been Sezincote's head gardener for 20 years, is not so sure.

'I don't like to contradict,' he says, deferring loyally to this family tradition, 'but I have me doubts, let's put it that way.' Loyalty is the quality Mrs Peake values most in Ted Carss and his two under gardeners. If this can be judged by results she has it.

'But we are conservers, not creators,' Mrs Peake says. At Sezincote, it is *she* who does the practical work of conserving, not only the gardens but a 3500-acre estate as well. Her husband, a banker, spends five days a week in London. 'Last week-end I actually made him do six hours weeding,' she says. 'That was a triumph. People ask why, with a place like Sezincote, he doesn't live here all the time. They don't understand that without what he earns in London we couldn't keep it going.'

Slightly built, constantly active, Mrs Peake is at one moment instructing Ted Carss about the suppression of Sezincote's rabbits, at the next moment showing a party of 25 visitors round the house, then driving about the estate planting notices to advertise the next open day. Mid-afternoon, she is knee deep in the hostas of the Thornery, filling plastic buckets with weeds. Clover, her black and white cat, follows her about the garden. 'She's good company when I'm working – except when she brings me one of her horrid trophies.'

Mrs Peake likes to work in the gardens not just to help the gardeners but because she finds it the only satisfactory way to check the health of her plants. 'No one's going to walk round a garden examining them in proper detail, but if you're pulling out weeds around them you can't help it.'

As a child she wasn't a gardener, and though she was brought up at Sezincote she assumed that one of her two elder sisters would inherit it. Living here after the war she enjoyed the freedom of this big estate and remembers how she and her sisters would dam and divert the stream in the Thornery – an activity which now seems sacriligious – but she also remembers how lonely she was, isolated here when petrol was rationed. She eventually came to live at Sezincote out of a sense of duty. 'I don't know what would have happened to the place. It's too small for an institution and the National Trust wouldn't have it because we wouldn't open at week-ends.'

Now that it is her own, Sezincote has captivated her. 'It's such a happy place to live and work,' she says. And gardening expertise has emerged which she never realized she had. 'How do I know that you must cut down the ornamental rhubarb's stems as soon as they've flowered? I suppose some time my mother must have told me.' This year she and her husband plan to go to Kashmir where they will be able to check their Indian garden in Gloucestershire against the gardens of the Emperor Babur.

DRUMMOND CASTLE

The great parterre at Drummond Castle is unique in Britain, this at least is certain. Such a creation on the continent would be remarkable enough but a formal and elaborately patterned garden on such a scale in Perthshire, 40 miles north west of Edinburgh, within sight of the Grampian mountains, is astonishing. As so often with British gardens, who made it and when is not certain. A pair of copper beeches were reputedly planted by Queen Victoria in 1842 – the spade she used is preserved in the castle museum. Paintings of this occasion show that by then the parterre existed in a form not too different from today's, but Lord Ancaster, whose ancestors have owned Drummond Castle since the 15th century, doubts whether she came specially to celebrate the garden's completion. 'It was part of her Scottish tour. In her journal she describes Drummond's rooms as nice but pokey.'

These were not improved till two generations later when a fire destroyed a large part of the 17th-century dwelling house. Two paintings which hang in the cloakroom at Drummond show Sir Charles Barry's proposals for transforming castle and house into a Moorish palace. Lord Willoughby had by then rejected these but he did rebuild the top two stories of the old castle, and almost certainly laid out the parterre.

Best evidence for this is a coloured plan, also at Drummond, by the son of Lord Willoughby's factor, showing the complete layout, its faded date reading either 1832 or 1838. A painting, of a slightly earlier date, shows the terraces below the castle, but only what appears to be a wooden palisade crossing the area now occupied by the parterre. A number of descriptions of the early 19th century also suggest that until 1820 it did not exist.

This great work was probably therefore carried out some time in the 1820s or 1830s. As for what garden, if any, had ever existed here, there is written evidence that John Drummond, second Earl of Perth made a garden in 1630. A clump of old yews bordering the parterre to the east could have been planted at that time. And some of the old copper beeches across the valley seem to date from the 18th century, but no more is known.

Although the parterre in outline, together with many of its statues, is about 150 years old, throughout the 19th and much of the 20th centuries it was very differently planted. It included typical large Victorian herbaceous borders, and its clean lines were obscured by dense shrubberies. Lord Ancaster remembers these from before the war. He also remembers how much work clipping them required, and that during the war they got out of hand. A photograph of 1942 shows only a tiny centre circle round the sundial surviving. Elsewhere a few isolated clipped trees stand in what looks like a

Above: Lord Ancaster, who remade the parterre at Drummond Castle. Left: 'Iceberg' roses surround a pool, central feature of the west end of the parterre framed here by the castle's arch.

1 Pond
2 Castle (the
Dwelling House)
3 The Old Castle
4 Terraces
5 Sun Dial
6 Vegetable
Garden

DRUMMOND CASTLE

ploughed field. When the war was over Lord and Lady Ancaster had almost entirely to recreate the parterre. Its many box hedges were planted again with cuttings taken from the few which remained.

Visitors approach Drummond Castle along a mile of drive through parkland, then enter the gardens from the cobbled courtyard between the old castle and the 17th-century dwelling house. At this point they step out onto the highest terrace with the whole 13-acre parterre spread below them. Photographs can give an impression of its size but fail to suggest the drop from castle to parterre. Because of its situation, Drummond Castle is sometimes compared to Powis Castle in Wales (see page 27), and they are indeed similar, though Powis's position is even more dramatic. But the real difference between the two is that at Powis the terraces are everything, and the parterre if it ever existed is a lawn, while at Drummond the parterre not only survives but catches the whole attention. 'The nice thing about this garden,' says Lord Ancaster – who is no longer young – 'is that you can see every part of it without taking a step out of doors.' The south windows of his library (a far from pokey room since the dwelling house was extended six feet to the west by the first Earl of Ancaster) give him a complete aerial view.

After the first impact and wonder, one pleasure in looking down on such a formal garden consists in picking out the different elements in its pattern, somewhat in the way instruments can be picked out from a symphony. Purple prunuses, clipped to balloon shape on four-foot trunks, are dotted evenly about the whole area. Small golden Irish yews stand in circles, suggesting Druid rings. 'We have terrible trouble with the snow crushing those,' Lord Ancaster says. And there are bigger hollies and cupressus, and many acers, either standing individually or planted in curves.

Beech hedges circle some of the statues. But it is the many low box hedges which form the more detailed parts of the pattern, in particular two crowns on either side of the central circle. Everywhere there are statues, brought at different times from Italy and for the most part representing Greek or Roman mythological figures. 'That one's meant to be rather good,' Lord Ancaster says, pointing down to a marble figure sitting on a globe.

The boldest lines of the design are three parallel paths which reach away from the terraces to the far hedge, and two diagonals running from corner to corner, appropriately representing St Andrew's cross. For edging, the aim is to use white and grey plants but precisely which is still a matter of experiment. 'We've tried santolina of various sorts,' Lord Ancaster says. Most recently euryops has been used.

"Euryops grows fine for a few years,' says Islay Allan, the short, wiry-haired Scot who has been Lord Ancaster's head gardener for 18 years. 'Then it just dies out. It's not the soil, but the nature of the plant.' He plans to return to anaphalis, used more successfully before.

Some of the intricate spaces among the box hedges are gravelled, though these need hand weeding for it is risky to use weed killer in such small areas. Elsewhere lavender is successful, but some experimental helianthomum less so. The decorative tops of the crowns are planted with red and white pelargoniums. 'They take a lot of work. And a lot of greenhouse space,' Islay Allan says. In general the aim is to use as little bedding as possible. He has only three assistant gardeners to manage not only the parterre but an extensive vegetable garden and several large greenhouses.

Beyond the crowns come circular beds of roses – 'All Gold', and 'Iceberg'. Small triangular beds radiating from the centre are now planted alternatively with white alyssum and blue ageratum. 'They use it in every municipal garden,' Lord Ancaster says, 'but it seems to hold the garden together. When Scottish nationalism was so strong I had them planted red, white and blue – red salvias, blue lobelia and white alysum.'

At the very centre stands the garden's strangest monument, a sundial pillar with sixty faces, some telling local time, some the time in different capital cities of the world. It was made by John Mylne, Master Mason to Charles I, and stands on a circle of pebbles laid in a pattern of black and white waves. 'From the Drummond coat of arms,' Lord Ancaster says. 'For the three rivers of Perthshire, that's one theory. Or because an 11th-century ancestor rescued a Hungarian princess from a storm in the Firth of Forth.' The Scottish king married the princess and rewarded this ancestor with lands, offices, a coat of arms and the family name of Drummond.

When Lord Ancaster recreated the great parterre after the last war he was uncertain whether to use gravel or grass as its overall background, and in a central section he experimented with an area of each. This is how they have remained, but elsewhere clipped trees stand on lawn and the paths are grass.

In autumn the parterre's many acers turn brilliant reds and crimsons, and give the colour which its flowers provide in summer, changing the emphasis of the pattern. It changes again in winter, when Lord Ancaster considers it most remarkable, its dozens of clipped trees rising from a blanket of snow.

Tall beech hedges bound the parterre to east and south. Further south, where the land dips into the valley, are Islay Allan's caged vegetables, and his greenhouses, filled with brilliantly colourful pelargoniums, begonias, coleus and many others. Here he also grows peaches and apricots, and there are productive white and black vines. Red spider on the peaches, a recurring pest, he controls by introducing predator wasps. Apples against the walls above the vegetable garden crop heavily – Coxes and a number of Laxton varieties.

Across the Drummond Burn, which runs below the vegetable garden, the ground rises and is well wooded, with a wide grass avenue up the centre. From the castle terraces the trees of this wood appear deceptively foreshortened, but the tall copper beeches along its lower edge are considerably taller than Queen Victoria's pair in the parterre, and cannot be less than 200 years old. A statue half way up the avenue is known to the family as Dagon, though Lord Ancaster considers this powerful figure, an eagle beside one leg, to be more probably Apollo. From here you have another view of the parterre, seen this time from the south with castle and dwelling house standing formidably above it.

From here too there is an overall view of the terraces, and of the hillsides to either side of them, where Portugal laurels – 17 on one side, 12 on the other – have been clipped to the shape of giant mushrooms. Until the war there were also Portugal laurels on the steep bank below the terraces, underplanted with common laurel, but the work of clipping these on such a

Detail of parterre: the box-edged beds are infilled with lavender.

Overleaf: the great 13-acred parterre at Drummond was probably created in the 1830s. Here it is viewed centrally from the terraces which rise dramatically above.

slope was heavy and the bank is now patterned with shrubs and other cover plants in large patches – purple and green *Cotinus coggygria*, cotoneaster, potentilla, *Vinca major* 'Variegata' and heathers – the steps up the centre lined with dark red fuchsia, the outer edges with tall white yuccas.

Bear away to the right to return towards the terraces and you pass first a small green hill with several tall conifers (a well-grown Lebanon cedar and a silver fir among them) underplanted with rhododendrons, then reach a castellated bridge which crosses the so-called pond, though in summer it is dry. Close above is the large clump of clipped yew which possibly dates from the early 17th-century garden. Islay Allan and his two assistants clip this 30-foot clump with no outside help, clambering over the top with ladders. A path now winds uphill to an area he has recently cleared to the bare rock and planted as a rockery. But it is a rockery with a problem. Nearby, a small oak tree is the roosting place of 18 peacocks. Colourful and appropriate as these seem when pecking about among the box-edged beds of the parterre, they are not Islay Allan's friends. 'Anything small they just trample into the ground.'

As a result his rockery is more of a shrubbery. Here he has small conifers, rhododendrons, hebes, fuchsias, red berberis and numerous others. 'That's quite a bonny thing,' he says about an abelia blossoming profusely in pink and white.

The path curves up to a grass court at the side of the dwelling house where white hydrangeas prosper, though other varieties on the terraces have proved less hardy. At the centre of the court is a stone pool, with central pillar surmounted by a stone dog. The dog is from the Drummond coat of arms, Lord Ancaster says, and no special breed, though there used to be a Willoughby pug. A verse is inscribed at the pool's side in Latin and English. 'When Trevor-Roper came he said the Latin grammar was all wrong,' Lord Ancaster says, 'but I've never put it right.' In English it reads:

> *May this pure fount perpetual streams supply*
> *To every thirsty soul that passes by*
> *May these shrubs flourish as the waters run*
> *Unchanged by winter's frost or summer's sun.*

The pool is dry.

Inevitably the terrace beds themselves take second place to the parterre at Drummond, but they are well planted with rugosa roses, mauve and white buddleias, huge clumps of bronze fennel, sedums, acanthus and agapanthus lilies, which do well here. Escallonias and desfontaineas thrived for a time, but have failed in recent hard winters. 'It's too far north for them.' Islay Allan considers. From the highest terrace 12 white marble busts look down on the parterre.

Climb again to the entrance gate, where in the courtyard between castle and dwelling house there are three sorbus, brilliant with scarlet berries in autumn, as everywhere in Scotland. Then look back again, first to the parterre, then to the wood across the valley, then above to a little gardener's cottage, so appropriately set on the hillside and attended by the odd cow that Kent or Brown might have put it there.

But the grander views are down the valley to the east where, below cloudscapes of black and white cumulus, two round hills in the distance are 25 miles away beyond Perth; and to the north where the whole skyline is filled by the dark and massive Grampians.

Shortly before 1820, Dr John Macculloch wrote to Sir Walter Scott that Drummond was a wilderness from which even the owners were excluded, but that 'Art might accomplish in a few brief years all which is here demanded and render Drummond Castle the pride of the Lowlands and the third jewel, at least, of Scotland.' Art and a 20th-century shortage of labour have done no less.

Statues from many periods, imported in Victorian times, are features of Drummond's parterre.

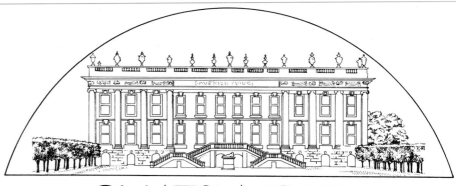

CHATSWORTH

On a Sunday afternoon in summer, when Matlock Band plays in the bandstand, the grounds of the Duke of Devonshire's palatial house at Chatsworth in Derbyshire seem pleasure gardens in the old sense, even if the company enjoying them is less aristocratic than once. Lovers sit side by side on the grassy slopes, small children bathe on the upper steps of M. Grillet's great Cascade and teenage girls with rolled jeans scare themselves by paddling near the lip of its lowest fall. This is the way the present Duchess of Devonshire, youngest of the well-known Mitford sisters, likes to see her gardens give pleasure.

Not that Chatsworth was always exclusive before she and her husband opened it to the public in 1949. In the 1840s when the head gardener Joseph Paxton completed his plant house here, it caused so much interest that 10,000 people a year came to see it and a special railway station was built to receive them. Paxton is still the best-remembered gardener to have worked at Chatsworth, but a gardening tradition began here many years before the sixth duke employed him, and has been fully maintained by the present duke and duchess.

'We've become rather stuck,' the Duchess says modestly, ignoring the five major features they have added during the last 30 years. 'Perhaps Chatsworth should have some new owners.' The duke is content with the theory that gardeners have five ages in which their interests progress from flowers, to flowering shrubs, to autumn colours, to leaves, to the backs of leaves. Today he surprises friends by expecting them to admire the velvety fur below hydrangea leaves.

Now that the plant house has been pulled down, no changes or additions can take away from M. Grillet's Cascade its position as Chatsworth's most splendid feature. This giant's water staircase can be seen the moment you turn from the public road to cross the grassy park where thousands of sheep graze, a bright streak on the valley side above the house. It is one of the oldest features to survive, created as part of the first duke's water garden in 1696. This also contained at least nine fountains, but only one, the Sea Horse Fountain, remains. At about the same time, George London of the well-known Chelsea firm, London and Wise, laid out elaborate parterres around the house.

Fifty years later Lancelot (Capability) Brown was the next important gardener to work at Chatsworth. He left the Cascade untouched on its hillside above and to the east of the house, and concentrated his attention on the park to the west, the direction in which the house was now made to face.

Opposite: pillars and roses in Chatsworth's west parterre, survival of its seventeenth century formal gardens.

70

Here, he brought the park up to the walls of the house and deepened and altered the course of the River Derwent which flowed below. Philistine though Brown may sometimes be considered, the great area of parkland which he established continues to provide the house with a splendidly expansive setting, whether seen from the approach drive, or from the house itself. James Paine's bridge over the Derwent, built during the same period and set at a perfect angle, provides the required architectural feature in so much contrived naturalness.

An uneventful period followed till, in 1826, the sixth duke employed Paxton, then a young man of 23 whom he had met in London, to be his head gardener. Paxton worked for the bachelor duke for 32 years, only leaving when the duke died. In his plant house he was the first gardener in Britain to make the great Amazonian waterlily, *Victoria amazonica*, flower. His daughter appeared on one of its leaves at the Great Exhibition of 1851. He also built the 'Conservative Cages' along the garden's south-facing walls, installed the Emperor Fountain, and introduced an assembly of huge boulders half-way up the valley side, which he named after such well-known figures of the day as the Duke of Wellington. For good measure he created the 'Sunian pillar' by importing blocks of marble from the temple of Minerva Sunias in Greece, on which his employer's statue now stands.

Calm again followed, and for nearly 100 years 80 gardeners sustained the gardens under successive dukes, making no major changes apart from the ninth duke's demolition in 1920 of Paxton's plant house. Eventually,

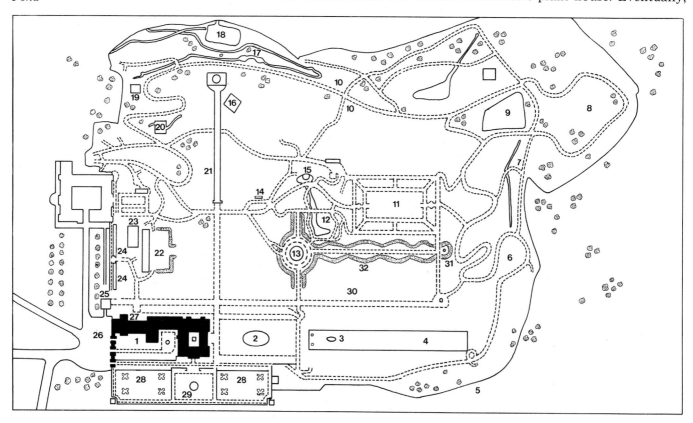

during the Second World War, a girls' school occupied the house, and the lawns reverted to long grass in which heather sprouted.

There is evidence of the gardening enthusiasm which the present duke and duchess brought to Chatsworth before you enter the gardens themselves. On the grassy slopes around the car park the Duke has planted bulbs which provide a continuous display from January to June – 16,000 in total, he estimates, including 60 varieties of crocus. They are now so thick underground that you can't dig to plant more without slicing those already there.

The entrance to the gardens proper is through another 17th-century survival, the temple of Flora. From here the Broad Walk stretches ahead for three furlongs, ending distantly with an urn to the memory of the seventh duchess against the skyline. This wide gravel walk is the axis to which the rest of the garden can best be related.

At once, as you advance along it, you pass below a complex of glass houses on the hillside above, and soon afterwards below the bandstand. At this point the Broad Walk is beset with problems for the Duchess. Her sister tells her that the multi-coloured roses which edge it to the right should all be ripped out and replaced with white ones. The golden yews, alternating with Irish yews, on the left, which she believes provide brightness under the grey Derbyshire skies, she is sure her son will remove. As for the newly-laid orange gravel of the walk itself, the contractor assures her it will mellow. She hopes he is right.

As soon as the Broad Walk passes beyond the house, two of the garden's

Above: gunnera and primulas in the Strid, Chatsworth's water garden. Below: Dennis Hopkins, head gardener at Chatsworth where he has worked for forty-three years.

*The Duke of Devonshire, an enthusiast
for greenhouse plants and tropical fruits.*

principal wonders appear. To the left you look directly up the great Cascade. Its size is astonishing: there are 24 falls, each 24 feet wide. So, too, is the engineering skill which makes the water flow continuously and evenly over every step, creating the water-staircase effect. At the top the Cascade emerges from another temple, around which woods – and in their season tall banks of mauve ponticum rhododendrons – finally close. Higher again, trees rise to the skyline. It is hard to believe that these dense and apparently natural woods, which stretch along the hilltop in both directions, were only planted in Paxton's time. When M. Grillet worked here, the hilltop was bare, like most hills in Derbyshire's Peak District. For years the surroundings of the Cascade were considered excessively rocky.

At this point along the Broad Walk the Sea Horse Fountain is close below. Its name refers to Cibber's sea horses round its pool. Today it is formally enclosed by two long avenues of pleached limes, planted by the present duke and duchess in 1952, some years before they finally took up residence at Chatsworth. But the second wonder is the Emperor Fountain, lying further ahead, which dwarfs the older fountain and competes for attention with the Cascade. It rises from a rectangle of water known as the Canal Pond – once used to make ice in the winter for summer use. The fountain was added to celebrate the visit of the Czar Nicholas to Chatsworth in 1844. Even at half cock, its single jet is remarkable. At full power it rises high above the mature limes which enclose the Pond, and reaches a height of 290 feet. The Czar never saw it for he cancelled his visit, so now it displays itself for today's special occasions: the visits of television filming parties.

For the whole of the rest of the Broad Walk the Canal Pond lies below – 315 yards in length. If you stand centrally at the pond's far end and look back, past the Emperor Fountain, past the Sea Horse Fountain, towards the house's formal rectangular south facade, the ground between has been land-scaped so that the house now seems to rise from the water.

It is best from here to climb in a wide half-circle through the woodlands Paxton planted, and eventually reach a point above the great Cascade. The path passes a deep valley of azaleas (Ghent, double Ghent, and Mollis), a wild ravine of harebells, *Inula bookeri* and other wild or naturalized flowers, Paxton's pinetum (he was the first in England to plant many North American conifers), and the Grotto Pond with lilies, bamboo, broom and witch hazel overlooked by the Duchess Georgiana's stone grotto. Where it crosses the upper hillside there are encouraging milestones, *e.g.* '1 mile from main front door, if Pinetum included add $\frac{1}{4}$ mile.' From among the trees on either side the continuous sound of running streams mixes with the distant rush of the waters of the fountains and Cascade which are out of sight in the valley below. Higher up in the woods are the reservoirs which provide their water. The force of gravity, unassisted by any engine, powers them.

From the top of the Cascade, beside its gushing temple, the view across the Derwent Valley is magnificent. Below, offset to the right, stands the house, massively formal with its roof top balustrade. A little beyond in the valley is the steeple of the church of Edensor emerging from among trees. This village Paxton designed too, after removing it from its previous position in the park. Beyond again, across a great sweep of countryside the ground rises to hills which were also forested along their crest in the 19th century.

If you descend on the grassy slope beside the Cascade and turn back the way you came you discover among tall hedges a series of enclosures which form the garden's secret core. No statistics successfully suggest their size, but in the biggest are the surviving remains of Paxton's wonderful plant house. All that is left is a stone parapet wall enclosing an area in which it would be possible to fit four tennis courts. Today massed michaelmas daisies and dahlias for late summer grow at one end, massed lupins for May and June at the other, while in the centre the recently retired comptroller, Dennis Fisher, made a yew-hedged maze for the present duke. The public can peer at it over the walls but may not enter because they get lost, and force their way through its hedges. The Duchess has considered reinforcing these with barbed wire, but fears for visitors' clothes, while her head gardener fears for his mechanical shears.

Nearby is the Ring Pond, surrounded by a double ring of fastigiate yews, then by a circle of 10-foot beech hedge. Perhaps this hedge gave the Duchess the idea for another of her introductions: two serpentine beech hedges which swell away from each other then close again for 100 yards as they ascend towards the statue of the sixth duke on its pillar of Sunian marble. The serpentine hedges are now as tall as those surrounding the pond. Elsewhere (to the west of the house) she laid out hedges of another sort: low ones of box which outline the ground plan of Chiswick House, once another Devonshire property. Landscape gardening, rather than plant gardening, is her enthusiasm, and she is excited by the sort of projects she describes as 'enormous gangs of people doing wonderful things.'

Paxton's great rocks lie close above the Ring Pond, overlooking a small watery jungle known as the Strid, named after a similar feature in Wharfedale near Bolton Abbey. Water flows over and around them, and the banks of the Strid itself, an L-shaped pond, are thickly planted with bamboo and many other water-loving plants. About such areas of lushness the Duke quotes Cecil Beaton: 'A good garden should be like a fat woman struggling into her stays.'

A little to one side is Chatsworth's greatest oddity, a metal fountain in the shape of a tree, known as the Willow Tree Fountain. It is hardly beautiful in itself, but said to be a sprouting wonder when it works. Lately it has had plumbing problems.

The way back towards the entrance now goes by tunnel below the Cascade (once used to bring coal to the furnaces of Paxton's plant house), passes the bandstand and arrives at the greenhouses. Of these, John Pearce's, built in 1970, is the strangest. Tall steel poles and stainless steel wires support it from the outside, leaving the inside entirely clear for plants.

Dennis Hopkins, head gardener at Chatsworth, where he has worked since he left school in 1939, has the keys. The problem with hothouses in public gardens, he explains, is that people want to go inside but can't be allowed to. Nor is it easy to make what they can see by peering look interesting. In the cool end of the house the Duchess has solved this problem with a long arch of brilliant fuchsias.

This end, as well as the two hotter sections, is largely given over to semitropical and tropical fruit, about which the Duke is enthusiastic. Lemons, oranges, apricots, grapes, bananas, pomegranates and limes all fruit successfully. So do pawpaws, of which, Dennis Hopkins says, His Grace is particularly fond, but he doubts whether the loquats (*Eriobotrya japonica*) will ever fruit – a not uncommon problem with tropical fruits grown from seed in greenhouse conditions.

Deeply sunk into the ground of the tropical section is a pool where one day Paxton's giant waterlily will flower again. Replacements are due from Birmingham and Australia, but the latest seedlings suffered in the post and failed.

More elegant if less ingenious than the new glass house are Paxton's 'Conservative cages'. These line the garden's south-facing wall, tall and narrow, and still house the fruit trees and camellias for which they were designed. Central are two magnificent camellias (*C. reticulata* 'Captain Rawes' and *C. alba plena*), now 140 years old, their trunks like those of trees.

A garden owner's relationship with the head gardener is a problem, the Duchess admits. Of course he must be given some independence or he has no pride in his work. But he must also be guided. The splendid gardens at Chatsworth are evidence of how successfully the Devonshires co-operate with Dennis Hopkins to solve this problem.

Neo-classical statue, typical of late seventeenth century garden design: in the background, M. Grillet's Great Cascade. It has 24 falls each 24 feet wide and is fed by gravity from reservoirs in the hills above.

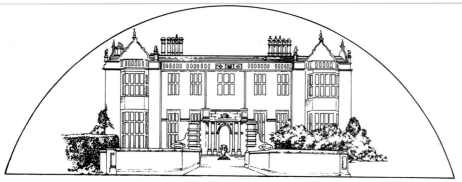

ARLEY HALL

The eight acres of formal garden at Arley Hall, near Knutsford in Cheshire, are best known for their herbaceous border, said to be the oldest in Britain, predating William Robinson's gardening theories by many years. They also have a unique avenue of gigantic cylindrical holm oaks. The history of Arley goes back to the 15th century – near the gardens there is a fine tithe barn of cruck construction which dates from 1470 at the latest. But the gardens themselves, including their two best-known features, were a 19th-century creation.

In 1813 the property passed from the direct line of descent to a nine-year-old great nephew, Rowland Egerton (to whose name the family name of Warburton was added). He grew to be a man of talents. With only the help of a local architect he took down the previous house and replaced it with the present neo-Jacobean mansion in dark red brick patterned with purple. As a keen fox-hunting man he wrote hunting songs and other verse which has recently been rediscovered. And from 1831 onwards he laid out the gardens at Arley in a way which was original for their period.

Gardening at Arley is not easy. 'With our cold Cheshire winds and water-logged soil we could never be a plantsman's garden,' says Lady Ashbrook, great granddaughter of Rowland Egerton-Warburton. 'What we try to be is an all-the-year-round garden of a family home.'

Despite her modesty, Arley was recently one of only two private gardens to be given premier awards in the British Travel Association's Landscape Heritage competition.

'The trouble was, we had no before-and-after photographs,' Viscount Ashbrook says, 'but I rang up the BTA and chatted to the girl for half an hour, and she said she'd enter us. Then we won.' The before-and-after photographs should have shown Arley's Walled Garden, where for 12 years after the war the Ashbrooks struggled to sustain a viable market garden. Today this huge enclosure with its 13-foot brick walls has been turned by Lady Ashbrook into an ornamental garden which competes with Arley's herbaceous border and ilex avenue.

'I always knew the garden had good bones,' Lady Ashbrook says. 'All the time we were growing vegetables I kept nagging at my husband to let us revive it. But I knew it would be a life work, and he was a chartered accountant, working in London. It was a big decision to abandon that. We came here in 1939 but it wasn't till 1960 that I convinced him.'

Arley's herbaceous border is reputedly the oldest in the country.

ARLEY HALL

1 Orchard
2 Walled Garden
3 Vinery
4 Flag Garden
5 Tea room
6 House
7 Chapel
8 Italian Garden
9 Herb Garden
10 Scented Garden
11 Furlong Walk
12 Herbaceous
Border
13 Tea Cottage
14 Sundial Circle
15 Ilex Avenue
16 Rootree
17 Fish Garden
18 Wild Garden
19 Tennis Court
20 Kitchen
Garden

Lady Ashbrook and her son Michael
Flower, to whom she is handing over
Arley's gardens.

The one part of Arley's gardens which has not yet been revived is the Eastern Garden. This was the only part closely connected to the house and was less original for the period. 'It was one of those grandiose Victorian pseudo-Italian gardens which were the fashion then,' Lady Ashbrook says. She remembers it well as a child. Today it is an abandoned expanse of grass, only its surrounding balustrade surviving. The stone-edged pool which was its central feature, Lady Ashbrook removed and placed at the centre of her transformed Walled Garden.

The remaining eight acres of Rowland Egerton-Warburton's garden ('the pleasure gardens, as old people here call them') are triangular, with only the triangle's apex coming close to the house. Here, forming one of the triangle's sides, the Furlong Walk begins. This wide straight pathway, 220 yards long (hence its name) is the feature of Rowland's garden to which all else can be related.

Stand on it and face one way, and you look across the ha-ha which runs beside it for its full length, to green parkland where the lower branches of stately limes have been so evenly nibbled by sheep that they suggest the model trees of a toy farm. Beyond and enclosing the park are dark woods. Face the other way and a succession of paths and avenues between tall yew hedges lead enticingly towards the garden's many enclosures and features.

The first of these paths passes a huge greenhouse (which Lady Ashbrook remembers when it had a curved glass roof, and where figs of a rare deliciousness grow) to the Walled Garden which she transformed in the 1960s. 'By then it was full of dreadful things like runner beans and pyrethrum – and bindweed,' she says. Its spaciousness is astonishing, and she has encouraged this effect by planting and decorating it with discretion, leaving much open lawn. Lawns of this sort, enclosed by old kitchen garden walls have a special charm, and Arley's competes with a similarly transformed vegetable garden at Rousham.

Lady Ashbrook gives the garden consultant James Russell credit for several of the features which she did introduce. Most notable, around the pool which she took from the Italian garden, are four tall fastigiate beeches. Close by are four stone heraldic beasts, rearing from their haunches. They were taken from the house in 1968 when half of it was demolished.

Around the beeches grow white 'Iceberg' roses and *Alchemilla mollis*. These pure white roses contrast with the Walled Garden's other prominent feature, placed centrally at one end: a bed of rich red 'Rosemary Rose', backed by only slightly less rich *Rosa* 'Bushman's Triumph', and surrounded by mauve catmint (nepeta). Around the walls are informal borders. 'Some things look right here and some don't,' Lady Ashbrook says. 'Delphiniums no, lupins yes. Mainly we use shrubby plants – buddleias, hydrangeas, fuchsias. But it's a wonderful place for growing things because the walls give shelter, and because it was a vegetable garden for so long it has marvellous soil.' Just the same she likes to follow the traditional gardener's adage and plant one specimen where you think it will grow, one where you hope it will and a third where you are convinced it won't. 'The result,' she says, 'is often surprising.'

Taking advantage of the shelter, she has planted against the walls themselves a number of special but risky favourites: *Abutilon vitifolium*,

Hoheria lyallii, Carpentaria californica. Just as she keeps in the borders a connection with the garden's vegetable past with a large patch of edible rhubarb, so there are still fan-trained apples, pears and cherries among the more exotic climbers. The walls are thick as well as tall, some with flues at their centres which were once used to warm them.

You can reach Arley's famous herbaceous border, either directly from the Walled Garden, or by the next turning off the Furlong Walk. A broad grass lawn divides it into two, one side backed against the reverse of the ex-vegetable garden's walls, the other against a yew hedge. On each side the borders themselves are divided into sections by sturdy buttresses of yew, and at many places the yew is topped with ornamental topiary shaped to suggest the pieces of an old-fashioned chess set. The borders to which all this is background justify their reputation. 'So many borders are too narrow,' Lady Ashbrook says. 'You can't have a proper one unless it has depth.' Those at Arley are 14 feet deep on one side, 16 feet deep on the other and 250 feet long.

The rootree at Arley, once a rockery, now a shrub garden where rhododendrons, azaleas and syringas create a small jungle.

The plants rise traditionally from front to back and are kept as far as possible to those which Lady Ashbrook can identify from a painting of the border by George Elgood of 1889. Early in the season she tries to restrict the colour range to blues and pale yellows, but by July such regimentation becomes impossible and giant thistle-like eryngium mix with the strange purple globes of *Allium giganteum*, the always startling heads of red hot poker and, nearer the front, sedums and multicoloured antirrhinums. The view outwards between the borders ends with the park, giving the sense of space which is all the time present at Arley. The view inwards leads to the Alcove, an arched shelter of classical design where you can sit and admire the borders at your ease.

Next along the Furlong Walk comes the Tea Cottage, a small brick and slate, honeysuckle-covered building below a dark yew, near a weeping willow. Inside are inscribed verses by Rowland Egerton-Warburton which he placed below each window of an octagonal tower on the house. Each verse celebrated the wife of a neighbouring landowner who lived in that direction.

Beside the Tea Cottage, Lady Ashbrook made another of her changes, replacing beds of hybrid large-flowered tea roses which never did well here with old-fashioned shrub roses which have flourished and are now among her most cherished plants. Of the many she has planted she finds the delicate pink of *Rosa Sancta* especially appealing. 'They mostly survived our terrible frosts too,' she says. 'The plants we did lose were always those with soggy feet.'

The ten 30-feet-high holm oak cylinders, which now appear to the right, suffered too. All through 1982 they were brown instead of green and seemed to hover between life and death. They were grown from seed, which Lady Ashbrook's great grandfather, who was an enterprising traveller, brought back from the continent. Here too, no doubt, he got the idea for their shape and arrangement; she knows of nothing like them in Britain, though she has heard that there may be a similar avenue somewhere in France.

Finally the Furlong Walk drops into the Sundial circle, Lady Ashbrook's most recent creation. Here species roses surround a sundial set on a clockface of stone. After so much formality the Rootree which lies immediately beyond is a complete contrast. The name no doubt came from a time when this garden was a jungle of old tree roots, and it retains a jungle quality, even if it is now an organized jungle. At first it was a rockery but alpines did not do well in such a shady situation and now there are rhododendrons here, and even more abundant azaleas. A maze of small paths runs among them, at one point reaching a green pool set about with huge-leafed *Peltiphyllum peltatum*, osmunda ferns and foxgloves. Like a true jungle, the smells make an even stronger impression, and in their season the syringas fill the air with a delicious sweetness, while the whole area hums with summer insects.

As a sight the Rootree is most impressive early in the summer, when you can climb a bank at its far end, stand below a yew tree there and look back towards the park. Then it appears as a densely overgrown ravine at your feet, brilliant with the blues of *Rhododendron* 'Blue Tit' and 'Blue Diamond', the pinky whites of *R. Williamsianum* (described by connoisseurs as the

Cheriton of rhododendrons) and the bright orange of *Berberis darwinii*, with many yellow *luteum* azaleas as a background. Surprisingly Lady Ashbrook finds that azaleas, which so often thrive in valleys beside streams, survive drought better than other rhododendrons.

If these are the garden's main features, Arley has many smaller gardens, tucked away like spare rooms among the grander apartments. One of these is the Flag Garden. This small square enclosure was created by Lady Ashbrook's mother to enable her to work close to the house. She was a lady of imagination and, after a notorious local murder, felt that she was dangerously exposed when gardening far away in the Rootree. Today this garden grows mainly cluster-flowered floribunda roses and lavender among its grey paving stones, but a stray heracleum stands six foot tall at the far end. All is so peaceful that a fly catcher may be found using this as a base for his insect forays.

Nearby, the Herb Garden is another small enclosure, where Lady Ashbrook had her own garden as a child. She has always, she says, been a compulsive grower. The stone ornament at its centre she bought more recently from a London antique shop, where the dealer told her that he had carried it down in his own arms from the top of a building being demolished at Piccadilly Circus. Beyond again is a small triangular garden devoted to scented plants. She has been surprised to find it easier to keep a continuous succession of different scents in winter than in summer.

In another area is the Fish Garden, most elegant and formal of all Arley's small enclosures, with lily pond, the statue of a boy with a fish at its centre, and eight neat little clumps of blue *Chamaecyparis* 'Ellwoodii' set around. Along one hedge are the burial stones of Rowland Egerton-Warburton's hunters, inscribed with his rhyming epitaphs. Of Saltfish who died in 1830 he wrote,

> *For hungry worms here lies a dainty dish*
> *Horseflesh by nature and by name Saltfish.*

And of his mare Goldmine in 1872,

> *Goldmine the name my chestnut bore*
> *Once good as gold but current now no more*
> *What of her worth and beauty now remains?*
> *The gold dust only which this grave contains.*

Elderly now, Lady Ashbrook handed over the running of the gardens at Arley a few years ago to her son, Michael Flower. He too was a childhood gardener, but abandoned it for a time, until he was living at home with nothing special to do, and his mother said to him, 'Why don't you clear that bit over there?'

The bit-over-there which Michael Flower began to clear in 1969 lies on the opposite side of the house from the formal gardens, and is reached below a clump of yews which have spread their lower branches along the ground for 30 feet in every direction. Here, as a boy not long out of school, he felled a motley plantation of silver birch saplings and cleared a tangle of brambles and fallen oaks to plant a small corner with such hardy hybrid rhododendrons as 'Pink Pearl'. Today the Grove, as it is now called, extends to five acres and is still growing.

Where the ground has been cleared, many varieties of specimen maple and prunus have been planted. 'I just love growing trees,' Michael Flower says. Here, too, are slim incense cedars and a few young Lebanon cedars, ready for the time when four or five ancient ones which date from his great-great-grandfather's time, finally fall. But on the whole the plantings are deciduous. Among other curiosities is a specimen of the prehistoric tulip tree, *Liriodendron chinense*. The trees are well spaced about roughly mown grass and he intends the Grove to provide an area where visitors can enjoy themselves with more freedom than they usually show in the formal gardens.

Further into the woodland, Michael Flower has cleared a churchlike glade, and planted little half circles of rhododendrons along its length, suggesting side chapels. A fine oak stands centrally at the far end. His next plan is a parallel glade running back towards the house. 'Otherwise they get to the oak and don't know what to do,' he says. 'I'm not sure where I'll stop. When the money runs out, I suppose.'

Returning, he stands looking over the gate at the meadow encircled by stone balustrade which was once the Eastern Garden, and admits that to turn this again into an Italian garden is an almost irresistable temptation. 'We need it too,' he says. 'Now the house is open to the public, they ought to be able to look down on a garden, not a meadow.' Like his mother, providing Arley's visitors with what they will appreciate has come to seem a justification for the work and planning which the gardens require. 'And our visitors do appreciate it,' Lady Ashbrook says. 'They've paid to enter, but they still come and thank me. I've made so many good friends.'

Arley Hall's walled garden. Opposite: 'Rosemary Rose' and cat mint at one end. Below: the central pool with 'Iceberg' roses, Alchemilla mollis, *fastigiate beeches and heraldic beasts.*

LEONARDSLEE

'A view is worth a thousand blooms, a lake is worth ten thousand.' So says Robin Loder, who at the age of 38 began recently to manage Leonardslee, probably the most splendid woodland garden in England and one of the finest in the world. Standing by the table made from a Sussex millstone which commemorates his great-grandfather, Sir Edmund Loder, who created the garden, he points down the valley to the string of lake-like 'hammer ponds' which lie at its bottom. 'Last December when I took charge that view was entirely blocked by a huge *Chamaecyparis obtusa* 'Crippsii'. It had to come down. The gardeners were horrified. All their work is about preserving trees. How could they destroy such a fine one? But when it had gone they agreed that I'd been right.'

He explains it another way: 'If the average age of the shrubs and trees at Leonardslee is 80 to 100 years, and the garden is 82 acres, then each year roughly an acre of ground has to be cleared and replanted. Sometimes a storm takes the decision for us and brings down a great beech, so we have to clean up the devastation. More often we must decide on our projects. This year we're clearing the lower valley to build another dam. That's where the beavers used to live. They died out in 1947.'

Beavers were only one of the exotic animals which his great-grandfather, Sir Edmund, brought to Leonardslee. Before 1900 coypu, capybara (gigantic South American guinea-pigs), ibex, mouflon, Japanese deer, Indian blackbuck, Tasmanian wallaby and even full size kangaroo could be found scuttling, grazing or leaping about its woodland glades. He won prizes for the best private menagerie in Europe. All the animals were either sold after his death in 1920 or died out later. Except *perhaps* the wallaby, Robin Loder admits mysteriously. But he prefers not to expand on this subject.

Sir Edmund was a true Victorian, with the money to devote his life entirely to what interested him and the intelligence and energy to pursue each hobby till he achieved excellence at it. Apart from animal collecting, these included astronomy, colour photography, rifle shooting and, above all, big game hunting and deer stalking. In the Scottish forest of Amat which he regularly rented, when filling a few spare moments by digging up flower specimens with his pocket trowel, he overheard the stalker say to the pony man, 'That scratching has begun again.' It was his scratching which in the end predominated. In his previous home in Northamptonshire he had already tried to make a garden, though without great success. Only in 1888 when he bought Leonardslee from his wife's family did he find the perfect setting for what is today his best-remembered interest.

Above: Robin Loder, who has recently taken over the gardens at Leonardslee from his father, Sir Giles Loder. Opposite: the view down Mossy Ghyl.

LEONARDSLEE

1 Entrance Drive
2 South Lawn
3 Loden Garden
4 Middle Walk
5 Dell
6 Magnolia Cambellii
7 Memorial Table
8 Rustic Bridge
9 Coronation Garden
10 Mossy Ghyl
11 Waterfall
12 New Lake
13 Camellia Grove
14 Rock Garden and Wishing Well
15 Temperate Greenhouse
16 House
17 Hammer Pond

Sir Edmund Loder, big game hunter, rhododendron enthusiast, creator of Leonardslee's gardens.

The house at Leonardslee stands 300 feet above sea level, at the southern edge of St Leonard's Forest – St Leonard killed a dragon here, and the lilies of the valley which flourish in the shadier parts sprouted where its blood fell – with magnificent views of the South Downs 14 miles away. Lancing school chapel, the Devil's Dyke and the Carthusian monastery at Cowfold can all be seen. But it was the deep valley which falls away to the east of the house, then rises as steeply on the far side which provided Sir Edmund with his opportunity.

Still thickly forested with native oak, beech, birch and conifer, it had once been a centre of the Sussex iron industry. The chain of hammer ponds (formed by digging out the ore, then used to power the forging hammers) are the picturesque remains. Its deep loamy soil, lying over sandstone and entirely free from lime, perfectly suited the rhododendrons and camellias which became his passion.

There was a garden of some sort at Leonardslee already. A sale note of 1855, some 23 years before Sir Edmund arrived here, mentions an American garden with magnolias and rhododendrons. Some of the sequoia certainly date from then. So do the old Cornish Red rhododendrons, which in early May form 30 banks of scarlet, and have trunks as thick as a man's body. Perhaps these were Sir Edmund's inspiration. Whatever the reason, he set to work with typical industry and thoroughness, crossing rhododendron species to produce better varieties. Of his many crosses the most successful was between *Rhododendron fortunei* and *Rhododendron griffithianum*. When in 1907 these finally began to produce their enormous fragrant white and pink blooms their worth was at once recognised, and they were soon winning prizes. They were the foundation for such now well-known cultivars as *loderi* 'White Diamond', *loderi* 'Sir Joseph Hooker' and *loderi* 'King George'.

This particular cross had been made by others, producing the indifferent hybrid, *Rhododendron* 'Kewense'. Sir Edmund's achievement was in part the result of thoroughness: he crossed both ways, using each of the two species in turn as seed-bearer; it was when *R. fortunei* was the seed-bearer that he achieved best results. But it was also the result of using the finest specimens of both parent plants. 'Working from the best specimens is a principle live-stock breeders would never dream of ignoring,' his great-grandson says, 'but for some reason plant breeders often forget it.'

Many of the original *Rhododendron loderi* can still be seen, the trunk of one 'Gamechick', for example, 45 inches in circumference, only a little less than those of the Cornish Reds. Their blooms are as fine, even if, as Robin Loder says, you now need a helicopter to see them. But Sir Edmund's planting would have made Leonardslee a remarkable garden without new species. All about the woodlands he set rhododendrons, azaleas, camellias and magnolias, to mention only the most obvious trees and shrubs, so that now in May, swathes of brilliant colour reach up into the forest, or stand out among the greens and tawny browns of early summer in pools of yellow, orange, crimson and mauve. The blending of these exotics from China, India and the Americas with oak and beech produces an unexpectedly harmonious result.

The death of Sir Edmund's son (an earlier Robin Loder) in the First

World War turned his attention increasingly to his garden, but his son's widow was more interested in the breeding of Dexter and Red Poll cattle. By 1946 Leonardslee was heavily overgrown, its lawns hayfields, all but the widest of its paths blocked by thickets of birch. This was when Sir Giles Loder, son of the Robin who had been killed, father of the present Robin, took over. Four years later a visiting journalist could not believe that there had ever been such disorder. All seemed again to be as Sir Edmund had made it, and this was how Sir Giles and his wife kept things for the next 30 years.

Sir Giles had his own enthusiasms and left his own impression. On the one hand he favoured camellias. He planted groves of them and filled three greenhouses with the more tender species. And he indulged the rhododendrons, allowing them to form impenetrable thickets. On the other hand the

Spectacular azaleas, introduced by Sir Edmund Loder below the native trees of St Leonard's Forest.

hardy palm (*Trachycarpus fortunei*) which flourishes and seeds itself at Leonardslee, he considered a weed, cutting many of them and using their durable trunks for edging paths. Even then some would not die but sprouted from the horizontal. His son preserves such curiosities, protects the seedlings with wire netting and in less guarded moments says that at Leonardslee today camellias are a disease.

He can enthuse over them too, and show with delight a 'sporty' *Camellia japonica* which flowers white on one branch, bright pink on another only a few inches away, as if one of the Queen of Hearts' gardeners has been at it with a paint brush. But their drawback is that too few of them bloom during Leonardslee's short opening period (late April to early June, then again on October weekends for the autumn foliage). 'We try to open only when we're fabulous,' Robin Loder says. 'That's one reason for our reputation.'

To sustain and if possible increase Leonardslee's reputation is his constant preoccupation, and he admits that its survival depends on his success. It is a disturbing thought for those who assume that Britain's many private gardens are a permanent feature of the country, that one of the finest is in danger, but Robin Loder leaves no doubt that this is so.

The house is his worst problem. 'Minimum winter heating costs £10 a day, the plumbing would have shocked the Romans, the wiring is pre Thomas Edison and we've run out of nails big enough to mend the fuses.' The house apart, a couple of wet weekends in May, or a miscalculation about the entry charge can make the difference between profit and loss. In 1981 it cost £1 to visit Leonardslee. In 1982, after fierce family argument, it was raised to £1.20. Robin Loder believes that it should have been £1.50, and that even if he continues to raise the price annually, it will always be 25 per cent below what it should be.

Meanwhile the emphasis at Leonardslee must be less on plant breeding, or the sustaining of rare species of interest to the few, than on providing the many with what they have come for. Fortunately there is ample space for the many, and even the 2000 who come on a good Sunday in late May seem thinly spread on the ground. Sunday is the busiest day, and one year Sir Giles tried charging extra to spread attendances. It had the opposite result: more came, as if believing that the flowers on Sunday must be special.

'What most of them really want when they arrive is a cup of tea. I don't blame them.' In earlier years tea (but little else) was provided by Women's Institute volunteers, boiling urns on gas burners. Now the newly equipped canteen is the responsibility of Robin's wife Jane, and when she drives up to the house the back of her station wagon will be loaded with 50 or 60 loaves of sandwich bread.

On open days everyone does everything, the gardeners manning the kiosks or staffing the car park. 'It's festival time for them,' Robin Loder says, 'but it's more than that: an important part of their reward for their work is having people tell them how much they admire the gardens.' There are four whole time gardeners at Leonardslee and three part time. All live on the estate and most have been here many years. There is no head gardener, as there used to be in Sir Edmund's time when Mr Whitner, in bowler hat and suit with gold watch chain, was in charge. 'Now it's muggins,' Robin Loder says, referring to himself. 'A head gardener who could take decisions would need a salary of about £10,000, and there's no way the gardens could support that.' So at eight every morning he sees all the gardeners and allocates work for the day.

Almost the first thing the visitor sees at Leonardslee is a tulip tree which must be one of the most magnificent in the country. Standing on the back lawn like a gigantic candelabra, it was 112 feet high when recently measured.

The lawn here also provides the first of many views down into the valley with its string of ponds; and, on the opposite slope, of the stream bed known as Mossy Ghyl. Here in May the yellow azaleas (*Rhododendron luteum*) are at their most intense, reaching up into the trees like a line of forest fire.

From this point most of the garden proper lies to the left. Here a number of paths follow the contours of the valley side, each lined with a different combination of brilliantly coloured shrubs, rhododendrons predominating but not excluding other plants. The maples are a feature, an *Acer palmatum* 'Dissectum Atropurpurum' for example, about four feet high, its inner branches so convoluted that they suggest a bad experience with knitting wool. Here are several handkerchief trees, a snowdrop tree and at the far end an exceptional 75-foot *Magnolia campbellii*. Other magnolias reach half way up the trunks of the beeches, oaks and conifers which stand above them. 'That one will have to go,' Robin Loder says, pointing to a 90-foot monkey puzzle tree growing too close to a huge *Sequoiadendron giganteum* with fine symmetrical tapering trunk. 'You have to be ruthless in this sort of a garden. It could never be run by a committee.'

All trunks, and especially those of the older rhododendrons, give him pleasure, and in many areas he has cleared away the great thickets which used to form their skirts and which his father tolerated. A garden like Leonardslee is especially in need of open spaces, he believes, not just for picnics, but to give relief from the forest and a proper sense of its character, instead of a feeling of being engulfed.

'We have roughly a descending pattern of flowering,' he explains. 'At the top come the more tender and earlier blooming species. The temperature is less extreme here. The medium hardy are half way down. The valley bottom is not exactly a frost pocket but it can get very cold. Similarly in summer it can be very hot. So we end up down there with all the yellow smellies,' he says, referring to the groves of *Rhododendron luteum*, 'which send our Women's Institute visitors into such ecstacies.'

Down in the valley bottom the scene was once so jungle-like that it was used in the 1950s for the making of 'Black Narcissus', a film set in the Himalayas. The Horsham fire brigade was hired to provide the necessary monsoon rain. Late in the summer when the company returned to complete shooting, the director was affronted to find no rhododendron blooms and ordered the bushes to be hung with coloured crepe paper. More typically at this time tall pines stand reflected in the smooth green surfaces of the ponds and the effect is peaceful.

They are not the end of the gardens. High up on the eastern valley side, close to the head of Mossy Ghyl, Sir Giles in 1953 created a garden to celebrate Queen Elizabeth II's coronation. Here many azaleas and younger plants of rhododendron *loderi* type have been planted. Here also stood the country's biggest sassafras tree till it lost its top in a recent gale. Gales are a woodland gardener's dread. While the visitor admires vast drifts of rain gusting up the valley, the gardener fears for his trees. The severest damage at Leonardslee occurs in the valley bottom, not because the wind is strongest here but because of its turbulence. Groups of rhododendron are literally twisted out of the ground. A few years ago three large oaks came down in a gale, each of them falling in a different direction.

Back in the vicinity of the house there are more things to see: the camellia houses and the rockery, now planted with shrubs – 'It would take four gardeners all their time to keep it as an Alpine rockery.' Here is the wishing well, where money is collected for the Gardeners' Royal Benevolent Society. One of Robin and Jane Loder's nightly duties on an open day is to dredge out, rinse and dry the coins. And close below the house there is a garden of once dwarf conifers. 'The trouble is they cease to be dwarf if you plant them in good enough soil.'

Nor are the shrubs and trees all: the woods in May are carpeted with bluebells among which grow three-leafed wake-robins, and from which *Peltiphyllum peltatum* poke their leafless flower heads; boggy areas have giant kingcups alongside the enormous-leafed *Gunnera manicata*. Among so much, what is Robin Loder's special obsession? 'Vintage cars. Well you can't garden after dark,' he explains.

His hobby is not so far removed from the garden as it might seem. Often he stands one of his cars in the public car park to create interest. 'It may be a pity, but we have to show something which stays in the memory and distinguishes Leonardslee from other gardens. Then when the time comes to decide which to visit the child says, "Let's go to the one where we saw the funny car."'

Robin Loder's reward for the work he has already put into Leonardslee and the vast amount more which he plans can be as direct as the admiring comments his gardeners get on an open day. He has many letters, even poems of gratitude. Only occasionally does he get the opposite kind, for example one which complained, 'There was nothing but rhododendrons.' 'Once we got a complete tape-recorded opera of praise. The thought was nice, even if it wasn't a work of musical genius.'

But the real urge which lies behind his work for Leonardslee is that he refuses to be known as the Loder who gave up. If he fails, that's too bad, but at least he will not have abandoned something so splendid without a fight.

'Growing up with all this, I had to join 'em or hate 'em,' he says. From an early age he joined them. By ten he had his own greenhouse with more than 100 cacti. He exhibited at Royal Horticultural Society shows and on open days sold cuttings by the entrance kiosk.

Soon afterwards came disaster. His greenhouse was pulled down to make room for one of the camellia houses. It left deep resentment. 'In the end the space wasn't even needed,' he says. For many years his gardening ceased. That he did not start to hate 'em after such a trauma suggests that he will always remain the inheritor of his great-grandfather's gardening enthusiasm. And his early success with cacti beside Leonardslee's entry kiosk is a good omen for its financial future.

Opposite: Leonardslee's one-time Alpine rockery is now planted with rhododendrons, azaleas, camellias and other early summer-flowering shrubs.

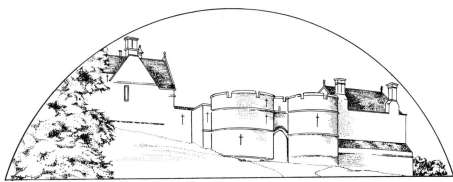

ROCKINGHAM CASTLE

The history of Rockingham Castle itself and that of its gardens are closely interwoven. Set on a rocky promontory high above the Welland Valley in Leicestershire, its position is both romantic and of great military importance. Britons, Romans and Saxons each in turn had defensive positions here, and in 1066 William I ordered a castle to be built. Throughout the Middle Ages Rockingham Castle was what the present owner, Commander Michael Saunders-Watson RN, describes as 'a Windsor of the Midlands.'

His ancestors have been in continuous occupation since 1530. Lewis Watson, second Earl of Rockingham, the owner at the time of the Civil War, was a Royalist, but Royalist forces failed to arrive to defend the castle and it was occupied by the Roundheads. 'Before they came up the hill,' Commander Saunders-Watson says, 'they were heard grunting like pigs down in what is now the Wild Garden.' The expelled Royalists attacked from the church. If you stand in Rockingham's forecourt (the Green Court), looking out across the Welland Valley, the church is a stone's throw away on the steep grass slope below the castle's outer walls.

These walls which once ran the full length of the north and west edges of the castle's promontory, are today a low parapet topped by Victorian stone cannon balls. At the time they were a formidable fortification 30 feet high and nine feet thick. When the fighting was over Cromwell demolished them, and as a result the part of the garden now enclosed by the Terrace Walk is three or four feet higher than it was in Tudor times. 'We haven't any proper soil there, just rubble,' Commander Saunders-Watson says. 'He brought in 500 hands, the 17th-century equivalent of a bulldozer, and levelled the walls to the ground.'

South of the castle, Cromwell also levelled the circular keep, which is now the site of Rockingham's Rose Garden. Further south the parkland known as the Tilting Lawn is where mediaeval knights practised for joust or battle. Between the Rose Garden and the castle, a strange dell has an odder historical explanation. King John stayed in the castle shortly before he lost his baggage in the Wash, and his queen returned to besiege Rockingham, but failed to take it. There had always been a family tradition that she had come back for the king's treasure which was buried somewhere in the grounds, and in 1935 King John himself appeared to the Rev. Plant, vicar of Rockingham, during a seance to confirm the rumour and reveal the place. Commander Saunders-Watson's grandmother at once began to excavate. The

Cross garden at Rockingham: beds of 'Pirneille Poulson' roses edged with lavender.

95

result was this flowery dell, and the discovery of one of the old gateways to the keep, but no treasure.

By this time Rockingham was owned by Commander Sir Michael Culme-Seymour Bt, RN. Thirty-five years later in 1971 he offered Rockingham to his nephew, Commander Michael Saunders-Watson. The decision to accept was a hard one. As a regular naval officer, Commander Saunders-Watson was about to be given his first command. Rockingham, he says, is like a beautiful woman, supremely selfish. Generation after generation of his family has been seduced by her. 'Give her enough admiration and she's enormously rewarding, but take your eyes off the ball and she's inclined to sulk.' His own seduction began in 1971.

Though his uncle left Rockingham in excellent repair, it was not financially viable. Since before the war it had been partly run as a market garden, but this was making a 'cracking loss'. So the Saunders-Watsons sacked the head gardener and concentrated on opening to the public. A period of expansion followed in the mid-1970s when there was money around. 'Now it's touch and go. I'm not using capital, but the overdraft goes up.'

Commander Saunders-Watson is captain of Rockingham Castle – he has opened a naval museum in one wing and the Terrace Walk has a distinct quarter-deck flavour with the valley spread below like the sea. He also manages Rockingham's 3700-acre estate which includes the 40 houses of Rockingham village. But his wife has charge of the gardens. 'We never succeeded in finding a new head gardener, so now it's Georgina,' he says. Georgina Saunders-Watson was an even more reluctant convert to Rockingham. 'Churches, houses and gardens, as a child I hated them in that order,' she says. 'All the things my mother was keenest on.' It was only when she had a place of her own that she became interested. Now, as well as being head gardener, she herself never gardens less than three days a week.

Rising steeply above King John's dell is the so-called Mount. Rockingham's is long, curved and terraced. It is also high, and adds yet another level to a garden in which the sense of being high up above the surrounding countryside is anyway so important.

At one end of the Mount an elevated arbour known as the Bandstand has been built above another gateway to the keep, the beams of its roof hung with honeysuckle. Replacing the broken coping of its low walls with genuine stone cost £100 a metre, Commander Saunders-Watson says. Composition stone would have been almost indistinguishable but he would not then have received help from the Historic Buildings Council. From the Bandstand you look across the Cross Garden (of which more later) to a long double yew hedge which is said to be as old as the Mount, though the present yews look a lot younger. The hedge certainly existed by the mid-19th century. Rockingham is believed to be Chesney Wold in Charles Dickens's *Bleak House*. Dickens was a friend of the Watsons and when writing in the Victorian wing which looks down the hedge's centre he conceived the ghost of Lady Dedlock walking there.

The hedge is known as the Elephant Walk because of the unusual way in which the yews are trimmed, not in straight lines with precise topiary shapes, but in a jumble of smooth humps which suggest elephants. Dromedaries would be a better comparison. These are the humps which Georgina

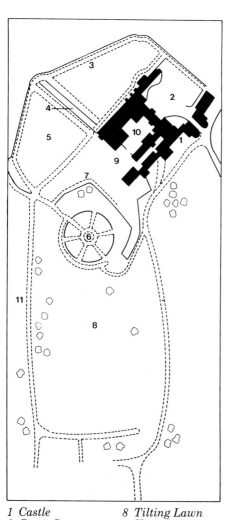

1 Castle
2 Green Court
3 Terrace Walk
4 Elephant Walk
5 Cross Garden
6 Rose Garden
7 Mount
8 Tilting Lawn
9 King John's Garden
10 Queen Eleanor's Garden
11 Wild Garden

Saunders-Watson tries to persuade her husband's foresters to shave before October each year, but which they are inclined to leave till February when they can do nothing in the estate's woodlands.

Between the Mount and the Elephant Walk, the Cross Garden is a roughly triangular lawn, now laid out in two long crossing rose beds. At the beginning of the century it was a mass of what Georgina Saunders-Watson calls jam-tart beds, and perhaps this was its condition in 1848 when Joseph Paxton, the great glasshouse builder and head gardener of Chatsworth, drew up a plan to build a large rectangular sunk garden here. The Saunders-Watsons have the plan but it was never put into practice. Today the crossing beds have a uniform spine of fine red *Rosa* 'Pirneille Poulson' edged with lavender on one side and matching mauve catmint on the other, a planting scheme said to have been suggested by the talented garden designer John Codrington in 1910 when he was fourteen.

Beyond the Elephant Walk is Rockingham's largest formal lawn, the one built on the rubble of the walls which Cromwell destroyed. All along one side beyond its low parapet wall the view over the Welland Valley is at its

Mrs Saunders-Watson, who takes active charge of Rockingham Castle's gardens. As a child, gardens, houses and churches were the three things she hated.

finest, with the hazy hills towards Uppingham and Beaumont Chase rising in the distance. Along the other side stand the residential parts of the castle, built in a mixture of grey limestone and orange-brown ironstone. This elevation, when seen from the valley in the evening, catches the sun and glows like pink coral. It is a text book sample of building style: Tudor wing, more severe Restoration wing, gabled Victorian wing where Dickens wrote, balancing castellated tower added by Anthony Salvin during the same period, then beyond, rising above the stone roofs, the square tower described by Commander Saunders-Watson as 'that misery which Great Uncle George added.' Great Uncle George, who died in 1900, had grandiose plans: colonades, ballroom, a great chapel, but fortunately his money ran out. Where do the Saunders-Watsons live today? In Great Uncle George's tower.

The large lawn which lies between the castle and the terrace wall is this morning being mown and rolled by David, the youngest of their three children, with the help of friends from the village. It is part of Rockingham's character that it remains emphatically a family home as well as a family enterprise. Georgina Saunders-Watson's hunters graze beside the public car park ('I'm so bad at selling them,' she says), and a small pack of pedigree liver-and-white cocker spaniels are continually being called to obedience by the whistle which hangs round the Commander's neck. The lawns are normally mown by outside contractors. This provides extra help in the summer when it is needed, and makes it possible to manage with only one part-time and two full-time gardeners. 'But I depend on him,' Georgina Saunders-Watson says, referring to the part-timer. 'When there's a big job it's a great psychological help to put two of them onto it.'

Along the foot of the castle walls are narrow beds where she struggles to get the planting right. In mid-summer she has settled conventionally for pink geraniums, edged with dark blue lobelia. She was better pleased with an earlier combination of dark red wallflowers, white lily-flowered tulips and forget-me-nots. But the beds are too narrow and she would like a proper herbaceous border, at least 12 feet deep. 'The trouble is, I take a long time to make up my mind.' Just when she had decided to establish one on the far side of the Rose Garden, a friend told her she would need another on the near side to balance it.

The Rose Garden lies beyond the Mount, in an area half circled by stone and brick walls. It is against one of these that she would like a border, but apart from the problem of decision, it would mean moving two favourite small trees – an *Acer griseum* with decorative peeling bark, and a *Magnolia x watsonii*. So at present only narrow beds for syringa, ceanothus, clematis and climbing roses lie at the foot of the walls, and the main feature of the garden is the Rose Garden itself. This large circle, on the site of the original keep, is surrounded by a tall yew hedge which, at least till 1921 when another great uncle, the Rev Wentworth Watson, illustrated it in Country Life, was trimmed with precision. Now, either in imitation of the Elephant Walk, or because it got out of control during the Second World War, it is similarly humped and bobbly.

Massed hybrid tea roses are seen at their most spectacular when you step through these yew hedges into Rockingham's Rose Garden. Georgina Saunders-Watson resists the advice she is sometimes given to reduce the number of beds. Pink 'Grace de Monaco', deep red 'Mister Lincoln' and 'Etoile de Hollande', creamy yellow 'Sutters Gold' and *grisbi* – there are a large number of varieties and a full range of colours.

More intimate than either the Rose Garden, the Cross Garden or Rockingham's lawns with their expansive views, are its two remaining formal gardens, one created in the excavation for King John's treasure. Here the stone surrounds are planted with grey santolina and swathes of thyme, and the sides of the dell with a mixture of campanula, purple acers, cotoneaster, rue and lavender.

Finally, within the walls of the castle (where there is also a complete mediaeval cobbled street) is Queen Eleanor's garden, a small courtyard overlooked by many parts of the castle but given character by the rough orange-brown ironstone of the servants' wing. Up the various walls grow roses, wisteria, clematis and a fig tree. The lawn is crossed by paved paths and there is a small box-edged bed at the centre.

The formal gardens at Rockingham measure four and a half acres, the mown park another four. Commander Saunders-Watson has increased this fenced-off area since he concentrated his efforts on opening Rockingham to the public. 'Animals and visitors don't mix,' he says. 'We've had as many as 5000 people here in a day without unduly crushing them.' Though at present his annual target is 30,000. The mown park begins with the Tilting Lawn, where in the mid-19th century Commander Saunders-Watson's great-great-grandparents, Richard and Lavinia Watson, planted many of the trees which are now well grown. Here are tall cedars, a grove of red-leafed prunus, a large tulip tree and catalpas. All are surrounded by two connecting avenues, one of limes and one of sycamores. But it is beyond, where the ground drops steeply into a further eight acres of forested valley known as the Wild Garden, that they planted most extensively.

In spring the upper banks of this are a mass of snowdrops, wild violets, primroses and aconites. 'Great Uncle George would never go out without a pocket full of seed to scatter,' Commander Saunders-Watson says. The trees themselves begin a little lower down the slope. In total there are some 200 different species. They make the long walk round the Wild Garden, where in summer a sultry heat collects, a rewarding one. There are vast beech, hornbeam, horse chestnut, sycamore and small groves of walnuts. Among many exotics there is a fine ash-like *Pterocarya fraxinifolia* and the biggest sitka spruce, *Picea sitchensis*, north of Kew.

All are more easily seen today, since 32 full grown elms died of elm disease in the 1970s. 'It seemed to give us a taste for clearing,' Commander Saunders-Watson says. 'We aim to make more vistas.' The Wild Garden is his own responsibility, and he admits that he hasn't been giving it the attention it demands. At present he spends three days a week in London, his particular responsibility chairing the tax committee of the Historic Houses Association. He has strong views about the country's confused arrangements for supporting gardens. The Historic Buildings Council makes grants for garden structures. The Countryside Commission is interested in parks and public access to them. The Forestry Commission may help with wild gardens. But only Kew is interested in purely horticultural and botanical gardens, and Kew has no money, so it is these which are often left without support. What is needed, he believes, is a central body which will look at a particular garden's needs as a whole.

The planting in the Wild Garden has continued and there are many interesting new trees in the valley bottom. Here, where it ends in fields, a large pool with yellow lilies is surrounded in summer by tropical growths of *Peltiphyllum peltatum* and gunnera. It was made by Great Uncle George in the 1870s to give work to local labourers during the agricultural depression of that time. Close by stands one of the finest of all the garden's trees, a gigantic 200-year-old copper beech.

Commander Sir Michael Culme-Seymour (the uncle who gave Rockingham to Commander Saunders-Watson) also planted extensively: cherries, crabapples, prunus (ornamental cherries) and many rarer trees and shrubs, for example the tall cotoneasters, *C. lacteus, C. simonsii, C. frigidus*. His final creation, known as Sir Michael's Bank, is an upper slope above the Wild Garden which he cleared for further shrubs. Unfortunately he introduced variegated lamium (dead nettle) as ground cover. Now this covers bank and shrubs alike. Georgina Saunders-Watson agrees that here she has temporarily taken her eye off the ball.

'I just need one completely free week,' she says optimistically. If there are a few small areas where Rockingham seems to be sulking, this is by no means general, and the formal gardens are immaculate. In any case Mrs Saunders-Watson refuses to be disturbed, believing that if you once start to worry about a garden you destroy all its pleasure.

Below: the sunk garden at Rockingham Castle, created in an excavation made by the present owner's grandmother when searching for King John's treasure. Opposite: Rockingham's rose garden stands on the site of the keep which Cromwell levelled.

TYNINGHAME

'If you see a piece of abandoned ground every time you look out of your window,' says the Countess of Haddington, 'you can't help thinking it would be lovely to make a garden there entirely of your own.' This was the origin of her Secret Garden, the most substantial addition she has made to the gardens at Tyninghame, on the coast of Scotland 25 miles east of Edinburgh, principal home of the Earls of Haddington for the last 350 years. The piece of abandoned ground where she created it lay just beyond Tyninghame's West Parterre, in full view from the house's library window. Here she decided to make a garden where she could work peacefully by herself, sufficiently small for her to maintain with little or no help.

Gardening, it seems, had already been going on at Tyninghame for at least 1600 years. On the site of a Roman village by the riverside small yellow tulips have been identified as *Tulipa sylvestris*, a variety the Romans are known to have first brought to Britain. They have apparently been flowering here ever since. And old yews which stand in the grounds and give good shelter against the east wind must have been planted in the 17th century. But the earliest garden event which can be dated with certainty occurred in 1707 when Thomas, sixth Earl of Haddington, encouraged by his wife Helen Hope, began tree planting on an extensive scale. His mile-long avenue of beeches, three deep on each side, starts some way to the north-west of the house, breaks as it passes across the front, then continues all the way to the sea. It remains Tyninghame's most impressive feature.

Near the start of the Sea Avenue, in an area known as the Wilderness, the sixth earl also laid out 14 straight woodland walks, radiating from a common centre, in the French geometric style of the time.

Little is recorded of what happened in the gardens between his death in 1735 and 1829, when the house was substantially remodelled by William Burn. Burn not only gave it its seven 'Scottish Baronial' turrets, each with its little slate steeple, but entirely refaced it with its present smooth pink sandstone, laid out the parterre to the west and created the formal terrace garden to the south.

Again for 60 years there are few garden records, though gradually the sixth earl's alleés in the Wilderness were obscured by Victorian plantings of newly arriving conifers from North America. All this time, certainly since 1735 and probably from much earlier, Tyninghame had had a typical Scottish walled vegetable garden, standing some distance from the house and so large that it had probably once been the parish glebe. It was here, in the 1890s, that the present earl's father and mother made the next important change, trans-

Above: the Countess of Haddington, an enthusiastic gardener since her Canadian childhood on the banks of the St Lawrence. Opposite: standard 'Iceberg' roses flourish in the parterre.

1 House
2 Grove
3 St Baldred's Church
4 Terrace Gardens
5 Secret Garden
6 Old Bowling Green
7 Obelisk
8 Wilderness
9 Walled Garden
10 Fountain
11 Apple Walk
12 Parterre

TYNINGHAME

forming this great walled garden (almost four acres in area) into a flower garden. At the same time, outside its south wall and running the full length of this, they made Tyninghame's famous Apple Walk.

Despite their interest in the gardens, the late earl and his wife only lived at Tyninghame for three summer months each year. The rest of the time the countess engaged in a lengthy correspondence with Arthur Brotherston, her head gardener. It was Brotherston, a learned man who wrote two books about Scottish gardening, who carried out their plans and subsequently maintained the results. He was Tyninghame's head gardener for 49 years. 'My mother-in-law was extremely knowledgeable,' Lady Haddington says, 'but she wasn't a working gardener.' In this she differed from her daughter-in-law, who was born a Canadian, brought up on the banks of the St Lawrence River and given her own plot to cultivate with herbs and annuals from early childhood.

She and her husband came to live at Tyninghame in 1953, and have probably made greater changes than anyone since Thomas, the sixth earl, planter of the Sea Avenue. Lady Haddington began with the parterre. The box-edged beds of this formal square were planted 'in the usual Victorian way, with pansies and things'. She kept the beds and their box edges, but swept away all previous plants and replaced them with yellow roses and white roses – yellow 'Golden Shower' climbing over pyramid-shaped wooden frames, white standard 'Iceberg' and yellow 'King's Ransom' in the beds around them. She believes that restricted colouring suits this formal garden. Dark Irish yews line the parterre to the north, and lilacs to the west. To the south the view is across parkland which slopes down to the little river Tyne.

When the Haddingtons first arrived, a heavy stone verandah (part of William Burn's reconstruction) hung out from the house over the parterre like the edge of some ornate tea tray. 'It was all falling down,' Lady Haddington says, 'and we rather encouraged it.' 'It was made of rotten crumbling Arbroath granite,' the Earl says. Predominantly blue and mauve flowering plants and shrubs grow in its place against the house: *Hydrangea villosa*, ceanothus, rosemary, and agapanthus lilies (the Headbourne hybrids).

Where the same tea-tray verandah was demolished to the south of the house, blue flowering and grey foliage plants continue. There is much lavender (a background plant in many parts of the garden) and a large *Garrya elliptica*, with its dangling grey tassels. Here too are big grey-green tumps of santolina. Below the terrace wall the beds are deeper and shrubbier, with white and mauve buddleias and many bush roses. At one end a little enclave among the shrubs, protected by a hedge of escallonia, suggests times when the sun shines here but cannot be enjoyed without shelter from the cold east wind. At the opposite end there are several island beds; two of them the shape of harps, planted entirely with lavender; another planted with purple *Cotinus coggygria*, shaped H for Haddington.

Central on this terrace lawn, below a low but ancient yew, a comparatively new lime walk extends the garden into the parkland, to the ruins of St Baldred's church. The church was largely demolished in 1761, when the parishes of Tyninghame and Whitekirk were amalgamated, but two dog-toothed Norman arches still stand; and during the 1930s the stone foundations of the nave were exposed. In and around the chancel a number of the earls of Haddington lie buried. St Baldred was an influential saint, with the power to move inconvenient rocky islands around, off the coast near Tyninghame. His church on its mown island in the park is a charming ruin.

To the east of the house the Haddingtons have also been busy, extending and extensively planting a long wide lawn known as the Grove. This is enclosed to the north by the Clock House (a modest-sized building to which they retreat in winter when the big house is expensive to heat) and by many tall deciduous trees. Among oaks, sycamores, limes and elms (Scottish elms, the Earl suggests, have proved partially resistant to Dutch elm disease) there are some especially fine Spanish chestnuts. But the trees which first catch the attention are several well-grown *Arbutus unedo* (Strawberry Tree). One of these makes a feature at the centre of the Grove.

Below the trees many shrubs have been planted: cotoneasters, fuchsias, small purple acers, hydrangeas, scarlet-berried sorbuses and, as everywhere at Tyninghame, lilacs. The scent of these still reminds Lady Haddington of her childhood duty to cut and arrange flowers for the house. Though she does not especially favour rhododendrons, there are two well-shaped, big-leafed *R. macabeanum*. At the bottom of the Grove another lime avenue has been planted, and near the house the Earl has lately started a new rock garden. So far this consists mainly of heathers. 'It hasn't quite taken off yet,' his wife admits.

Cornucopial urn of geraniums beside Tyninghame's parterre.

Terrace beds of lavender and Cotinus coggygria *symbolically shaped as harps or as 'H' for Haddington.*

Back to the west of the house, beyond the parterre, lies the Secret Garden. Lady Haddington admits that she cannot now manage this single handed; it is astonishing to think that she ever did. It justifies its name, not merely by being secret in itself, but by being filled with such well-grown plants that every corner seems hidden from the rest. The fact that it is more or less rectangular can easily be missed.

In designing its layout, Lady Haddington consulted 17th-century French gardening books. She was also continually encouraged by a contemporary French gardener and friend, the late Comte de Noäilly. When digging began, she came upon all manner of rubbish and discovered that her Secret Garden had been a Victorian tennis court. But she persisted, and planted principally old-fashioned roses. Here are 'Bourbon', 'Hybrid Perpetual', 'Centifolia', 'Damask', 'Hybrid Musk' and 'Gallica' – some growing in the beds, others supported by wire arches or climbing (with purple clematis) over a central lattice-work arbour where a statue of Summer stands.

At the north end of the Secret Garden a stone mask is set in the wall of a small stone alcove. 'This is rather fun,' Lady Haddington says, disappearing into a still more secret corner and turning a switch. Water pours from the mask's mouth. Mask, and the ancient stone basin into which it pours, were found in the gardens.

Beyond an apple walk (also created by Lady Haddington as part of her Secret Garden) stands a tall horse-chestnut, and here, as elsewhere at Tyninghame, are the grave stones of loved dogs: 'Smokey, died 12 Jan 1980.' 'Ruff, Golden Labrador, died 19 March 1979, aged 15 years.' Dogs accompany Lady Haddington everywhere – a black-and-white border collie frolicking among the shrubs, an older brown dog of less certain breed attached to her by an extending and re-winding clothes line. 'Otherwise they escape and go hunting,' she explains.

It is a longish walk from the Secret Garden to the Walled Garden. No doubt recognizing this the Haddingtons have lined the way with trees and shrubs. Right at the start the oak, planted by King Edward VII in 1902, shows the growth an oak will make in 80 years. Lady Haddington is almost sure the present Queen also planted a tree at Tyninghame, but she can't remember where. Soon afterwards comes a remarkable horse-chestnut, with outer branches which have rooted themselves 20 feet from the central trunk and grown into substantial trees themselves. Beyond are many prunuses, lilacs, acers, hybrid thorns, buddleias, escallonias and extensive plantings of shrubby potentillas and *Berberis darwinii*. In autumn, below an ancient sycamore, areas of pale mauve colchicum appear, astonishing as always for their leaflessness. The shrubs end with many *Hydrangea macrophylla*, the common hydrangea, flowering on the sandy soil a reddy mauve rather than blue.

A left turn now leads to the best approach to the Walled Garden and comes first to the Apple Walk. This has lately been replanted, using mainly 'Golden Hornet', with its tiny brilliantly-coloured fruit. The archway is only seven feet wide and eight feet high at the centre so in a year or two the trees will meet overhead and create again this unique 120-yard tunnel.

Entering the Walled Garden from a point mid-way along the Apple Walk you get an instant impression of its size. On each side its ancient brick walls,

15 or 16 feet high, reach away out of sight. They were once warmed by internal flues for the benefit of the fruit trees they support.

Ahead, up a gentle slope, there are wide lawns between clipped yew hedges. Thirty years ago, when the present earl and countess arrived, these lawns were edged with wide herbaceous borders, four in total, each about 200 feet long. With only two gardeners where there had previously been six or seven, these were impossible to maintain. Impressive as they must have been, Lady Haddington thinks she prefers the present simplicity. In niches on either side stand statues representing music and the seasons. 'We got them in Vicenza,' she says. 'Luckily we had a friend in shipping who brought them home for nothing.'

Far away at the top of the lawns, an elegant white-painted greenhouse makes the Walled Garden's central feature. Its only plant is a prolific trumpet vine, *compsis grandiflora*. Close below is a knot garden, also one of Lady Haddington's creations. Beds of lavender are edged with box and have weeping mulberries at their centres. From the doorway of the greenhouse, facing south, is the garden's finest prospect. First the Walled Garden is spread at your feet, then the park with its winding river, where the Earl's Highland Cattle sometimes graze, then beyond the purple Hills of Lammermuir rising in rounded humps against the skyline.

The Earl's own part of the Walled Garden lies below to the right. Here he has planted a large number of trees, in particular eucalyptus, the common Tasmanian *E. gunnii*, the longer leafed *E. perriniana* and *E. parvifolia*, both from New South Wales. Here too are a number of pinus (*P. pinea*, *P. leucodermis*). 'We brought them back as seeds from Portugal,' he says, referring to the *P. pinea*. 'As tiny seedlings actually,' the Countess admits. Also a number of brilliant berried sorbus, many acers, a well-grown *Paulownia tomentosa* tree, with lower leaves the size of rhubarb (though it has not yet produced its foxglove-like flowers), and a *Rhus potaninii*. 'That's the finest colouring tree in the garden,' the Earl says. 'Like a fire engine.'

Against the west wall a row of *Eucryphia* x *nymansensis* 'Nymansay' has survived despite recent hard winters, and higher up, close to the greenhouse is a *Cercidiphyllum japonicum*, believed to be the tallest in Britain. The first few years in the lives of trees planted at Tyninghame are always anxious ones. In spring there are long dry periods which they may not survive – the annual rainfall is only 21 inches. Once established they flourish.

The Wilderness lies between the Walled Garden and the house. Lady Haddington has established many beds of shrubs here too, below 19th-century plantings of tall conifers (*Pinus nigra*, *Thuja plicata*). But it is the ancient beeches in the Wilderness which are most impressive, many of them now a remarkable 275 years old. Among them is Tyninghame's bowling green, where the Earl remembers as a child the local bowling teams playing their matches.

Beyond the Wilderness an obelisk marks the inland starting point of the Sea Avenue. It was put here in 1856 to commemorate Thomas, the sixth earl, who planted the avenue and records that he was also 'an active and successful promoter of agricultural improvement.' Many of the beeches of the Avenue survive from his 1707 planting. Others date from the 19th century, for half the original ones were blown down in the great gale of 1885, which destroyed hundreds of thousands of trees in this part of Scotland. Others the present earl planted as replacements during the last 30 years. Standing at the obelisk, looking down the full length of this great beech avenue, a tiny triangle of blue is the sea where St Baldred adjusted the disposition of the local rocks.

Tyninghame has not long been open to the public, and at present only some 2000 visitors come each year. Lord Haddington is not concerned. Visitors could never make more than a small contribution to the cost of its upkeep. The point, he says, is that the gardens ought to be open because they are worth seeing. They justify his claim.

Right: a corner of Lady Haddington's secret garden which she created on the site of a Victorian tennis court. Opposite: the lavender walk in the walled garden.

BODNANT

Bodnant is the best known of all Welsh gardens. Situated high above the valley of the river Conwy with views towards the mountains of Snowdonia, the various parts of the garden are said to blend so well together that they seem to have been designed as a whole. Yet no garden could be more clearly divided into formal and informal parts, and the two blend only in the sense that opposites complement each other when set side by side.

This lack of uniformity is perhaps surprising since Bodnant's gardens are almost entirely the creation of one family of owners and another family of head gardeners. Henry Ponchin bought Bodnant in 1874, and almost immediately began to plant here. Today his great grandson, the third Lord Aberconway, lives in the house and, although the gardens belong to the National Trust, he has responsibility for them. In 1920 F. C. Puddle became Bodnant's head gardener. He was succeeded in 1946 by his son Charles Puddle who still holds the position 63 years after his father first accepted it.

There had been some tree planting at Bodnant before Henry Ponchin's time. From the north-east corner of the house a broken ring of ancient beech trees still marches down the hillside, circles below and returns to the house's south-east corner. They are reaching the end of their lives and many have fallen or been felled in recent years. Charles Puddle counted the rings of one and found it to be over 200 years old, suggesting that they were planted around 1760. But from that time till Henry Ponchin arrived in 1874, no significant gardening was done and Bodnant seems to have been a farm.

Exactly how much Henry Ponchin contributed is uncertain. Less than the guide book suggests, Charles Puddle says. 'These things get copied down and no one checks them.' There is no doubt, however, that he planted trees in the Dell, mainly conifers which are now reaching their full height and which include today's leader in the height tables for Britain, an *Abies grandis* of 184 feet. More significantly, in 1876 he planted two cedars much closer to the house, one a Lebanon cedar, the other a blue Atlantic cedar, well spaced apart, half way down what was then a sloping meadow.

Henry Ponchin's daughter, who married Henry Duncan McLaren, later to become the first Baron Aberconway, was a gardener with wider interests than her father. When she and her husband inherited Bodnant in 1895 she planted herbaceous borders and many shrubs. But her really important contribution was made 20 years later, at second hand. Then, in 1905, she handed over the running of the gardens to her son. It is to him, the second Lord Aberconway, that by far the most credit must be given for creating Bodnant as we know it today. His mother not only gave him the freedom to

Above: Charles Puddle, second-generation head gardener at Bodnant, with his son Colin who appears likely to carry on the family tradition. Opposite: the shrub beds.

develop the gardens as he chose but also the money for his grandiose plans.

No lesser word will do. In simple terms, he took the grassy slope where his father had planted a couple of young cedars and transformed it into the most splendid of this country's terrace gardens. He began in 1905, drawing up the plans himself and personally supervising the work. The work required was enormous since the terraces are wide and three of them very tall. Photographs taken at the time show scores of men wheeling barrows. Every bit of the stone needed for the terrace walls was quarried on the estate, and the bricks for their paths baked here too. By the start of the First World War four terraces had been completed and the lowest one planned. After the war, in 1919, the fifth, now called the Canal Terrace, was finished. Its most famous feature, however, was not added till 1939. Then Lord Aberconway found in Gloucestershire an 18th-century garden pavilion which had more recently been a mill for the manufacture of pins. He bought it, sent his workmen there to demolish it, numbering each stone, then had it brought back and re-erected at one end of the Canal Terrace. 'Experts say it's out of place in Wales,' Charles Puddle says. 'Nothing's right for experts.'

Between the completing of the terraces and the addition to them of the Pin Mill, Bodnant developed in another way. It was a period when such well-known collectors as Frank Kingdon Ward, George Forrest and J. F. Rock made expeditions to the Himalayas, China and Australasia, and a number of these were organized and financed by Lord Aberconway. New areas of the

The pin mill, brought here by the second Lord Aberconway to be the main feature of his lowest terrace.

gardens at Bodnant were opened up to make space for the plants which they brought back.

These were the years when F. C. Puddle made his special contribution to Bodnant. He had previously specialized in the hybridization of white orchids, but now worked on the hybridization of rhododendrons, which had become one of Lord Aberconway's special interests. The many rhododendrons which make the woodlands at Bodnant so spectacular in early summer are largely their joint work.

In 1949, four years before he died, Lord Aberconway gave Bodnant's gardens to the National Trust on the condition that he and his heirs should continue to live there and have charge of the gardens. Do the present Lord Aberconway and the National Trust garden consultants differ about the management of the gardens? Never, says Charles Puddle, because the Trust's consultants don't come to Bodnant. Puddle works for both, but his loyalties are to neither, he says, they are to Bodnant.

White haired now, short and broad, the build of a traditional Welshman – though in fact his family came from Yorkshire and he was born in Berkshire – he has worked at Bodnant most of his life, his only long spell away when he was a glider pilot in the Second World War. As a small boy he well remembers the second Lord Aberconway, creator of the gardens. Today he is in continuous collaboration with the present Lord Aberconway. The suggestion that either of his employers has ever been dictatorial he emphati-

Bodnant's laburnum arch, where 48 laburnums are trained on an iron frame to form a golden tunnel.

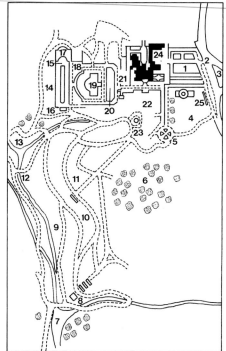

1 *Glass Houses*
2 *Entrance*
3 *Car Park*
4 *East Garden*
5 *Round Garden*
6 *Old Park*
7 *Mill Pond*
8 *Mausoleum*
9 *Dell*
10 *Yew Garden*
11 *Shrub Borders*
12 *River*
Hiraethlyn
13 *Rock Garden*
14 *Magnolia*
Borders
15 *Canal Terrace*
16 *Pin Mill*
17 *Stage*
18 *Lower Rose*
Terrace
19 *Lily Terrace*
20 *Croquet Terrace*
21 *Rose Terrace*
22 *Front Lawn*
23 *Formal Pond*
24 *House*
25 *Laburnum Arch*

cally denies. 'Everything that's done here is by agreement. Lord Aberconway may suggest something, or I may. When we've agreed about it, he never interferes – now that's a rare thing.' But Charles Puddle agrees that Lord Aberconway is a keen businessman, and the gardens at Bodnant rarely make a loss. This is not surprising, perhaps, since Bodnant's nurseries, which are Charles Puddle's second responsibility, propagate half a million plants a year.

Any description of Bodnant's gardens must begin with its terraces. At once they present a problem. Lord Aberconway might have been expected to set them centrally below the house's eastern facade, but this is not what he did. Instead they are offset, their centre beyond the house, so that a visitor coming past the north face arrives precisely at the mid-point of the top terrace. Perhaps the original shape of the sloping meadow made this a better position for them, but it seems a fair guess that this surprising arrangement was suggested by the two cedars which his grandfather had planted, by then 30 years old. They stand now at either end of the third terrace, their branches reaching out to overlap the lily pond between them, not only dominating their own terrace, but visible from each of the others and giving form to the whole of the design.

On the top terrace they are matched by two splendid *Arbutus* x *andrachnoides* (strawberry trees). The peeling chestnut stems of the larger are twice the size of a man's body. By comparison, the rectangular beds of hybrid roses on this terrace are a background. The arbutuses were planted in 1905, right at the start of Lord Aberconway's terracing. They fruit about every fifth year, and Charles Puddle well remembers him picking and eating the mushy red and yellow berries.

Next below comes the Croquet Lawn terrace, largely grass as its name suggests, but with a *Magnolia campbellii* and *Eucryphia* x *nymansensis* 'Nymansay', among other plants, against its terrace wall. At the centre, two large white wisteria, *W. venusta* and *W. floribunda* 'Alba', envelop a baroque fountain. Continually, as you descend the terraces, shrub-lined tunnels lead off to the right with forest trees at their far ends. In early summer these tunnels are bright with rhododendrons and azaleas in many colours; in July and August they are more delicately decorated with purple maples and *Eucryphia glutinosa*. At Bodnant there are many of these (the only deciduous eucryphia) with their briar-like white flowers and bristly stamens. Unlike other eucryphias, they are fully hardy.

The drop to the third terrace, where the two cedars frame the large lily pool, is more dramatic – 20 feet at least – showing what a formidable task the building and infilling must have been. The tall walls were as important to Lord Aberconway as the levels because they gave shelter to the tender plants in which he was interested. Hydrangeas are a feature against this wall and in the bed below it. Here too are *Buddleia colvilei*, *Camellia reticulata*, another strawberry tree, and a number of clematis.

The large pool itself is planted with many varieties of waterlily, among them off-white *Nymphaea colossea*, and *N. atabopurpuria* – Charles Puddle's favourite for its well-shaped bright red flowers and curling red leaves. This pool and the Canal Pool have to be drained every third year and the lily plants thinned. Even without such special tasks, Bodnant's combination of

Shrubs and water plants in the deep valley of the river Hiraethlyn.

informal gardens, formal gardens and nursery requires much labour. Everywhere about the terraces gardeners are at work weeding, planting and clipping in Victorian profusion. Charles Puddle is unsure how many, but discovers on checking that there should be nineteen.

The drop to the fourth terrace is still greater, perhaps 25 feet, but the effect is modified by elaborate pergolas of lattice construction which look frail but have now survived for 70 years. This is the main rose terrace, glowing and sweet-scented in summer, the roses set off by large clumps of *Stachys olympica* (syn. *S. lanata*) with its grey foliage and looping spikes of pale pink-purple flowerlets. Already, the fifth terrace, lying close below, is in full view and so picturesque that it catches most of the attention.

For the greatest impact, you descend to it at the theatre end – where there is an elevated grass stage complete with wings and small dressing rooms formed of yew hedges – and look up the long narrow Canal Pool towards the Pin Mill. You will then see not just the mill but the inverted mill reflected in the smooth green water of the canal; all but its ends is kept clear of lilies for the purpose. If this classical building with its cream rendering and five romanesque entrances is not especially Welsh, it is a beautiful and successful anomaly. From the mill, looking back along the canal, a Monterey pine appears centrally behind the stage at the opposite end. It is the fastest-growing species of pine and inclined to become untidy, Charles Puddle says, but care and skilful lopping have made this a perfect specimen.

You have to stand beside the canal pool at its centre and look up the terraces to get the full effect of their grandeur. The house, set off a little to the left, crowns them. Built of grey stone with grey slate roof and many gables, it could never be beautiful, but its fabric can barely be seen for its deep clading of creepers. Of these a vast growth of *Pyracantha coccinea* 'Lalandei' is most impressive: all winter it keeps its red berries. Two families of kestrels preserve them, Charles Puddle believes, by driving away the small birds which would eat them. In summer the young kestrels can be heard squealing in the tops of the tall beeches beside the house.

This view also suggests the contrast between Bodnant's terraces and other parts of its garden. On all sides stand tall and enclosing trees, so that the terraces seem to exist precariously, a civilized rectangle in so much that is more rugged and natural to this mountainous region. The view in the opposite direction confirms this impression: the pale green leaves which show above a low yew hedge are the top branches of a grove of magnificent magnolias, planted on still more steeply sloping ground below. Among them, two *Magnolia veitchii* are the most remarkable, so like forest trees that they could at first glance be taken for full-grown walnuts.

The descent to the Dell, as the informal part of the gardens is called, begins behind the Pin Mill and passes at first through a grove of camellias. These, too, grow well in Bodnant's acid soil, and are one of Charles Puddle's special interests. Some years ago he took in hand the confused nomenclature of camellias and formed the International Camellia Society to straighten it out. The Dell itself is less a dell in the normal sense than a deep valley, down which flows the Hiraethlyn, a tributary of the Conwy river. At its lower end stands an old flour mill, its roof picturesquely moss-covered. The stream up to this point is tidal. At the top end, 500 yards away, a mill pool discharges

115

over a wide cascade. In between paths run beside the stream, but the Dell is most impressive if seen from a higher path which runs half way up the side of the valley.

In early summer when the larches are still bare this gives a view to the opposite side where the woods are densely planted with Bodnant's spectacular rhododendrons. Among them are the hybrids for which Bodnant is famous, in particular, reds which used *R. griersonianum* and *R. forrestii repens* as parents. The important thing in such work, Charles Puddle says, is to know what you're aiming for. Since before the war the aim at Bodnant has been to produce hybrids which are compact, free flowering, with good foliage and therefore suitable for small gardens. It is time-consuming work. In any hundred seedlings he would be well-satisfied to produce five good ones. Even small rhododendrons take three years to flower and prove themselves, large species up to 10 years.

From the valley bottom grow the conifers which Henry Ponchin planted 100 years ago, now magnificent trees. The fact that his *Abies grandis* is the tallest in the country, Charles Puddle considers unimportant, and recommends that Alan Mitchell, the well-known authority on trees who comes to measure and watch over it, should list *best* trees instead of single qualities such as height.

The banks of the stream itself have been planted with bright blue varieties of the common hydrangea, (*H. macrophylla* 'Blue Ware' and 'Generale Viscomtesse de Vibraye') which in late summer are a compensation for the rhododendrons and azaleas. At Bodnant, as in so many gardens with a reputation for rhododendrons, the aim now is to extend the range of plants and thus the garden's flowering period.

Back on the level of the house, three special garden features are properly part of the formal gardens, though they are set well away from the terraces. The first is a small oval pool entirely surrounded by low pink-white *Rhododendron williamsianum*, its water covered by white-flowering Cape pond weed. The second and most recent is a circular shrub garden, where daphnes predominate, at its best in early summer. Finally there is Bodnant's Laburnum Arch. The idea is so simple that it is no wonder other gardens are now copying it. An avenue has been created by training plants – about 24 each side – to meet on a curved iron frame. The frame is only about eight feet tall at the centre – photographs are misleading. From it, for a few weeks in May and June, many thousands of bright yellow racemes hang. Even on a dull day the golden tunnel they create is remarkable, and when the sun shines through them still more spectacular.

'No garden stands still,' Charles Puddle says. He certainly does not mean to let this happen at Bodnant. Eighty acres are at present open to the public. A walk round the Mill Pool, as well as another 17 acres of woodland beyond the Dell would already be included if the winter of 1981–82 had not set him back; winter is the time for development. A heather garden, across the north lawn beyond the ha-ha is underway and in the sloping meadow behind the Canal Terrace's stage, specimen trees have already been planted. Charles Puddle's achievements at Bodnant and his plans for the future are evidence of more determination and ambition than his slow, precise and reflective manner might suggest.

Opposite: nineteenth century conservatory at Bodnant.

HIDCOTE

The Gloucestershire farm house which the wealthy and twice married American, Mrs Gertrude Winthrop, bought for her son, Major Lawrence Johnston in 1907 could hardly have been a less suitable place around which to make a garden. It stood, with its tiny hamlet of Hidcote Bartrim, 600 feet up at the northern end of the Cotswolds, in an exposed position on thin chalky soil. So few records survive that it is not even certain that Johnston meant to garden when he and his mother arrived in Gloucestershire. He had fought in the Boer War and briefly studied farming, and at Hidcote he is remembered often ploughing. But here, over the next 40 years, he created a garden which became not only one of the most lovely in the country, but the most important influence on other English gardens of any in this century. Vita Sackville-West's garden at Sissinghurst Castle, to name just one, owed much to Hidcote.

Nor is there any evidence that Johnston had a theory of gardening before he began; it seems more likely that the garden which he created, made up of separate gardens, came about as a response to the difficulties he faced. In this way it resembles Lutyens's garden at Great Dixter (page 126), begun a few years later, but whereas farm buildings provided Lutyens with a structure round which to make his 'compartments', Johnston found no such help at Hidcote. There was a wall enclosing the old farm's kitchen garden and there was a single Lebanon cedar and two clumps of beech trees; but by far the greater part of the 10 acres which the garden now covers was open field. The hedges he began to plant here had one clear function: to give shelter to his plants.

Hidcote thus became what it remains today, a garden of many hedges. But the hedges are not mere background and protection for the plants which Johnston gathered inside them. He turned them into features in themselves, using beech, box, yew, holly and hornbeam, either on their own or mixed, to produce what have been called his tapestry hedges. Most successfully, he mixed holly with copper beech, the rich red of the beech blending with the shiny dark green leaves of the holly.

Though large parts of the gardens were completed before the First World War (in which Johnston was twice wounded and once laid out for dead till a friend saw his body twitch) he continued, between the wars, to expand the garden across hill-top farmland. Some of the features which come closest to landscape, as opposed to plant gardening, probably date from the

Hidcote's renowned red borders and, in the background, hornbeams on 'stilts'.

HIDCOTE

1930s, though again there are few records. Of these, the Long Walk, a 300-yard, broad grass avenue between tall hedges of hornbeam, is most impressive.

By 1948, however, Johnston's interests had become split between Hidcote and another garden on the French-Italian border, and he was persuaded to give Hidcote to the National Trust. Until his death in 1959 he continued to live at Hidcote for three months a year, but would say sadly that it was no longer his baby.

The National Trust has done its best to maintain the garden as Johnston made it and for more than a decade Paul Nicholls has been the head gardener responsible for this work. 'That's the aim,' Paul Nicholls says, 'but we do get people saying, "That's a Graham Thomas touch,"' (a reference to the National Trust's garden consultant). 'Well you'd expect it, wouldn't you?' Slightly built and moustached, still in his 30s, Nicholls comes from the urbanized Black Country near Stafford, but after working so long at Hidcote would never return to city life.

Much can be learned about Hidcote, Johnston and his garden from its

1 *Manor House*
2 *Front Courtyard*
3 *Chapel*
4 *Old Garden*
5 *Lilac Circle*
6 *White Garden*
7 *Red Borders*
8 *Stilt Garden*
9 *Pillar Garden*
10 *Winter Garden*
11 *Mrs Winthrop's Garden*
12 *Bathing Pool Garden*
13 *Fern Dell*
14 *Lower Stream Garden*
15 *'Westonbirt'*
16 *Rock Bank*
17 *Pine Garden*
18 *Future Paeony Garden*
19 *Old Tennis Court*
20 *Kitchen Garden*
21 *Beech Wood*
22 *Rose Walk*
23 *Theatre Lawn*
24 *Long Walk*

Paul Nicholls (right), head gardener at Hidcote for the past ten years, with one of his assistants.

front courtyard. Ahead is the old stone-built, stone-roofed farm house, dating from 1600, and the new wing which Mrs Winthrop added 75 years ago, now blending with the original. To one side is the little stone chapel which Johnston built, incorporating old church windows which he collected – he was a Roman Catholic convert. Opposite are stone barns, in one of which he made a squash court. Against the buildings grow creepers and shrubs which give a foretaste of the gardens to come: a blue *Clematis macropetala* rising up the house to its gutters, a strawberry tree (*Arbutus unedo*) and next to it a large *Cotoneaster serotinus* hybrid below the stable wall, a blue *Wisteria sinensis* near the chapel. Mother, religion, sport, gardening – and a pack of dachshunds – these were the framework of Johnston's life. Inside one of the barns, now the National Trust's shop, old photographs show Mrs Winthrop, a grey-haired old lady by then, and Johnston with his dogs.

The photographs also show Hidcote as he found it. The contrast between the farm tracks, fences and stone walls of 1910 and today's gardens is astonishing. But they leave many questions unanswered, and make Hidcote for the garden historian an exercise in detective work. The first enclosure you

Above: hostas in Hidcote's stream garden. Below: Mrs Winthrop's brick-paved garden. She was the mother of Lawrence Johnston, and provided him with Hidcote and his opportunity.

reach, known as the Theatre Lawn, provides one puzzle. The only feature of this large empty lawn is a raised circular 'stage', with a fine beech tree at its centre. The tree is the puzzle. Its trunk spreads naturally at ground level, showing that earth was not artificially built up around it to make the stage. Was the stage, then, given its height by removing several feet of earth from the whole area around it? Paul Nicholls thinks this possible, but no one is sure.

The Theatre Lawn is important at Hidcote for the contrast it provides with the rest of the formal enclosures, where plants grow so thickly and give such complex impressions. Here all is simple, the grass auditorium seems to wait for its audience and the stage for its play. Once a year the Gloucester Drama Association provides one.

If you step through the side hedge of the Theatre Lawn to reach the main garden, and stand between two little brick gazebos with pagoda-style stone tile roofs, you get an overall impression of its form. Its backbone is an irregular T. Straight ahead, looking from one gazebo through the other, the Long Walk forms the T's stalk. It has a bold simplicity, dipping at first, then rising towards unseen and tempting views at the far end. Only when you start along it do you discover that a deep and densely-planted stream bed, entirely hidden from the gazebos, crosses it in the dip.

To the right, one arm of the T rises more steeply towards a brick gateway with wrought iron gates and ends even more temptingly in space. From the gateway, parkland drops away, planted with dark clumps of holm oak. Like the garden's hedges, they were probably put here by Johnston to modify the westerly winds, though at this time there were many elms round Hidcote which also gave shelter. Since they were destroyed in the mid 1970s by Dutch elm disease, Paul Nicholls has found the winds noticeably stronger. Set off towards the holm oaks in the park and there is another surprise. Almost instantly a hidden ha-ha opens at your feet.

This arm of the T also contains Hidcote's strangest and most described feature: the avenue of hornbeams on 'stilts'. It is a double avenue, 14 trees on each side in two rows of seven, their trunks bare for the lowest six feet, their tops clipped on both sides. Standing inside either group of 14 you look up into a rectangular tree room, your hair at the level of its missing floor.

Turn and look down the other, much longer arm of the T and you see first the Lebanon cedar which was here before Johnston's time, then the yellow-brown stone walls of the farm house. Closer and more compelling are Hidcote's famous red borders. By July they could hardly be finer. Here are red dahlias, red cannas with their big purple leaves, *Potentilla* 'Gibson's Scarlet', *Salvia neurepia* and *Salvia fulgens*, scarlet *Lobelia* 'Queen Victoria' and a dozen other red or scarlet flowering plants with big patches of purple sage in the foreground and purple prunuses and acers behind. In total these borders seem a horticultural rebuke to all those timid gardeners who find red plants hard to accommodate and resort to pastel shades.

Beyond the red border, around the Lebanon cedar, the garden is at its most compartmented: some of its 'rooms' created inside the brick wall which once surrounded the farm's back garden, others outside it. Here, to start with, are three huge herbaceous beds which rise mountainously at their centres. Johnston's method was to plant densely so that his plants would suppress weeds. It is true, Paul Nicholls says, that in some areas, after a spring weeding the plants take control. But the garden is nevertheless labour intensive, and he and his five gardeners are only just able to manage it. To name a few plants in these great beds would fail to suggest the variety, but to give a comprehensive list would fill a chapter. The colours are soft, in contrast to those of the red border, but the sense of luxuriance greater.

Nearby is a white garden with little box hedges and squatting topiary hens. Where the box seemed to be dying, Paul Nicholls suspected an unknown virus but discovered it was a cat's privy. Beyond is an acer garden, with several small green and purple maples and centre bed of artemesia with bedded purple heliotrope. It is in this area that Johnston made his tapestry hedges, many of them for good measure decked with brilliant red rivulets of Scotch Flame Flower.

Strictly outside the old garden, but similar in character, are the Round Garden surrounded by many lilacs, a small square garden entirely devoted to varieties of fuchsias, and the Bathing Pool Garden. Here is a planting of *Meconopsis grandis* described by Paul Nicholls as of the 'oo how lovely' kind. Here were two fine *Magnolia* x *soulangiana*; one flourishes, one died. Perhaps its roots went through to the lime, he suggests. There are so many areas in the garden where lime-hating plants grow successfully that the tradition that Johnston had a train-load of acid soil delivered to Hidcote seems probable. It was near the Bathing Pool Garden that he kept flamingoes, wintering them in warm sheds; but they didn't like the public, Paul Nicholls says, and took off. They can't have seen the public often for neither was Johnston fond of it and he rarely opened his garden.

Immediately beyond the pool a simple, circular grass 'room' hedged with box and yew marks the southerly limit of the formal gardens, and an entirely different, less-often described Hidcote begins. If it were better known, the impression that Hidcote consists exclusively of little hedged enclosures would be less common. First comes a fern garden, then a wooded area described by Paul Nicholls as his 'herbaceous Westonbirt', after the well-known arboretum.

Here are more holm oaks, miraculously unharmed by the winter of 1981–82, when so many were killed or almost killed in the west of England. The frost, it seems, rolled off this 600-foot Cotswold hilltop. Johnston is said to have planted so many holm oaks because he associated them with France where he had spent part of his childhood.

Below the trees the stream begins, running diagonally from here, across the Long Walk and out into parkland at the garden's south-west corner. The lushness of its planting parallels that in the herbaceous beds above but is of a wilder, more watery kind; hostas, *Lysichitum americanum* (bog arum), astilbes, bergenias, *Peltyphyllum peltatum*, *Cardiocrinum giganteum* (the giant lily), and many more, ending near the bottom with a plantation of huge-leafed *Gunnera manicata*. When they are in flower in July and August, clumps of orange *Ligularia clivorum* attract more peacock and red admiral butterflies than any buddleia. This small scented valley on a Cotswold hilltop, humming with summer insects, its shrubs alive with the birds Johnston encouraged, is as remarkable an achievement as his hedged gardens above.

Back at the start of the stream, but staying to the east of the Long Walk, 'grassy Westonbirt' stretches away to the south. Like the Long Walk, this area was only taken into the garden in the 1930s. Its lawns rise and fall in a succession of waves, created by ridge and furrow ploughing of the arable land it had been before.

Its trees are of modest size, making it something of a suburban arboretum, but this is appropriate to its modest area. The central mown avenue swells and contracts, just as it rises and falls. Silver birches, rowans and other ornamental trees predominate, and there are rarer ones, including two well-grown *Acer griseum*, with their decorative red trunks and peeling bark. In late summer, large hydrangeas are a feature, a splendid pure white Hydrangea *macrophylla* 'Veitchii' the most spectacular. Here too are big bushes of *Viburnum opulus* 'Compactum', with berries turning from yellow to bright red, of *Berberis thunbergii* (also red-berried in autumn) and many other ornamental shrubs.

At its southern end there is a view over farmland to another Cotswold ridge. Following the boundary fence to the west, you reach the end of the Long Walk for finer views down the valley to Chipping Camden, Broadway, the Malvern hills, and on exceptional days as far as the Black Mountains in Wales.

These are by no means all the gardens at Hidcote. In the armpits, as it were, of the T are the Pillar Garden, where 22 tall pillars of yew stand above paeonies, hardy fuchsias and roses; the Winter Border; the Terrace Garden, and Mrs Winthrop's Garden – a small terracotta-coloured square with brick paths, golden shrubs and ground cover, purple cordylines in red earthenware containers and two hardy palms.

And on the opposite side of the Theatre Lawn another group of separate gardens begins. Most spectacular here, for two or three weeks in June and July, is the Rose Walk, where old French roses bloom below tall lilacs and more pillars of yew. To extend its flowering season there are early pulmonaria, and later lupins, and sweet peas on frames. At the far end, a white-painted metal seat encourages you down its ash path. Elsewhere in the garden the benches are the blue-green used by Johnston, a colour the National Trust has trouble in blending today.

Throughout the gardens many of the most colourful and frequently recurring plants are named after Johnston or Hidcote: *Campanula latiloba* 'Hidcote', *Verbena* 'Lawrence Johnston', *Rosa* 'Lawrence Johnston' and *Rosa* 'Hidcote Gold', and among commoner plants, Hidcote's rich golden St John's wort, and dark purple lavender.

Close to the Rose Walk is Johnston's tennis court, now sadly derelict, its red sand flaking and moss covered, where each year he would employ a professional to coach him. It needs only a little imagination to hear them still at play here, the sound of ball on racket caught by the tall beech avenue which runs beside the court, the only occupants of his 10-acre garden.

Today 77,000 visitors a year come to Hidcote. For their benefit, Paul Nicholls and his gardeners labour to make it one of the country's best kept. But, resting on the steps of the theatre from shifting the huge aluminium ladders needed for clipping the hedges, he admits that he enjoys it best on its two non-visiting days, when he and his gardeners can work on their own. Perhaps he has caught something of Major Johnston's views on the subject.

Opposite: the rose walk at Hidcote, where old French roses are backed by lilac and pillars of fastigiate yew.

GREAT DIXTER

Major Lawrence Johnston at Hidcote in Gloucestershire, and Vita Sackville-West at Sissinghurst Castle in Kent, are commonly said to have brought back into fashion the room-like garden lay-outs which were normal until Tudor times but almost entirely swept away by later fashions (in particular the great 18th-century landscape garden movement). Less often credited with setting this trend is the architect, Sir Edwin Lutyens. But at Great Dixter near Northiam in Sussex, Lutyens designed and virtually completed a garden in 1910 – long before Hidcote became an important influence – while, at Sissinghurst, Vita Sackville-West did not begin her transformation till the 1930s. Great Dixter's garden is at least as roomy, in the literal sense, as either of the other two. Even if its nursery is excluded, it has at least 18 separate or partly separate compartments.

The nature of Great Dixter as Lutyens found it, rather than gardening fashion, dictated his design. Though the house is a fine example of a timber-framed 15th-century manor, it was empty for 10 years before he began to work here; and before that, probably since the 18th century, it had been a farm. As a result all around it were barns, sheds, cattle drinking troughs and, most picturesque, a line of three old oast houses. Far from sweeping these away, he used them as the framework for his many garden 'rooms'.

Lutyens often worked with Gertrude Jekyll. She must have been aware of what he was doing at Great Dixter, but there is no evidence for the theory that she assisted him here, either professionally or privately. The second influence on his design was a more obvious one: his employer, Nathaniel Lloyd, the architectural historian and authority on topiary. Lutyens's garden designs would typically include many walls and stone terraces – there are some of these at Great Dixter, new as well as old. But Nathaniel Lloyd insisted that by far the greater part of the garden's structure was to be formed by hedges. These, largely of yew, are tall, thick and mostly cut square at the top with square battlement-like turrets. There are also many free-standing clipped yews topped with geometric or naturalistic topiary specimens. Nathaniel Lloyd's standard work, 'Garden Craftsmanship in Yew and Box', was based on his experience at Great Dixter.

'Walls were also much more expensive,' says his son, Christopher Lloyd, the well-known gardening correspondent who now manages the gardens at Great Dixter. But Christopher Lloyd has found Lutyens's clipped hedges a marvellous framework. Though he has made changes during the last 28 years he has never wanted to alter the garden's structure.

After the First World War, Nathaniel Lloyd turned one of the en-

Christopher Lloyd, well-known gardening correspondent, who manages the family's gardens, created by Sir Edwin Lutyens in 1910. Opposite: the long border.

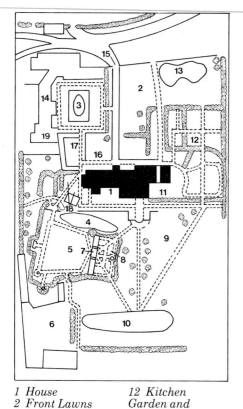

GREAT DIXTER

closures into a garden entirely of his own design: the Sunk Garden. Today this is one of Great Dixter's most delightful features. He died in 1954, leaving the house and garden in trust for his children. While Christopher manages the garden, Quentin is responsible for maintaining the house, and for the business side of the enterprise. Their mother lived on till she was 91, and was still actively gardening in 1972, a week before she died. Mrs Lloyd's special interest was what she called 'meadow gardening', and at any time from early spring to late summer a meadow-like front garden of grass and flowers is the first thing a visitor sees at Great Dixter. Christopher Lloyd maintains it in the way his mother intended.

In the Thirties he remembers helping her make it. Together they would go, with Sussex trugs and trowels, to nearby woods and meadows to dig up wild plants and bring them back for planting. Today conservation laws forbid such practices, but in retrospect Christopher Lloyd does not regret what they did. On the contrary, he believes that they preserved wild species – the green winged orchis for example – which were once common in this part of Sussex, and then disappeared but are now beginning to spread again from Great Dixter's transplants.

This first 'meadow' (it is more in the nature of an orchard, planted with walnuts, two grey-leafed thorns, *Crataegus tanacetifolia* and *C. orientalis*, and the green leafed *C. prunifolia*) is crossed at its inner end by hedges which include tall bay and pear trees. Apart from the trees in the main orchard, this pair and one fig tree were the only plants in the garden when Nathaniel Lloyd came here. The house is now close ahead. It is an important feature in all except the outermost gardens at Great Dixter, and even in these its five tall brick chimneys and expanses of red tile roof can usually be seen over the hedge tops. Here at the front its large, timbered porch and timber-framed or tile-clad walls dominate.

But the plants already compete. At the foot of the walls are dark green ferns, an arrangement which seems appropriate as soon as you see it. Ferns were another of Mrs Lloyd's interests. In a centre bed is the Chilean bamboo, *Chusquea couleou*, and at the end known as the Solar Garden (overlooked by the house's solar) a border of pink *Verbena hybrida*. Christopher Lloyd grew them from seed, and something different will be here next year. It is just one place where he favours bedding. 'You don't get as tied down as you do with shrubs and perennials. Certainly it makes more work, but the gardening which needs work is the interesting sort.' He punctuates progress round his garden with such often unfashionable opinions on accepted practices.

From the Solar Garden it is simplest to circle the house in an anticlockwise direction. 'When you walk round the house, you walk round the garden,' Christopher Lloyd says. But the circuit is complicated because its different 'rooms' are as irregularly connected as those of an old house. First comes a small rectangular garden, protected by tall brick walls. Walls don't give the shelter they are supposed to, Christopher Lloyd says. The wind can get inside them and whirl around in a vortex. Hedges are better because they absorb the wind. This little Walled Garden, planted among other things with bold groups of white *Veratrum album*, mauve *Hosta ventricosa* 'Variegata' and 'Tall Boy', forms an antechamber to the Sunk Garden.

Here Christopher Lloyd's wide interests are fully displayed. Though he has not changed the structure of Great Dixter's garden, he has dramatically increased the interest of its planting. 'It was full of rather dull and conventional things,' he says. Today plant after plant stops a visitor as he passes, either because he has never seen one like it, or because he has never seen so fine a specimen.

Alongside the jungle-like path which circles above the octagonal pool are plants of every shape and every sophistication, from petunias, pansies, solomon's seal, pink-leafed fuchsias and a large purple lilac ('Souvenir de Louis Späth'), to a sky-blue clematis ('Perle d'Azur'), blue-stemmed eryngiums and New Zealand grasses. Prostrate conifers (*Juniperus sabina tamariscifolia*) soften the corners of the garden's well, the flags within the well are carpeted with red *Acaena novae-zealandiae* and the pool itself decorated with pink waterlilies.

Luxuriant planting behind the timber-framed manor house.

The Sunk Garden is overlooked by the three *square* oast houses and by tile and weather board barns. (Square oasts are either, like these, the oldest, or the most modern – round ones coming between.) Wisteria and red-berried *Schisandra grandiflora rubiflora* climb over the tiles of the barns, and their tallest wall is covered by two large 'Brunswick' figs, this variety chosen by Lutyens because it has the largest and most indented leaves. Inside one barn a rusty man-trap is a reminder of Great Dixter's mediaeval past.

The second exit from the Walled Garden leads into the Blue Garden. Only a few of the garden 'rooms' have names and these often seem surprising. Appropriate names will no doubt be devised when Great Dixter's gardens have a guide book, but Christopher Lloyd is waiting for Quentin to draw a plan and Quentin is waiting for Christopher to write the text. 'Anyway, blue plants on their own aren't satisfactory,' Christopher Lloyd says. 'They need contrasting colours to set them off.' So in the Blue Garden in mid-summer there is a white, late flowering *Magnolia* 'Maryland' (*grandiflora* x *virginiana*), and in another border, yet one more of Christopher Lloyd's enthusiasms: hydrangeas. 'They grow well here,' he says. 'A gardener *should* grow what grows well for him. So many spend their time trying to do the opposite. If I lived on chalk I could survive without rhododendrons.' Most showy is the bright red *H.* 'West Falen', but there are also big clumps of *H.* 'Bluebird', 'Veitchii' and 'Bluewave'. Here too are the first of the garden's topiary specimens: a pair of large yew tea pots.

To the right now is an odd-shaped ilex enclosure, its hedges some 20 feet high, a single conifer at the centre (*Pinus patula*). Though not so tall as those at Arley Hall in Cheshire (where they are shaped into huge cylinders), these hedges show how effectively clipped holm oak can be used, something which Continental gardeners know but English ones seem to forget. The ilex hedges and a belt of ash trees give shelter to the Topiary Lawn, largest of the garden's compartments.

On stout pillars of yew, nine of Nathaniel Lloyd's geometric shapes and creatures stand about it. Christopher Lloyd maintains them, though he is not a topiarist, conforming in this at least with contemporary taste. 'They're easy to keep clipped,' he says, 'but we have no one with the skill to create new specimens.' Here, too, are some of the round brick cattle troughs which Lutyens preserved, and a long outhouse which he used to form one side of the Topiary Lawn.

Beyond the outhouse, enclosed by more curved yew hedges, Christopher Lloyd has made a new rose garden, mixing in with roses, wisteria, clematis, a bottle brush tree, *Callistemon subulatus*, and a planting of the pink-white flowering annual, *Impatiens balfourii*. Between the house and the Rose Garden, a long hollow in the ground (once part of the house's moat) was transformed by Mrs Lloyd into another meadow garden. In spring fritillaries are a feature here. She was afraid that the bottom would be too wet and planted them on the banks but they seeded downhill and now flourish in the bottom too. Surprisingly, Christopher Lloyd does not find invading nettles and docks a problem, provided you use good turf at the start, or first eliminate them by close mowing.

As well as creating the gardens at Great Dixter and restoring the house, Lutyens added at the back a complete second house. It was a 16th-century timber-framed yeoman's house, which he found in the nearby village of Benenden and bought for £70. Close beyond the moat, this second house rises high above the garden. To go with it he arranged a vista down curved stone steps, along one side of the orchard, leading to dark oaks which reach out above a piece of moat still filled with water. The main bedroom of the added house looks down this vista, but it leads up to no doorway. Instead, much of the lower house is hidden by magnolias, and a peach climbs high up its walls. A black mulberry tree beside the steps is the most essential feature

of this arrangement.

From here the orchard slopes down the hillside – bright with swathes of daffodils in spring, where specimen trees have now replaced many of the old apples and pears. Though the garden is not high (180 feet), this is the slope which provides useful frost drainage. Across a shallow valley, the ground rises and there is a view of a typical Sussex ridge of hills. Christopher Lloyd is grateful for the frost drainage, but not for the view. 'People who are interested in the views from their gardens aren't interested in their gardens,' he says. All along the top of the orchard is the Long Border.

'It's a *mixed* border,' he insists. 'That's what Gertrude Jekyll wrote about, not a herbaceous border. The term "herbaceous border" occurs nowhere in her writing.' His Long Border contains several small trees (*Escallonia* 'Iveyi', *Gleditsia triacanthos* 'Elegantissima', *Genista aetnensis*) and many more shrubby plants than usual.

Shrubs, he says, provide solidity, texture, different types of leaf and something to look at in winter. Among the trees and shrubs are not only hardy perennials but annuals like nasturtiums and tender plants for bedding out. Where oriental poppies bloomed one week, dark purple cannas replace them the next. 'It's laziness that makes people keep things all in one place. They like to say, "This is my bedding area, these are my perennials".'

North of the Long Border lie several closely-integrated yew-hedged

Annuals, perennials, shrubs and small trees all have their place in Christopher Lloyd's long border. It is a mixed, not a herbaceous border, he says.

enclosures, the first containing Nathaniel Lloyd's best known topiary display, the 'Conversation Piece'. On individual pyramids of yew, 18 birds seem less to be conversing than – with heads down and tails erect – to be about to charge each other. 'They're mostly turning into peacocks, I'm afraid,' his son says. Their presence everywhere about this small enclosure is slightly sinister. Tall wand flowers (*Dierama pulcherrima*), with their delicate arched stems and dangling purple flowers lighten but do not dispel the effect.

Close by are two typical Edwardian vegetable gardens, espalier apples and pears edging the paths, the vegetable beds hidden behind. Some of the fruit trees survive, climbed over for example by the yellow *Clematis orientalis* x *tangutica* hybrid 'Bill Mackenzie'. Elsewhere they have been replaced by hebes, roses, small conifers and many other shrubs. One hebe here ('Watson's Pink') won a Royal Horticultural Society Award of Merit recently. A single white rose, *R. rugosa* 'Alba', is fine, both in bloom and when covered in red hips as large as crab apples. 'People like to grow the double, *R.* "Blanc Double de Coubert",' Christopher Lloyd says. 'But if you look closely almost every flower has a mouldy centre. What they really like is to show they can pronounce the name.'

Where the vegetables once grew there are now orderly rows of tall white *Galtonia candicans* and delicate blue *Limonium latifolium* – some for sale in the nursery, some for planting in the garden. Not that Christopher Lloyd despises vegetable gardening. In another enclosure he enthuses over celeriac, globe artichokes, autumn raspberries and waxy potatoes. He cooks for himself since his cook died six years ago and as a natural result wants to grow his own vegetables.

The enclosures end finally in a large pond formed in an old excavation for iron stone. Red water lilies have been introduced, and a number of other colourful plants which one would be lucky to find round a farm pond, but the effect remains natural. This is where Christopher Lloyd likes to come after lunch to drink his coffee and watch the continuous pond life. Swallows skim the water, moorhen play in the reeds, dragonflies hover, goldfish and carp swirl among the leaves of the lilies. His life is busy and it is not surprising that he needs to relax. Apart from managing this seven-acre garden and its nursery, with only three gardeners, he writes four regular gardening columns and today returns to entertain to a vegetarian lunch the editor of his next book.

Meanwhile at the garden's front gate his brother Quentin works with a screwdriver to mend the latch. Maintenance is his role, and he also looks after nearby Bodiam Castle. He won't reveal how many visitors come to Great Dixter, and disapproves of National Trust visitor rating tables, but is keen to increase Great Dixter's appeal. A house and garden are not sufficient in themselves, he believes, but need an extra attraction. Lions, perhaps, or, as at Great Dixter, a plant nursery.

In 1928 Great Dixter's gardens were among the first to be opened to the public, only preceded, he believes, by Sandringham. On the first open day he remembers how every London quality paper from The Times downwards, had photo features. Why did his father open his garden? Because he wanted to share it with other people. His two sons work conscientiously to maintain this tradition.

Christopher Lloyd had no complaint about the structure of Great Dixter's garden when he took over its management, but the planting was dull. It is this he has tried to improve, as the rich variety of colour and texture opposite shows.

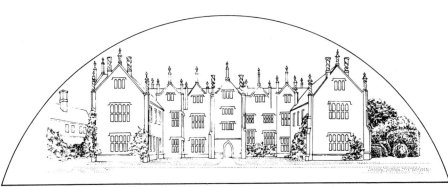

BARRINGTON COURT

For years Barrington Court's gardens have occasionally been open to the public to raise money for charities. Now they are open regularly four days a week; even the Lyle fortunes, based on the sugar business founded by Andrew Lyle's great-great-grandfather, can no longer support this National Trust property in the generous way they have for the last sixty years.

Andrew Lyle still works in the family business, lives in London Mondays to Fridays and at week-ends is pre-occupied with the 1000-acre dairy farm which forms part of the Barrington Court estate. The houses (there are two of them) and the garden he delegates to his wife, who manages them, as well as four children under eleven, with a surprising appearance of ease. By local advertising it was only two months before she was getting 500 visitors on a fine day at a week-end.

'Barrington was one of their first great country properties when the National Trust acquired it in 1907,' Mrs Lyle says. 'And incidentally one of their last to be let on a full repairing lease,' she adds ruefully. Colonel A. A. Lyle (Andrew Lyle's grandfather) took the letting 13 years later in 1920. The Trust could hardly have been luckier. Colonel Lyle had been severely wounded on the Somme, and Barrington Court became his life's work; the family tradition is that it was the large doses of morphine he had to take which inspired his restoration of the property. The main house, a 16th-century manor built in grey Ham stone, was a ruin, occupied by one ancient farmer, and the gardens didn't exist.

'It's all a sham,' says Mrs Lyle, showing a sepia photograph of farmyards with cows, wagons and Somerset farm hands where today herbaceous borders flourish in walled courtyards. 'But what a marvellous sham.'

Colonel Lyle and the National Trust, with the advice of the architects Forbes and Tate, reconstructed on a grand scale, treating nothing piecemeal but the estate as a whole. 'At one time there were 400 men working here,' Mrs Lyle says. 'In winter the mud was three feet deep.'

Central to their plans were two crossing avenues of horse chestnuts, one 415, the other 240 yards long. These are now 80-foot trees. At three of the avenue ends, new farm houses and cottages were built in traditional style and local stone. At the fourth end the 16th-century house stands side by side with its 17th-century stable block. Here Colonel Lyle not only restored to the manor house the grandeur it had once had, using panelling he had picked up in junk shops all over Europe, but turned the brick stables into a dwelling

Typical Gertrude Jekyll brick paving at Barrington Court.

135

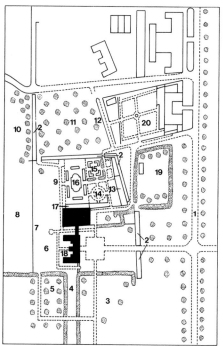

Mr and Mrs Andrew Lyle, National Trust tenants of Barrington Court. Andrew Lyle's grandfather rebuilt the two houses and created the gardens.

1 Avenue	12 Herbaceous
2 Moat	Border
3 East Orchard	13 Ox Stalls
4 Lime Walk	14 Rose Garden
5 Arboretum	15 Iris Garden
6 Lawn	16 Lily Garden
7 Ha-ha	17 Stable House
8 Park	18 House
9 South Border	19 Tennis Court
10 Cricket Pitch	20 Kitchen
11 Orchard	Garden

house. 'He was a perfectionist,' says Mrs Lyle. 'If the best locksmith lived in the north of England, that was the man he sent for.' The two houses, and above all the brick stable block, standing almost as tall as the stone manor, dominate the gardens.

Forbes and Tate also made elaborate garden plans, but Colonel Lyle and the National Trust modified these and, more significantly, consulted Gertrude Jekyll. Miss Jekyll was already in her eighties and probably never visited Barrington Court, but she took a keen interest in the proposed garden, sent for biscuit tins of its soil to analyse and drew up plans which are preserved among her papers at Berkeley, California. The garden's finest features are her invention, and although borders with carefully chosen plants, which were so important in her garden designs, are by their nature less permanent than other garden features, those at Barrington Court have been well preserved and in many parts are still planted as she meant them to be.

The two houses were Colonel Lyle's principal interest. Though he approved plans for the gardens he did not live to see them fully carried out. His wife Elsie was anyway the more enthusiastic gardener. She survived him, living until 1947. She was able to see the gardens completed and to have them kept in good shape during the war when so many British gardens deteriorated (Barrington Court was used by an evacuated school).

She was followed by her son, Sir Ian Lyle, who was forced to become a gardener when his own wife died young. He maintained the gardens and acquired a keen interest in plants, but never much sense of design. The golden chamaecyparis and prostrate conifers he planted to the east of the manor house, interesting as they may be in themselves, look distinctly odd alongside a Somerset apple orchard. 'We're discreetly reducing them,' says Mrs Lyle. When Sir Ian died four years ago the gardens suffered their only period of decline. 'Appalling to see how overgrown they became in just a year.' It is the present Lyles' achievement to have restored the gardens to the order and elegance they had in the 1930s.

Much as Mrs Lyle loves the gardens, she admits that she is no plantsman. She is a farmer's daughter from Hampshire, and was perhaps over encouraged by her grandmother who would keep her, as an impatient child, standing for ten minutes over a plant while she explained its botanical subtleties. She tries never to bore her own children in this way and only to draw their attention momentarily to colour or shapes. She, like her husband, believes in delegation, and has delegated the professional running of the garden. Three years ago Chris Middleton, still in her early twenties, came to Barrington Court as head gardener. 'We are unbelievably lucky,' Mrs Lyle says. 'It is she who has made Barrington what it was again. But you can't tell her so because she's hopelessly modest.'

Mrs Lyle interferes as little as possible. 'People prefer not to be hustled. Anyway there isn't any need. Chris is highly professional. She has an incredible memory. She'll remember the latin name of a particular plant she saw at Chelsea three years ago. And she's excellent with the three gardeners under her because she works harder than any of them.' Today Chris Middleton is helping to lay three-foot-square concrete paving slabs as a floor for a second propagating house. She first came to Barrington Court as a horticultural student, then returned, studies completed, to take her present job.

As part of the redesigning of the Barrington estate the two houses were turned back to front. The chestnut avenue now leads up to what were once their backs. At their fronts the old approach drive was abolished and a vast lawn, 150 yards wide and 75 yards deep, was made. Nothing could better set off the two houses, each now fine examples of their periods, than this simple lawn, which runs right up to their walls and has as its only artificial feature a tall 10-sided sundial.

Across the lawn the houses face gently rising parkland, set with native and a few exotic trees. If Barrington Court does not quite have Cranborne Manor's snug sense of being set in a dell, the ground here too rises on several sides and the warmth of summer is held in its low lying courts and orchards.

Above: ox-stalls at Barrington. Where much of the brickwork is modern, these are genuine 18th century. Below: the lavender walk runs alongside the iris garden.

Box-hedges supplement walls to make Barrington Court a typical 20th-century garden of many outdoor 'rooms'.

The garden is only 100 feet above sea level.

Neither house has been left stark: Virginia creeper softens parts of the manor's walls, and against the stable block's brick facade, around the tall doorways where the coaches once entered, there are two fig trees, and a vine which rises to the roof. They face south and in good summers all fruit. In 1976 the vine produced an exceptional crop of sweet white grapes.

To the west of the lawn, in an angle of tall brick wall, is the first of the garden's borders. Here shrubs – *Daphne striata* and *Cotinus coggygria* 'Royal Purple' for example – and small maples are planted with peonies, variegated hostas, *Euphorbia griffithii* 'Fireglow', *Yucca gloriosa* and many other hardy perennials. They are backed by a vast wisteria, reaching its arms 30 feet in each direction.

From the lawn the old main gates lead to the West Orchard – not the one where Sir Ian planted conifers, but the one which Colonel Lyle wisely left out of Forbes's ambitious plans. It is a pleasant enough feature, grazed by a flock of white geese. Separating it from the village cricket field to the south is an arm of the so-called moat, though it is not a moat as moats are normally imagined, but in many places a fast-running stream. A first-time visitor can find little pattern in its lay-out, discovering it where he least expects it, or discovering where he expects it, only a dry ha-ha. It provides a home for another of the garden's features: the many mallards who puddle the mud of its shallower reaches in fluffy families, appear suddenly in flight above a courtyard or land with a splash in a lily pond at your feet.

A second way from the lawn leads directly into the first of Gertrude Jekyll's courts, known as the Lily Garden. It is her most important creation at Barrington. The dark red facade of the stable house dominates it at one end. Ten-foot walls of mellow brick form the other sides. Even those which Mrs Lyle would call sham have been built with such carefully chosen brick that it is almost impossible to tell them from the older.

At the centre is the lily pond with white and pale yellow waterlilies which gives the court its name. Surrounding this come raised beds with brick edges of the sort so favoured by Gertrude Jekyll's Surrey School of gardeners. To provide a suitable habitat for the azaleas she wanted here she required them to be filled with imported lime-free soil. 'We had to top them up once,' Chris Middleton says, 'but that's all.'

Outside again come typical Gertrude Jekyll paths of patterned brick, and then against the walls a wide border which, for all her reputation for subtlety and the careful blending of shades, is quite simply in wallflower time a riot of glorious colour. Among the wallflowers are pansies in pure white, blue and gold polyanthus and great splodges of bergenias with their big red and green leaves. At the corners of the azalea beds are the delicate crinums which Gertrude Jekyll suggested, though they are not exactly in her chosen position. Over all hangs the heavy summer scent of the azaleas and wallflowers, making this courtyard as intense an olfactory experience as a visual one.

Beyond the Lily Garden comes a Lavender Walk, Chris Middleton's favourite feature. Here subtle shadings of mauve and pink are sustained by lavender in front, roses at the back and summer bedding of ageratum, *Verbena rigida* and *Aster* 'Milady Pink' and 'Milady Blue'. This walk is separated by a sturdy box hedge from the Iris Garden, the area which most excites plantsmen, and which preserves a valuable collection of iris cultivars from the Twenties and Thirties. '"Alcazar", "Prairie Sunset", "Wedgwood", "Edward of Windsor",' Chris Middleton identifies, 'or is it "Prince of Wales"?' Tall and clean-shaped – each variety a separate group – these irises seem a more distinguished plant than the often scruffy examples which fight for space in a border. The effect is of great elegance, and also draws attention, if this is needed, to their inate strangeness. When they are over they are cut down, and every fourth year the clumps are split. Later in the summer *Clematis jackmanii* flower here on tall pyramid supports around a statue of Pan on a plinth.

Beyond the Iris Garden, fitting round another court (the Rose Garden) there was once one of Barrington Court's vaster herbaceous borders, backed by a row of brick ox-stalls. Where so much has been skilfully constructed in the 1920s, it is a surprise to discover that these picturesque stalls are genuine 18th century. The border however was too big for today's four gardeners (there used to be nine) and half of it has been replaced by a lawn with a weeping laburnum.

Alongside the new lawn a rose pergola has been built, of brick pillars supporting heavy crossbeams, very much in the Lutyens manner. Mrs Lyle is unhappy about the colour of the bricks but hopes they will fade and blend. Where the border has been retained there is a sweet-scented rugosa rose, 'Roserie de l'Haÿ', said to be the largest bush of its kind in the country. Overhanging ox-stalls and border is a many-branched ash, which gives summer shade and adds to the feeling that all has been as it is for many centuries. It was this area which Mrs Lyle's sepia photograph shows as a muddy farmyard.

Across the moat again the path runs between the orchard with its white geese and the largest border of all, this one predating Gertrude Jekyll. Horse-tail and bindweed are Chris Middleton's problems here, as perennial weeds are in all borders, but she appears to have them under control. The path crosses the border at its centre and leads past the new propagating houses to a walled vegetable garden which, by comparison with Miss Jekyll's modest sized courtyards, seems enormous. Though large, it is kept in cottage garden style, the paths which cross it from side to side lined with gaily flowering perennials: alyssum, lupins, peonies and delphiniums.

Around the walls are fan-trained pears, peaches and nectarines which all ripen here in the warm west country, and over the walls tall lilac bushes, white and lilac, add colour. 'It needs a lot of work, keeping a vegetable garden this size,' Mrs Lyle says. 'It partly pays for itself with its produce. Last year we started self-pick raspberries. But we really keep it because visitors like it.'

'It's where the men always come,' Chris Middleton says. 'Till the women drag them off to the flowers.'

The women are no doubt right. Enjoyable as the vegetable garden is, the flower-filled courtyards and the Iris Garden are what make Barrington Court memorable, and what are likely to make it increasingly celebrated. Nowhere else can two such fine period houses be seen surrounded by a garden from a third and entirely different period.

KIFTSGATE COURT

At least 100 feet in height separate the upper part of the garden at Kiftsgate Court from the lower part. As the garden is also comparatively small (about 2 acres), parts of it are therefore very steep. Mrs Binny, who took over Kiftsgate from her mother in 1955, describes the cultivation of these parts as like gardening on the face of a cliff. The cliff is dry too, since the steepest slopes are overhung by many tall radiata pines. Her success in growing plants here among the pine needles is remarkable. As for the tender and semi-tender plants in the lower garden at the foot of the bank – 'Visitors,' she says modestly, 'can be surprised.' For Kiftsgate stands high up on the most northerly spur of the Cotswolds. From the upper garden Bredon Hill and the Malverns can be seen to the west, and on occasional very clear days the Wrekin, 70 miles away in Shropshire to the north.

Here, at the summit of the garden, there seems to be a genuine Georgian stone house, complete with Palladian portico, but until 1887 the hill top was empty. A photograph taken 100 years ago shows what appears to be the same house standing a mile below in the village of Mickleton, and named Mickleton Manor. When Sidney Graves Hamilton, the local lord of the manor, finally decided to move uphill to Kiftsgate and build a house there – something he and his ancestors had long intended – he took his manor's Georgian facade with him.

Partly, no doubt, he was tempted by the hill-top's fine views. But the site had other advantages. One hundred and fifty years before, in 1750, William Shenstone, poet and landscape gardener, had stayed at Mickleton Manor and suggested to his host the planting of trees at Kiftsgate. These were an elm avenue which reached from the manor to the hill top, a line of Scots pines to edge the escarpment to the north-west, and a lime avenue running along a right of way which also led to Kiftsgate. The elms died of Dutch elm disease in the 1970s, and seven of the limes have fallen during the last 60 years, but those which survive, as well as the gigantic bolls of some which haven't, still line Kiftsgate's front drive. Many of the Scots pines also still stand.

Apart from its trees, a walled kitchen garden and a paved court behind the house, the gardens were still undeveloped when the Graves Hamiltons eventually sold Kiftsgate to Mrs Binny's parents, Mr and Mrs J. B. Muir, in 1918. As they exist today the gardens are largely the creation of Mrs Muir; in the 30 years between the wars she gardened here with such success that

Kiftsgate's Palladian portico, brought here by railway in 1887.

David Hingley, one of Kiftsgate's gardeners, at work in the propagating house. Plant sales are economically important for Kiftsgate.

Rosa 'Cornelia', one of Kiftsgate's many spectacular roses.

Kiftsgate came to rival Major Lawrence Johnston's nearby and better-known gardens at Hidcote.

There seems little doubt that Mrs Muir had advice from Johnston about the design of her garden. It was the plants and their arrangement which she contributed. She was above all a plantswoman, Mrs Binny says, interested in botany from the time when she had made a child's wild-flower collection.

Her first extension at Kiftsgate was in the upper garden around the house where, below the original court, she established a semi-circular lawn – this later became the Wide Border. At the other side of the house she made another court – the White Garden – and, reaching away from this, a long narrow garden somewhat the shape of a metronome, with a lawn running up its centre, edged, as far as Mrs Binny can remember, with beds of anchusa. It needed to be this shape because it ran along the edge of the steep drop into the valley below. Within a few years this area was completely re-designed and became what it is today, the Yellow Border and the Rose Border, backed by yew and copper-beech hedges. Across their base – the metronome's base – the Bridge Border was made, named after a stone bridge which is located at one end.

Beyond again, where there was slightly more space, she made that garden necessity of the Thirties, a tennis court. Only then, when the level

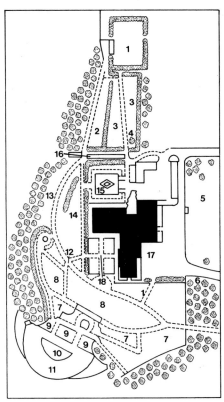

ground behind the house had been exhausted, did she begin on the steep banks below the radiata pines. Here, as well as planting extensively, she made zig-zag paths of staddle stones inverted or set on their sides, and built a tall retaining wall with a summer house. All this work, apart from the building of the last two, was done by her five gardeners. By 1939 she had reduced these to two, and two are all Mrs Binny has today.

So in 1955 it was Mrs Binny's good fortune to inherit a thoroughly established garden, full of well-designed features and a great variety of interesting plants. It was also her problem, because for some while she did not dare introduce ideas of her own, or indeed make any changes. Gradually she gathered the courage.

The courtyard, for example, which her mother had made as a white garden, has lost its white purity. 'Graham Thomas tells me I'm frightfully naughty,' Mrs Binny says, referring to the distinguished garden consultant. In early summer white roses still predominate. One of the earliest to flower is *Rosa sericea* 'Heather Muir', named after Mrs Binny's mother. Next to it is an even larger bush of white *Rosa soulieana*. The grey-green leaves of this continue to be a feature throughout the season, but later there are flowers of many colours, from lavenders, dark red hardy fuchsias and blue agapanthus lilies to the always remarkable spiky-headed *Allium christophii*. A tall white-flowering *Eucryphia* x *nymansensis* 'Nymansay' conforms; so does the white-flowering *Escallonia* 'Iveyi'. (There are a large number of unusual escallonias at Kiftsgate, defying the general belief that they are a semi-tender shrub which only grows well near the coast.) But by August the shrubs which dominate the White Garden are hydrangeas, in particular an enormous purple-mauve *H. villosa*, spreading from an angle of the house where it gets little sun. Next to it is an almost equally fine *H. sargentiana*.

Though this small court is formally sunk within low stone walls, the luxuriance of the planting largely hides them, so that its most noticeable architectural feature is an octagonal pond with a fountain rising out of a church font, copied from a mediaeval original in the Pyrenees. The pond was dug for Mrs Binny by an Italian gardener she once had.

'He was more of a builder than a gardener,' Mrs Binny says. The next job she gave him was the building of a wall close below the Wide Border, to support a new grey-foliage bed. When she began to plant here she found thick yellow clay, dumped from excavation for the foundations of the house. But she persisted, using quantities of peat, and in the great drought of 1976 this was the area of the garden which looked least devastated. Here are grey-green *Phlomis fruticosa*, white variegated *Cornus controversa* 'Variegata', the white-flowering grey-leafed bramble, *Rubus thibetanus*, white *Lychnis coronaria* 'Alba' and the grey-green *Berberis dictyophylla* – its leaves much the same colour as those of an overshadowing *Eucalyptus gunnii*. The *E. gunnii* at Kiftsgate are of a fully hardy strain, Mrs Binny claims, unlike some of the Continental strains now sold in garden centres.

In the Bridge Border Mrs Binny has made fewer changes. Throughout the summer it is dominated by a formidable yellow *Hydrangea xanthoneura wilsonii*, 12 feet high, its girth in proportion. A tall hedge of copper beech separates it from that long tapering pair of gardens, the Yellow Border and the Rose Border. Mrs Muir's colours and planting have been retained here

1 Hard Tennis Court	10 Swimming Pool
2 Yellow Border	11 Ha-ha
3 Rose Border	12 Zig-zag Path
4 Rosa Filipes 'Kiftsgate'	13 Grey foliage bed
5 Car Park	14 Wide Border
6 Bluebell Wood	15 White Garden
7 Middle Banks	16 Bridge Border
8 Banks	17 House
9 Lower Garden	18 Cross Garden

143

Avenue of Rosa gallica *'Versicolour' bordering Kiftsgate's rose garden.*

too. In the Yellow Border there are, for example, yellow-leafed acers, four sorts of hypericum (*balearicum*, 'Hidcote,' *kouytchense* and x *moseranum*), gold-variegated *Elaeagnus pungens* 'Maculata' and *Ligularia dentata* 'Desdemona'. Gold would indeed be a better description of the colour which predominates. Here, through the tops of the trees, are the finest views, but the sense of gardening on a cliff top is always present in the upper garden.

The beds of the Rose Garden are edged at first with curves of pink *Astilbe* 'Sprite'. Coloured edgings and hedges are a feature at Kiftsgate, and elsewhere there is a hedge of the red berberis 'Rose Glow' which is lightly clipped in April to make variegated pink and white shoots by the end of July. Next comes a low avenue of pink/red *Rosa gallica* 'Versicolour'. Backing this are many more roses, from the sweet-scented purple *Rosa rugosa* 'Roseraie de l'Häy' and the carnation pink *R. rugosa* 'Frau Dagmar Hastrop', to the Bourbon *Rosa* 'Fantin Latour'. But none can compete with Kiftsgate's greatest wonder: *Rosa filipes* 'Kiftsgate', which spreads and climbs rampantly over a vast area of this bed. It is the biggest rose in England, Mrs Binny claims, measuring 80 by 90 by 50 feet, and would be bigger if it weren't regularly cut back. Heather Muir bought it in 1938 as *Rosa moschata*; it was given its own name in 1951. Ten years ago, when Mrs Binny first opened Kiftsgate to the public, she publicized her prize plant with a notice outside the front gate reading 'Home of Rosa Kiftsgate', but removed it after a visitor had asked her when Rosa Kiftsgate died.

A few years before, this great rose *had* nearly died. Hormone weedkiller, sprayed on the fields below, rose up with a warm air current, then settled on the whole garden. Mrs Binny wept, she says, to see the appalling destruction. 'We kept the hose on Rosa Kiftsgate for weeks. Gradually she returned to life.'

Back near the house, the Wide Border leads to the original small court behind the house, known as the Cross Garden. It is as densely planted as the White Garden. In such a small garden, Mrs Binny and her mother had little choice, but by continuous care and attention they have made lack of space into an asset, and the concentration of planting at Kiftsgate is one of its features. Caring is the first essential in gardening, Mrs Binny says, and she believes that in any garden the degree of care will show. She also attributes her achievements to a determination inherited from her Scottish ancestors.

Mrs Muir must have had similar qualities because it can only have been lack of space and a determination to attempt the difficult that persuaded her to garden on the slope below the radiata pines. In many places tree trunks have been laid and staked horizontally to retain what soil there is. In others the plants seem to cling precariously to their positions. Here at the start of the descent, in what seems one of the most arid places, is a circle of *Cyclamen hederifolium*. Lower there are cistus, rosemary, euphorbia, golden lonicera, *Trachycarpus fortunei*, *Ilex aquifolium* 'Handsworth New Silver' and several bushes of the shrub *Indigofera gerardiana*, with its small, pink-purple vetchlike flowers. Among many, the two most important plants, Mrs Binny says, are *Hebe hulkeana*, and an evergreen ceanothus.

Where the ground flattens, come some of Mrs Binny's most valued plants, including abutilons, a collection of tree peonies, pittosporums and the difficult white-flowering, sweet-scented *Carpenteria californica. Abutilon vitifolium* seeds itself everywhere and comes true from seed, but the white *A. vitifolium* 'Veronica Tennant Alba' does not. Here too are well-grown magnolias. For 25 years a tall *M. dawsoniana* didn't flower, but was shocked into bloom by the severe winter of 1963. 'It must have thought it was in the Himalayas,' Mrs Binny says.

Centrally here at the bottom – it has been visible the whole way down – comes Mrs Binny's boldest introduction into her mother's garden: a swimming pool. Swimming pools are almost, but perhaps not quite, as hard to introduce tastefully into gardens as tennis courts. Kiftsgate's must be one of the most successful. This half moon of blue water is set on a small lawn which reaches out above the valley, the view framed by two elegant clumps of feathery bamboo. Though the pool looks blue even in the greyest weather, the colour comes from the sky, for the pool is painted white.

The climb back to the house passes another steep slope, thickly planted with acers and rhododendrons. This slope is waiting to be gardened, Mrs Binny says, but Kiftsgate is large enough for her already. Perhaps her daughter, Anne Child, who now lives in the house, will be tempted.

At the front of the house (clothed in white-leafed *Schizophragma integrifolium* and *Lyonothamnus floribundus aspleniifolius*, among other climbers) Mrs Binny's sister sells plants from a well-stocked stall. Occasionally, as you move round the garden, one sister will be heard calling to the other, 'Is the *Deutzia monbeigii* still on?' Plant sales are important at Kiftsgate, where they contribute twice as much to the garden's upkeep as the entrance tickets. Mrs Binny believes that she gets the fall-out from Hidcote, where fewer plants are offered. Mostly people buy what they see flowering in the garden, but she has knowledgeable customers too. 'A pot of something rare can sit there a couple of weeks looking small and uninteresting till someone who knows comes along and cries out, "Ah, you've got it!"'

Two further tennis courts – these ones grass – which the Muirs made in front of the house have become Kiftsgate's car park. 'I just dumped railway ballast on them,' Mrs Binny says. 'My friends were horrified.' But lawns don't interest her. 'The more moss the better – it means less mowing.' Here, as well as planting new limes to replace those lost there are new exotic trees – a ginkgo and two of the garden's taller eucryphias; an avenue of these has been planted outside the old vegetable garden.

Inside this large, walled enclosure half the area is used for propagation, where David Hingley, the young man who has been her head gardener for two years, has complete charge. 'That's where he can show his independence,' Mrs Binny says. She has had a number of head gardeners, including one with whom she could not agree. 'It was a great relief when he sacked himself. He begged me to take him back but I wouldn't.' The problem, she admits, is that she is bossy. 'Nothing gets planted in the garden unless I agree to it. If packets come for the head gardener, that's me.'

She is also ticket collector, and never regrets the financial necessity of opening her garden to the public. It forces her to keep it tidy, weeded and properly staked – and to extend its range. One of her aims is to stop people thinking of Kiftsgate as purely a rose garden. She won't show visitors round, but on open days sits at the entrance, talking to them if they want, or smoking a cigarillo and listening to their comments.

The wide border, densely planted, as all Kiftsgate's borders must be, since the garden has all too little horizontal ground.

HOWICK

Much would seem to conspire against the making of a woodland garden on the bleak coast of Northumberland with its limestone soil, northerly situation and bitter east winds. So the creation by the Grey family over the last 50 years of the gardens at Howick, five miles from the little town of Alnwick and not far from the Scottish border, might be thought something of a miracle. But Howick has two advantages. 'The first is our micro-climate,' says Lady Mary Howick, who has managed the gardens since 1963.

This is the result in part of Howick's position near the sea, but more importantly of its belts of shelter trees. The Greys, she says, like so many great Whig families at the beginning of the 19th century, retired to their country estates when they were out of office for 30 years, and planted trees. Everywhere around the house they stand: oaks, Spanish chestnuts, sycamores, even elms. These last have so far escaped Dutch elm disease (just as Howick's red squirrels have not been replaced by grey). Most numerous of all are the beeches. They are now reaching the end of their lives (about 200 years), so they were probably in fact planted slightly earlier, around 1780, at the time when the present house was built. But dozens of fine specimens still stand round the house and line the Howick Burn which flows through the garden.

Whether the trees or the sea are the more responsible, the fact is that together they temper Northumberland's northerly climate. During the last few disastrous winters Howick was far less severely affected than gardens in such normally milder areas as Wales, Gloucestershire and Somerset.

Howick's second advantage, only discovered by Lady Mary's father, Earl Grey, in 1930, is that the soil of about three acres of land close to the house is acid, and thus suitable for the growing of the rhododendrons, azaleas, magnolias and other lime-hating species which form the core of so many British woodland gardens. Lord Grey and his wife had always been keen gardeners and both remained so, but from this moment their interests divided, she remaining essentially a plantswoman, he becoming chiefly interested in the landscaping and planting of his discovery. The 1930s was a period when there was a fraternity of English gardeners, Lady Mary says: among them Sir Giles Loder of Leonardslee, Lord Aberconway of Bodnant, the Rothschilds of Exbury, Gerald Loder of Wakehurst and her father. They all knew each other and gave each other help and advice. They also organized and financed the collecting expeditions of the time. Many of the plants

'Sarabanda' roses surround the central pool of Howick's terraces.

147

Lady Mary Howick, who took over the management of Howick from her father, Lord Grey, and made his woodland garden her special concern.

Spectacular white blooms of the auratum lily in Howick's front garden.

which now thrive in Lord Grey's woodland garden were brought back as seeds by these expeditions.

Though Lady Mary favours different parts of her garden in different seasons, she has made her father's woodland garden her particular interest. The flowers planted around the shrubs may have altered, she says, sometimes from necessity. Candelabra primulas which were once a feature are now less numerous. Primulas, she now realizes, need frequent moving. But the shrubs and tree which are the backbone of the woodland garden, some now over 50 years old, she has kept as her father planted them.

The area which Lord Grey discovered was already forested, mainly with native hardwood trees and Scots Pine. He thinned these to create the sort of half-shade which rhododendrons like, and below them planted, as well as newly-imported varieties, such well-tried hybrids as the pink-white *R. x Loderi* and the many red hybrids which have *R. griersonianum* as one parent. He also planted many large-leafed varieties (*R. sinogrande, R. falconeri*) and blue-leafed varieties (*R. concatenans*). 'The exciting thing about rhododendrons,' Lady Mary says, 'is that each summer you can tell by the buds how they are going to flower next spring.'

As part of the woodland garden she has developed a small extension which she calls the Punch Bowl, planted chiefly with the strongly-scented

yellow and orange azaleas (*Rhododendron luteum*) which visitors so enjoy. Like many garden owners, she never regrets that her garden is open to the public, as it has been since soon after the Second World War, and she frequently finds herself considering how to plant things they will enjoy.

Just as spectacular in early summer in the Woodland Garden are a number of magnolias (*M. campbellii*, *M. wilsonii*). In July it has a quiet period but by August hydrangeas make it colourful again – there is a particularly large group of mauve *H. villosa*. Escallonias flourish too, as they are supposed to by the sea, and brooms (*Genista aetnensis*), but at this time the most impressive plant is a wide-spreading *Eucryphia glutinosa*, some 25 feet high, entirely covered in delicate white flowers. In the autumn many acers produce brilliant orange and red leaf colour, and there are pink-berried *Sorbus hupehensis* as well as the familiar orange-berried rowan (*Sorbus aucuparia*).

Around the trees and shrubs there are hostas, hypericum, kniphofia and agapanthus. These blue African lilies are everywhere in the gardens and Lady Mary is sorry for earlier gardeners who did not have such hardy strains. 'It was my mother's brother, Lewis Palmer, who bred the Headbourne strain. He called it after his house near Winchester.'

For the whole length of the Woodland Garden the Howick Burn runs below it, in the sort of small valley known in Northumberland as a dene. The burn, together with the untamed woods on its far bank, gives the area a pleasing naturalness, emphasized by the narrow and not overmown paths which wander among the shrubs.

Cross a track and you are in Howick's East Garden. This is divided into a meadow and a mown area, the meadow left uncut till July. Lady Mary describes herself as a conservationist rather than a plantswoman and here she encourages wild flowers as well as bulbs. First in spring come many snowdrops, then daffodils planted by varieties in swathes. Daffodils and

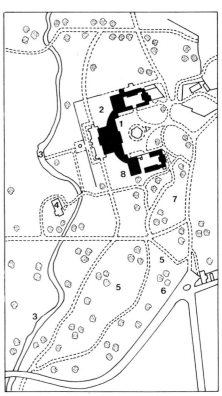

1 *House*	5 *Woodland*
2 *West Garden*	*Garden*
3 *Howick Burn*	6 *Punch Bowl*
4 *St Michael's*	7 *Acer Glade*
Church	8 *East Garden*

Earl and Countess Grey planting a cedar to celebrate their golden wedding in 1956. It was Lord Grey who in 1930 discovered three acres of acid soil near the house which he made into a woodland garden.

narcissuses were one of her mother's enthusiasms, 'until everyone else started to grow them,' and Lady Mary remembers that it was her autumn occupation as a child to plant the bulbs. Today she still naturalizes 100 tulip bulbs a year. Tulips succeed the daffodils, then come clovers, poppies and ox-eye daisies. The grass cannot be left uncut beyond July because finally hundreds of autumn crocuses (colchicums) appear.

Here too in spring there are profusely flowering Japanese cherries, the white *Prunus serrulata* 'Shirotae' and *P. serrulata* 'Tai Haku', and the yellow *P. serrulata* 'Ukon'. But the tree which dominates this area is a massive holm oak, estimated to be between 300 and 400 years old, its ancient limbs held together with metal shafts. Close below this east garden, among the trees across the burn, is Howick's small parish church. The village was here too at one time, but in the early 19th century the Greys had it removed to a decent distance a mile away.

If you descend below the holm oak to the burn – here dammed to make a long narrow pool – and stand centrally, you get the best view of the house itself. It stands at the summit of a low rise, an imposing stone mansion, wings curving back to east and west. The low stone terraces and lawns which lie below match its formality. Against one terrace wall there is a mixed border, but for the most part colours and plants have been kept separate. There are white 'Iceberg' roses below another terrace, and bright red 'Sarabande' roses round a central stone pool. Lavender tops the lower terrace and agapanthus the upper.

Facing away from the house, the banks of the burn are a complete contrast, informally planted with areas of monumental gunnera or left to flower naturally with proliferating willow herb.

Yew hedges enclose another formal garden to the west of the house, where it makes an angle with the west wing. In the beds are mauve and white buddleias among other shrubs, and among herbaceous plants, one of Lady Mary's particular interests, meconopsis.

The way round the house, keeping always within Howick's sheltering belts of woodland, leads to an area where seven or eight ancient beeches have fallen or have had to be felled over the last few years. Their stumps present a problem, and Lady Mary has tried burning them out (not very successful) and hiding them with bush roses. Meanwhile she has planted between them many acers to make an acer glade. Early in the year the whole glade is floored with forget-me-nots, only a narrow path mown through them.

The acer glade is just one area where new trees are being introduced at Howick. Outside the present shelter belts, others have been planted for the time when the present ones fail. Inside the old woods, more and more areas are being cleared to make space for new specimen trees. These are all signs that ambitious developments are planned. Howick has been made a charitable trust and Lady Mary's son, Lord Howick, has left his banking career in London to return to Howick and manage it.

The period of reducing the garden and the work it required is over. At one time a single gardener did what 14 had done between the wars, but already there are three again and soon there will be more. Lord Howick intends to make Howick a Westonbirt of the North (his great grandmother was sister of Sir George Halford, for many years owner of the famous

Gloucestershire arboretum).

Certainly Howick has what Lancelot Brown would have called great 'capability'. Not only are there 15 acres of garden round the house, still mainly untouched woodland, but its lands include the dene of Howick Burn, for its full length from the house to the sea. It is a pleasant scramble down here below ancient beeches to an unspoiled sandy cove; if this mile-long valley were planted as interestingly as the woodland garden above, the result would be remarkable indeed.

Left: agapanthus lilies at Howick. The hardy Headbourne strain was developed by Lady Mary Howick's uncle, Lewis Palmer. Above: detail of the only mixed border on Howick's terraces.

RODMARTON MANOR

At the centre of Mrs Anthony Biddulph's white border, like some inflamed cyclop's eye, stands a single scarlet poppy. 'I try to keep it all white and grey, then this happens,' she says.

The white border is a tiny section of the seven-acre gardens at Rodmarton Manor near Tetbury high on the Cotswolds, which Mrs Biddulph fights to maintain with astonishingly little help – just one girl and one man where there used to be 10 gardeners. In many parts she is clearly winning the battle, in others the issue still seems in doubt. 'But it's going to be all right on the third Sunday of June,' she says. That is the first of the three Sundays a year when she opens it for such causes as the National Garden Scheme.

'Kind friends give you plants,' she says, 'which you put in trustingly, like the *Buddleia mentha* we planted in the Leisure Garden. Buddleias grow well here, but it wasn't a buddleia at all, just a variety of mint. Now it's everywhere.' On the whole Mrs Biddulph takes the misguided generosity of friends with good humour. The late Margery Fish, author of 'We Made a Garden' and creator of the garden at East Lambrook Manor (page 176), is an exception. 'She came here, and she apparently liked what she saw because she sent me a thank-you present of lamiums [dead nettle]. Now look at them.'

The circular bed below the weeping ash is entirely full of lamiums and they are fast spreading through its 18-inch-high stone edging to invade a lower bed. 'I don't want Mrs Fish here. Over there' – Mrs Biddulph points ahead to the Wild Garden – 'she's all right, but *not* in my Cherry Garden.' Though she admired Margery Fish's professionalism; 'She had a photographic memory. She'd look at a border, go home and remember every plant in it.'

White Border, Leisure Garden, Cherry Garden – because it is divided into many room-like enclosures, Rodmarton has inevitably been compared to Sissinghurst and Hidcote, but Mrs Biddulph denies that she was influenced. 'Yes, I read Gertrude Jekyll and William Robinson, and visited gardens in England, Scotland and Australia. But I followed my own inclinations.'

At the centre of Rodmarton's gardens, and because of their architectural nature, forming their most essential feature, is the Cotswold manor house which the Hon. Claud Biddulph, the present Mrs Biddulph's father-in-law, began building in 1910. 'Though it was really my mother-in-law who did it,' Mrs Biddulph says. 'She loved craftsmen of every sort, because they were

Box topiary garden at Rodmarton, with Mrs Biddulph's stone troughs for Alpines.

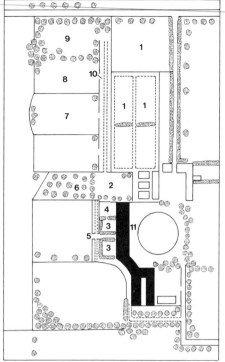

1 Vegetable
Gardens
2 Leisure Garden
3 Terrace Garden
4 Topiary Garden
5 White Border

6 Cherry Garden
7 Swimming Pool
8 Tennis Court
9 Wild Garden
10 Long Garden
11 House

happy people.' Rodmarton Manor is the final achievement of the Cotswold Movement, which had its origins in William Morris's Arts and Crafts Movement. It was designed by Ernest Barnsley. Sidney, his brother, was responsible for the fittings.

'Everything was made on the premises. The stones were cut by a mason, two old men sawed up whole oak trees for the beams, using a cross-cut saw in a saw pit.' Claud Biddulph, a stockbroker who worked all week in London, was a good deal surprised by his wife's creation as it developed.

It was because William Scrubey was a garden craftsman, not a plants-

Mrs Biddulph, who took over the
neglected gardens at Rodmarton in 1955.

154

man in the modern sense of the word, that the late Mrs Biddulph employed him as her head gardener. With Scrubey she worked for 50 years to make the gardens at Rodmarton. He became her closest ally, 'though they had terrible quarrels,' the present Mrs Biddulph says. 'For days they wouldn't speak to each other. Whole hedges were uprooted, then had to be replanted.'

Scrubey, by then in his eighties, was still head gardener in 1955 when today's Mr and Mrs Biddulph moved in. 'He was past it, but still very much in charge. I proudly brought my little spade and fork from where we'd been living a mile away and put them in the tool shed, but he wasn't having that, oh no. It was *his* shed. He locked up the potting shed and took away the key.'

In the past 29 years Mrs Biddulph has restored the gardens at Rodmarton to what they were in the Thirties, when Mrs Claud Biddulph was alive and Scrubey was younger. 'He was a very short man. One of the first things we realized was that everything in the garden was short too, and the house in contrast seemed too tall. He'd pollarded all the trees to his own height.' Today the first thing a visitor sees, after arriving down one of two long drives hedged in beech and holly, is the tall Cotswold stone house forming an arc round part of a big circular lawn. Facing it and now balancing it is an arc of Scrubey's once-pollarded limes which have been allowed to grow into good-sized trees.

Below them stand 30 genuine pyramid-shaped staddle stones, each one a different shape, each with its stone mushroom top. 'The concrete ones they sell at garden centres make me shudder,' Mrs Biddulph says. 'All these were found on the farm. They were used to support corn ricks. The mushrooms were reversed, pieces of wood laid across them, and then the rick balanced on top. The rats couldn't climb past the mushrooms. Though I bet they did.'

In her long, beamed sitting room Mrs Biddulph describes the problems of gardening 500 feet up in the Cotswolds. 'First there were the rains of 1980, then *twice* in 1981 we had the snow. Seven feet of it each time. Bushes and even trees were crushed to the ground. It's hard enough at the best of times, making a garden on brash.' Anthony Biddulph, who describes himself as purely a *destructive* gardener, looks up 'brash' in the dictionary. 'Rock disintegrated into small fragments.'

'You need a pickaxe to plant a shrub,' Mrs Biddulph says. 'In the village where the cottages have had gardens for centuries they've got a bit of friable topsoil; there wasn't any garden here before the 1920s and we still have precious little. But our snow did have advantages. Some of our roses survived when other people lost theirs. They were buried and protected. One night we had 42 degrees of frost.

'I knew I wanted a Terrace Garden,' Mrs Biddulph says, describing how she remade the gardens bit by bit from a condition in which you had to disturb nesting pheasants to prune the raspberries. The Terrace Garden is immediately outside the sitting room windows. Neatly trimmed yew hedges with topiary peacocks divide it into sections, where 'Coachman' fuchsias flower in wooden tubs and geraniums in stone urns. The grey Cotswold stone, as everywhere in the garden, provides the background colour. The terrace ends in round Portugal laurels which have also been allowed to grow into shapely trees.

Beyond the terrace, one of the garden's many dry-stone walls drops to a

Pollarded limes in a small court beside the grey Cotswold stone of Rodmarton Manor.

daffodil meadow, and beyond this the advantage of Rodmarton's height becomes clear. The view stretches away 20 miles to tree clumps on the top of the Marlborough Downs. To right and left, plantations of shelter trees frame it. Mrs Biddulph is convinced of the importance of protecting plants from the wind; up here it is particularly necessary. To the east are birch, ash and quick-growing conifers. 'That's where the cold winds always used to come, straight from Siberia. Now that's changed. The west wind is just as cold as the east. Ever since the icebergs got among the Azores a few years ago, so we're told.' Fortunately she seems to have foreseen this meteorological deviation because more birch, silver poplar and a decently hidden but hugely grown belt of *leylandii* cypress give protection to the west.

Between the meadow and the Terrace Garden, at the foot of the dry stone wall, comes the white border. That poppy apart, it has white agapanthus, white arum, white campion, and above all snowdrops. 'I am a galanthomaniac,' says Mrs Biddulph. *Galanthus elwesii*, *nivalis* 'Atkinsii', *nivalis reginae-olgae*, *nivalis* 'Scharlokii' ... 'I'll go miles to see a new variety. I can't explain it. I just love them.' All over the garden in different beds, rare varieties appear in spring. Does she ever try to naturalize them? 'I wouldn't dare, they're far too precious.'

West from here is the Cherry Garden, where in late May the ground is hidden by the pink snow of blossom. 'How badly we plant,' Mrs Biddulph says. 'However much we look ahead we always set plants too close together.' Certainly there are many interesting trees in this smallish area, but she is still adding to them. She has always wanted a handkerchief tree, for example, and a newly planted one flourishes, saved from the snow by a circle of strong wire netting.

Close by is the garden's only rhododendron, a bush of *R. luteum*, the strongly scented yellow azalea. How does she manage it on such limey soil? 'Tea bags,' says Mrs Biddulph. Its base is deeply mulched with rotting tea bags, and this anomaly indeed flowers successfully.

Now a succession of three large rectangular gardens stand side by side, each encased by tall yew hedges. The hedges were never allowed to deteriorate even in Scrubey's decline, though there was a problem when another old gardener was given a mechanical hedge clipper. He quickly and intentionally broke it – hedges should be clipped by hand, as they had always been.

Mrs Biddulph believes in machines. Without them, and with so little help, her garden would be quite unmanageable. Her Honda plough, Merrytiller cultivator and Little Wonder hedge trimmer she describes as her best friends. For 27 years however she resisted sprays and weedkillers, fearing what might become stored in the soil for the future. Reluctantly, on paths and lawns, she now uses them.

In one of the hedged gardens she has set a swimming pool. With rounded steps and mosaic at the water line, it is an example of how a swimming pool can look well in a garden and not be an incongruous sky-blue rectangle. Centrally at its far end is a trellis of clematis below a tall silver lime and an ancient ash. These gardens end with the Wild Garden where she is indulging the second of her special interests: variegated hollies and ivies. These are planted around another of Scrubey's pollarded avenues, this one of hornbeams, now grown to 50 feet, like a double row of close-branching candlesticks.

Nothing in this range of gardens is an adequate preparation for the Long Garden, which runs parallel to them to the north for their whole length. It was almost certainly designed by Ernest Barnsley, who set at its outer end a small stone summer house. Whichever way you look, whether from the summer house towards the east where the house rises tall and grey, or from the house towards the summer house, the Long Garden is equally impressive.

On one side it is enclosed with a yew hedge, on the other with a tall stone wall. Between lie herbaceous borders of formidable dimensions, planted in traditional style to rise from front to back. At the front, for example, grow begonias, various eryngiums and hostas – these are another of Mrs Biddulph's enthusiasms. 'I cannot describe the pleasure variegated hostas give me,' she says. Half way back are peonies, delphiniums, alliums and brilliant clumps of *Polygonum bistorta* 'Superbum'. Tallest are shrub roses – 'Nevada', 'Bonn', 'Penelope', 'Pax' – hardy fuchsias and supported clematises.

These beds Mrs Biddulph weeds herself by hand. She doesn't dare trust others to do it for fear that precious species will be grubbed out when dormant in winter. 'That's the way we lose so many plants.' To prevent herself making mistakes she tries to label every plant. 'Labels are essential for any serious gardener.' The vista is saved from over simplicity by a central pool surrounded by benches which, with stone seats and yew arms and backs, suggest tall basket chairs.

North of the Long Garden come two enormous walled vegetable

Benches of stone and yew surround a pool at the centre of Rodmarton's long garden.

gardens. The outer of these Mrs Biddulph is abandoning. Partly it needs too much labour, partly she has new plans for it: lawns grazed by Jacob sheep, with a few specimen trees. Anthony Biddulph is discouraging about so much additional grass. 'Up here on the Cotswolds a good lawn needs as much work as any other sort of garden.' He is thinking of all the dandelions, clover, moss and invasive rye grass he will be required to destroy.

The inner vegetable garden is still productive, with ancient apple hedges, apple arches, fan-trained peaches that ripen even at 500 feet and a wall of morello cherries. Here, too, is the potting shed which Scrubey locked, now containing Mrs Biddulph's favourite toy, a mist propagator.

Below the west wall of the house comes the last-but-one of Rodmarton's garden 'rooms', though it was the first Mrs Biddulph created: the so-called Leisure Garden. In parts it justified its name. Until it was devastated by snow, the large gold bed, with *Thuja* 'Rheingold', *Elaeagnus pungens* 'Maculata' and *Taxus* 'Dovastonii Aurea', used never to require weeding. And some of the twenty small beds set into paving have followed her plans for them: roses surrounded by groundcover plants. Most successful is a bed smothered rather than covered in the white and yellow *Limnanthes douglasii*. 'It should be an annual,' Mrs Biddulph says, 'but it behaves like a perennial'. Ajugas, artemesias and Japanese anemones make groundcover for other beds.

Overhanging the Leisure Garden are two weeping birches and on another side a bush of the strange contorted hazel, *Corylus avellana* 'Contorta'. 'It's best in winter when you can see the branches,' Mrs Biddulph says. 'I like to have it because it was discovered in a hedgerow near Tetbury. But there's no way I can get it to propagate.' The Leisure Garden is given form and protection by the tallest of the garden's stone walls.

Finally, between the Leisure Garden and the Terrace, comes the smallest and simplest enclosure, a garden of box topiary. Once made, this has proved still less demanding; an annual clipping of its bushes is the only work it requires.

'I'm no Alpinist,' Mrs Biddulph says, but nearby stand two dozen stone water troughs which she uses for any small plant that would get lost in the rest of the garden. The troughs range from sink size to huge tanks which had to be moved on rollers. Like the staddle stones, they were collected around the 1800-acre Rodmarton farm by one of her sons. Her sons and her husband between them manage the farm, the sons responsible for sheep and arable, her husband for the dairy herd. 'So I get all the manure I want,' she says. 'That's the answer to weeds: mulch and mulch again.'

Its vistas and rare plants apart, the secret of Rodmarton's appeal is that Mrs Biddulph can run her garden just as she pleases. As a result it reflects one person's special tastes. Since she was a child (when she collected 1400 different wild flowers and claims to have found the rare wild tulip in the company of a gaitered bishop) she has loved flowers. Everywhere at Rodmarton her delight in them shows.

Despite her freedom to please herself, this Saturday afternoon, in green waterproof jacket and plastic sou'wester, Mrs Biddulph is at work beside her Leisure Garden with fork and huge weedladen trolley. The third Sunday in June approaches.

Opposite: the summer house, a feature of the long garden designed by Ernest Barnsley of the Cotswold Movement, who was also the architect of the house.

PUSEY HOUSE

The gardens of Pusey House near Faringdon, in what used to be part of the county of Berkshire, have the classic features of an English landscape garden, if on a more intimate scale than they are sometimes found; a lake masquerading as a river, acres of smooth lawn, groups of tall native trees and splendid views across miles of open countryside to distant hills. They were in decay when Mr and Mrs Michael Hornby moved here in 1936. The Hornbys had not wanted so large a house but it had been empty for two years and cried out to be lived in. The garden was also crying out to be gardened.

Wellingtonias impeded the view, the lawns were cut up with paths and rose beds, the woodlands were impenetrable, there was laurel everywhere and the lake was so silted it was just a trickle of water running through mud.

Destruction was the first essential. For three years Mrs Hornby made bonfires. The only constructive work at this time was the filling of a large sunken rose garden immediately behind the house, where, on the advice of the garden consultant Geoffrey Jellicoe, she made a stone terrace instead. Then the war came and all her plans had to be suspended. She grew vegetables, the lawns were ploughed for a cornfield, and the house became a soldiers' convalescent home.

Who first made the gardens which the Hornbys, as soon as the war was over, began to revive, is uncertain. The Cotswold-stone Georgian house was built in 1748 by John Allen. Like so many inheritors of English country estates, Allen was not in the direct line of descent, but added the name Pusey to his own. Some of the trees in the garden were certainly planted by him, and it seems probable that he made the lake too, a garden feature so much in fashion at the time, and built its wooden Chinese bridge.

Pusey House went to his sister, but when she died unmarried she chose for her heir Philip Bouverie, who also took the name Pusey, though he was only related to the family by an aunt's marriage. Philip Bouverie-Pusey was so dominated by his mother that he did not marry till she died, by which time he was 52, but then had nine children. He is remembered today, if at all, as the father of the second of these, Dr Edward Bouverie-Pusey, who became the Oxford Movement's leading figure. Philip Bouverie-Pusey was also, however, a keen agriculturalist, founded the Royal Agricultural Society and at Pusey installed the first mechanical reaping machine. The age of some of Pusey's trees suggests that he, too, planted in the gardens. Nothing of note was done between then and the Hornby's arrival.

To clear the lake was their first need. 'We hired an old puffing-billy,' Mrs Hornby says. 'It worked a chain backwards and forwards from side to side,

Above: Ken Cotton, Pusey House's head gardener. He and three others do what six did before the war. Opposite: Lysimachia punctata *beside the lake.*

161

attached to a big wooden scoop.' She also demolished an enormous box hedge which ran the whole length of the garden's longest stone wall. Old photographs show that this hedge must have been 20 feet high. The wall now makes the backdrop to Pusey's biggest herbaceous border. The planting of borders, and the transformation of Pusey into a flower garden as well as a landscape garden was the Hornbys' second task. A pair of colourful borders are the first thing a summer visitor sees.

They run across an old walled vegetable garden (vegetable gardening continues here, screened by espalier apples) and are described by Mrs Hornby as her rainbow beds. She tries to make the plants follow a rainbow succession. Few gardeners find it easy to uproot a flourishing plant, even if it doesn't fit into their scheme – last year a huge clump of white-flowering tobacco competed with red *Salvia grahamii* and brilliant scarlet *Spirea* 'Gold flame' – but on the whole she is successful and red plants are followed by purple, by yellow, by blue, by white as you advance between the borders. Mrs Hornby uses her sensitivity to flowers and their colours in another way: she is a self-taught water-colourist, who has had three shows in London and two in New York. She took to flower painting because she 'could always fill in the odd 20 minutes with another leaf.' She has painted only one general picture of the gardens at Pusey. As a subject she finds them too extensive.

Their full extent becomes clear the moment you emerge from the rainbow beds into the garden proper. Smooth green lawns run down to the lake which lies close ahead and reaches away to the left where the white Chinese Chippendale bridge tempts you towards it. Beyond the lake are grassy walks below the trees planted by 18th- and 19th-century pseudo-Puseys. Even more enticing, to left and right is the border which replaced that huge box hedge.

The planting is now well established, but Mrs Hornby remembers how she originally designed it, with bamboo stakes, string and leafy branches stuck into the ground to suggest the size and shape of the plants she was

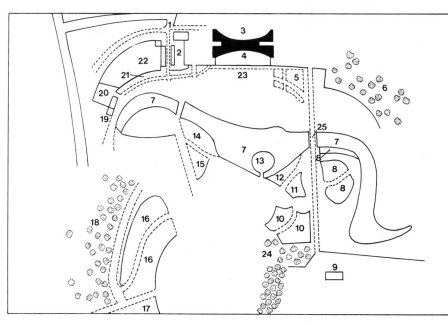

1 Entrance
2 Rainbow Borders
3 House
4 Terrace
5 Shrub Roses
6 Orange Bed
7 Lake
8 Water Garden
9 Church
10 East Pleasure Garden
11 Compton's Glade
12 Irish Yew Bed
13 Island
14 Walnut Bed
15 Variegated Bed
16 Main Shrubbery
17 Stubbs Corner
18 Wood
19 Temple
20 Lady Emily's Garden
21 Herbaceous Border
22 Kitchen Garden
23 Croquet Lawn
24 'Westonbirt'
25 Chinese Bridge

considering. A hosepipe she found particularly useful. Laid flat, it was clearly visible and easily kicked into a different shape. The border is edged with a gravel path, another of her principles. Plants like catmint and pinks inevitably spread forward as the summer advances and make a lawn alongside a border impossible to keep tidy. The border itself is densely planted. She believes that the plants should support themselves. Among dozens of different species, tall yellow evening primroses and single yellow hollyhocks are prominent at the back, and bright red *Potentilla* 'Gibson Scarlet' at the front. The curved stone wall provides a cool grey backing to this remarkable 360-foot bed.

Turn right, away from the Chinese bridge, then right again to return through the stone wall and you reach Lady Emily's Garden. It was Lady Emily who married Philip Pusey, when his mother eventually released him by dying, and became Dr Edward Pusey's mother. In this small walled garden, also created by Mrs Hornby, lawns, flag paths and eight formal rose beds are set in a geometric pattern round a central sundial over which clematis and roses climb on a wire frame. One wall is stone, but it is the other three tall red brick ones which dominate this flower-filled enclosure. As well as more clematis and roses, they support honeysuckles, magnolias, japonicas, and a 10-foot specimen of *Hydrangea sargentiana* with its furry stems, clusters of mauve buds and little white flowers. The low rounded doorways

Gunnera manicata *in one of Pusey's several water gardens.*

Overleaf: the lake at Pusey, a silted ruin when the Hornbys arrived in 1936.

Pusey's 360-foot herbaceous border replaces a tall Victorian box hedge.

163

which lead in several directions to potting sheds and vegetable patches add, curiously, to the sense of seclusion. There are white wooden benches on which to sit and enjoy so much colour and elegance.

Further away from the house and the Chinese bridge, the herbaceous border ends at the garden's only sizeable classical feature, a temple erected by the 18th-century spinster Pusey who once owned the house, in memory of her sister. Towering above is a giant plane tree, said to be the second largest in England, which must pre-date the temple. Here, at one end of the lake, you look down the length of the garden, and have the choice of crossing a small stone bridge into the woodlands, or of taking the smooth green lawns towards the house.

These are the lawns from which the Hornbys cleared the laurel, rose beds and sequoiadendrons. Today, at their centre, immediately below the house, the croquet lawn is sited, from which wide steps lead up onto Geoffrey Jellicoe's terrace. This is informally planted with lavenders and helianthemums which emerge in mauve and yellow clumps from between the paving stones. The Georgian house towers above, rough stoned at the back in contrast to its smooth facing at the front. 'Perhaps they ran out of money,' Mr Hornby says. Turn away from the house and you see for the first time Pusey's view, across the lake, up a grassy glade as wide as a football field (where the corn grew during the war) across eight miles of countryside to the Berkshire Downs around Lambourn.

Beyond the house, the lawns presently reach a gravel path which leads to the Chinese bridge. To one side two low oriental planes spread far across the water. When the Hornby's children were small, the larger of these was the perfect place for a tree house, from which they could fall harmlessly into the lake. On the other side, two large weeping willows meet over the water, so that it seems to wind out of sight below them. Between the bridge and the willows are colourful water gardens.

Here in mid-summer the bright golden *Lysimachia punctata*, and many shades of fuzzy-flowered astilbes, pink, white and mauve, are most prominent. Earlier there are primulas, hostas, arum lilies, ornamental rhubarb, polygonums, bergenias, euphorbias, aquilegia hybrids, huge-leafed *Gunnera manicata* and giant heracleum, backed by berberises and purple maples.

Across the bridge the path leads into the woodlands, but the lake still circles to the left. From these less tamed reaches a heron may rise with heavy flapping wings. They are also the haunt of a pair of Australian black swans, which Mrs Hornby hopes one day to persuade to nest, but haven't yet. 'We're not entirely sure about their sexes,' she says. They are so tame that they will take bread from your hands, but are less well-behaved towards the occasional white swans which visit from the Thames. On Pusey's lake there are also moor-hen, mallard and less common ducks including Carolinas, making it something of a small nature reserve.

Here, on land, are many well-grown trees, in particular ancient Lebanon cedars with contorted trunks, large holm oaks (hard hit by the 1981 frosts, but recovering) a tulip tree and a tall *Taxodium distichum* – the deciduous swamp cypress with leaves which resemble those of an acacia. Here too is a clump of box which escaped Mrs Hornby's bonfires, or was so formidable that it deterred her: the shape of a massive toadstool, it is some 25 feet tall at the centre and 55 paces in circumference. Among these trees Mr Hornby will arrive on a garden tractor and go to work with his scythe. Retired now from managing the W. H. Smith bookshop business, he has become as active a gardener as his wife, and skilful with a scythe. Here he is at work in Compton's Glade, named after Eddie Compton, the friend who suggested it.

The group of trees beyond are 'what we somewhat pretentiously call Westonbirt', says Mrs Hornby, referring to the forestry commission's famous arboretum in Gloucestershire. But the different parts of the garden are named for practical reasons, not snobbery. 'It's no good telling a gardener to plant something in "that big bed in the far corner." It's certain to end up in the wrong place.' Thus, there are the Irish Yew Bed, the Orange Bed, and the Variegated Bed (all self-explanatory), the Walnut Bed (for less obvious reasons since its big black walnut tree died) and Stubbs Corner (after the keeper who used to live in a nearby cottage).

Set among them is the Main Shrubbery. It was here that Mrs Hornby would extend the planted area, rather than create new beds, so that her husband should not realise how the garden was growing. 'He was always trying to stop me,' she says. But she had the urge of a true gardener to be forever civilizing new areas. More of these await her. 'There's no limit to this garden,' she says, pointing towards the natural woodland into which it shades beyond the lake in all directions.

The result of this policy of expansion by stealth has been an accumulation in the Main Shrubbery of a great variety of shrubs and small trees. Only the lime-hating rhododendrons, azaleas and camellias are missing, for they won't grow in Pusey's poor, light alkaline soil. Abutilons, cotoneasters, hydrangeas, viburnums, philadelphuses, hebes, buddleias, escallonias, berberises, acers, mountain ashes and whitebeams form the core, with euphorbias, silvery senecio and other foliage plants around the edges.

The way back to the lake leads below the oldest of the garden's trees – huge clumps of beech, horse chestnut, yew and plane – then to a stone bridge which pauses briefly on a small island, planted with purple and green acers. Here and elsewhere planting continues and new specimens flourish. Mrs Hornby admits that at first she used to think you merely needed to make a hole and stick in the plant. Now bonemeal, leafmould and peat are used in ample quantities, and the ground thoroughly prepared. And for the last eight years she has had a marvellous head gardener, Ken Cotton from Norfolk. He and three other gardeners do the work six would do before the war. 'Of course a lot of the time they used to do nothing,' Mrs Hornby says.

The Hornbys began to open Pusey House's gardens in 1973. They also sell plants which, unlike those sold by some gardens, are entirely grown on the premises, but the ticket receipts rather than the plant sales contribute most to the upkeep of the gardens. On a fine Sunday 300 visitors may come, and in a year around 15,000.

The Hornbys have found that opening to the public stimulates their gardening. 'It makes us keep the gardens up to the mark,' Mrs Hornby says. Tall and gaunt today, a Virginia-Woolf-like figure in pudding basin hat of dark green felt, she still strides purposefully about the garden which she and her husband began to resurrect 45 years ago; they too remain very much up to the mark and justifiably proud of their achievement.

KNIGHTSHAYES COURT

'Eleven months of hard labour and one month of acute disappointment.' This is how the late Sir John Heathcoat-Amory described gardening. 'He didn't really mean it,' Lady Amory says, and Sir John was no doubt exaggerating about the disappointment. But about the hard labour he should be trusted, as Lady Amory herself admits. 'There are those gardeners,' she says, 'who like to work on the ground with their hands, and this was our way.' Together the two of them laboured with their hands for 26 years to turn their garden at Knightshayes Court from something comparatively undistinguished into one of the most delightful in the country.

'I'm just a barrow boy,' Sir John would add, and certainly his wife's gardening enthusiasm came first, but he learned fast, acquired an extensive knowledge of plants, not to mention a phenomenal memory for their names, and by 1968 had lectured to the Royal Horticultural Society and received their highest award, the Victoria Medal of Honour.

He and his wife had been sportsmen when younger. Sir John was a dangerous fast bowler, and in the 1920s Lady Amory was four times British Ladies Open golf champion and five times English Ladies Open champion. White haired now, she still has the tall and upright carriage of a sports-woman. For many years they kept a putting green at Knightshayes, and the shape of two tennis courts can still be seen on the green hillside below the house. Gardening was not in their minds when they came in 1937 to this Victorian Gothic mansion, built of the brown local stone, set 450 feet above the small Devon town of Tiverton.

It stood in a park of trees, some native, some exotic, the latter added when it had been built. To the north west was a wooded area of mixed oak, beech, birch and commercial conifer, but of actual garden there was little more than some formal terraces below the house, laid out in Victorian style for bedding.

Here Lady Amory presently inserted colourful roses. Then the war began; Knightshayes became a casualty clearing station, and later a rest home for American airmen. It was only in 1946 that she started to garden in earnest and to discover that what she had already done was mistaken. The roses detracted from a view which is one of the garden's finest features. First she substituted less bright, cream and magenta roses for red, then these were also removed and the beds grassed over.

Now nothing distracts the eye, which is led between a tall Scots pine and the trunk of a wonderfully weather-distorted Lebanon cedar, down the hillside past what is probably the largest Turkey oak in the country, down

Above: Sir John and Lady Heathcoat-Amory, creators of the gardens at Knightshayes, where they arrived in 1937. Opposite: glade in the woodland garden.

again to Tiverton in the valley of the Exe, then up to the rolling green Devon hills beyond. Clearly – and appropriately – to be distinguished in Tiverton itself is the square red building to which Knightshayes and its gardens owe their existence: the lace factory founded here by Sir John Heathcoat soon after 1816, when his Loughborough factory had been wrecked by Luddites. It became the largest lace factory in the world and remained a family business till a few years before the late Sir John's death.

Between the house and the commercial wood there had also been two small enclosures, one a paved court, the other a bowling green. It was here that the Amorys now began to make positive changes. From the paved garden they again removed roses and substituted soft grey carpeting plants. At its inner end they set a large lead urn and later added, at the sides and the open end, small figures representing the four seasons. They planted standard wisterias in the back corners.

These in mauve flower, together with the silver foliage of the carpeting plants, mostly blooming in mauve and pink, and the red-brown paving stones make a rare colour combination. It is as if the court is being seen through a filter which eliminates the usual bright greens of a garden. All is enclosed by dark yew hedges, while beyond on rising ground, silver birches form a contrasting background.

The bowling green, also enclosed by yew, they changed more radically, creating for its main feature a circular pool 40 feet in diameter. Here large gold fish swim below four colours of waterlilies – red, white, pink and yellow – each allowed a quarter segment. A lone silver weeping pear overhangs the pool, frail and delicate, like some melancholy long-haired girl. The effect is as secluded and peaceful as the Amorys hoped, even if this has to be artificially sustained. The branches of the frail pear need constant thinning or they become as matted as wire netting.

Opposite these two hedged gardens, a final yew hedge completes what the Amorys first found at Knightshayes. Along its top, leap the animals of the well-known Knightshayes topiary Fox Hunt, looking more natural than might be expected of such an oddity. It was made in the 1920s to celebrate the family's passion for hunting (Sir John's father died from a hunting accident). Beyond this yew hedge the garden ended with the gate to the wood. It was here that temptation lay, a temptation to which the Amorys gave way, cautiously at first, then with increasing abandon, till virtually the whole wood had been taken into the garden.

They might never have begun this great work but for an odd chance: near the end of the war an American pilot buzzing his fellow airmen in the house, crashed into the near side of the wood, destroying a number of trees. It was the clearing of these which first gave the Amorys the idea for their new garden.

Soon they were advancing each year by a piece of woodland about the size of a tennis court, Lady Amory says. But always it was the piece beyond which they schemed to include. She remembers vividly the excitement of anticipation as they embarked on these expansions, the crash of the falling trees and the smell of bonfires burning the brushwood. One hundred and sixty full size trees were cut and two or three hundred smaller ones. The felling was essential to provide the Amorys with the space for the sort of

1 Willow Gardens
2 House
3 Holly's Wood
4 Sir John's Wood
5 Michael's Wood
6 Arboretum
7 Glade
8 Garden in the Wood
9 South Garden
10 Paved Court
11 Lilypool Court
12 Topiary Hunt
13 Terraces

garden they now planned.

It was to be less a woodland garden than a garden in a wood. To make this possible, they were probably the first gardeners in England (though not in Britain, for the idea came from Scotland) to establish below the remaining trees, beds edged with peat blocks. Stone edging would have looked incongruous and timber would have become quickly infected with honey fungus, widespread in Devon. Into these beds they set 'the plants we fell in love with.' The result is the fine collection to be seen here today which delights plantsmen and amateurs alike. At the same time native wild flowers were encouraged, so lamiums (dead nettle) grow alongside rare euphorbias, blue bells with three-leafed trilliums, primroses by hellebores and foxgloves next to hostas of many varieties.

Roses, low-growing purple maples, variegated strawberries, bergenias, rare snowdrops, tiny-leafed rhododendrons and hollies ... it is not merely the plants themselves but the circuitous way the paths wind in among them which creates an impression of an endless variety of different beds containing different species.

Deeper into the woods the Amorys made wide grassy glades and – more of a problem – left them empty. 'That needs a great deal of self-discipline,' says Lady Amory. 'The temptation is to make use of any open space for some interesting new plant.' But she restrained herself, believing that too much can cause indigestion and there should be intervals for relaxation.

Set around these grassy glades are rhododendrons, azaleas, mahonias, magnolias and many other shrubs commonly found in woodland gardens. But her aim has been to avoid the kind of colourful rhododendron garden so commonly found in the West Country, which has a single dramatic season in May. After her husband died she realized that there was barely a bloom to be seen in the garden from the 12th August till the end of September – these six weeks they had always spent in Scotland for the grouse shooting. She put this right with late-flowering New Zealand species.

Always she has tried to show by careful planting how much pleasure the shapes and foliage of shrubs and small trees can give when they are not in bloom. So, for example, one area is devoted to large-leafed rhododendrons and another slope is clothed in prostrate pines, junipers, abies and yew to give an effect of a water-like flow of plants down the hillside. She believes that a garden should lead a visitor from surprise to surprise, constantly provoking exclamations of wonder. If a group of plants is regularly passed without comment she realises that they are dull and changes them.

The Garden in the Wood, and its surrounding glades, were completed by 1972, when Sir John died suddenly. Fortunately by then he had made Knightshayes a trust, and this trust, together with the National Trust, has managed house and garden for the last 11 years. In charge of the gardens during this time, as well as for nine years before Sir John died, has been Michael Hickson.

'He came to us in 1963,' Lady Amory says, 'as a very young head gardener, full of enthusiasm and at the same time talented and efficient.' If the Amorys created Knightshayes, Michael Hickson can take credit for a great deal of what can be seen there today. No longer *very* young (and secretive about his exact age) he has not lost his enthusiasm and manages the gardens

Above: detail of the 'garden in the wood'.

Overleaf: heathers, acers and rhododendrons in the woodland garden. Everywhere at Knightshayes the emphasis is on soft colours and foliage textures.

Michael Hickson. 'He came to us in 1963' says Lady Amory, 'as a very young head gardener'.

with an anxious, even fastidious care.

Below the house's tall stone walls (clothed in blue *Ceanothus thyrsiflorus*, rich yellow *Fremontodendron californicum*, a large white wisteria and a still more impressive *Rosa brunonii* which climbs as high as the roof), he notices with disapproval that benches have been positioned in front of the doors and makes a note to have them moved. In the woodland glades he admits that he wishes he could exclude visitors who wear red clothes. Red is the hardest colour to use well, and at Knightshayes the usual red rhododendrons are rare. Everywhere the emphasis is on delicate shades. Where the prostrate pines and junipers should be flowing downhill, he points out that some are obstinately refusing to be prostrate and are thrusting up vertical shoots, the result of crude grafting by some nursery.

But he is modest, emphasizing that whatever he may have done at Knightshayes has been in co-operation with the Amorys. 'I wouldn't want it any other way.' He daily consults Lady Amory, who still lives in part of the house, and describes how, for example, they recently sited a bench made from the trunk of a huge beech, at the bottom of the park. 'We knew we wanted it somewhere here. We walked about trying different positions.' Once its place was fixed he explains how they planned its vista, forseeing changes over the years ahead. 'That Brewer's weeping spruce is only just becoming a feature. The rhubarb is spoiling it. That will have to go. And we've decided to move the bamboo. We'll put it behind the bench, where it will give a little shelter from the wind. But we want to keep it. Bamboo is always chattering. Hardly anybody notices sounds in a garden but they're as important as scents.' At Knightshayes, Michael Hickson and Lady Amory make all such decisions, and in this way it differs from other National Trust gardens, which the National Trust garden consultants manage more directly.

Above all, the aim is to create vistas which end in uncertainty. 'Secrecy is vital in a garden,' Michael Hickson says. 'People are lazy. You've got to make them want to discover what's out of sight.' Wherever you go at Knightshayes there is evidence of their success. It is a garden which you never cease to want to explore.

The bench suggests a less purist view of the total experience which Michael Hickson would like Knightshayes to provide. 'We want visitors to go home and say what a nice afternoon they had sitting under a tree in the shade. Outside the garden – there's another 15 acres of grass and woodland – we hope they'll have picnics, put up stumps, play ball games.'

Beyond the new bench at the bottom of the park, one of Knightshayes's four gardeners is putting up a badger-proof fence. He has worked for the Amorys since 1958 and remembers with affection how Sir John would drive about the gardens on his electric trolley, stopping to ask his workmen how they were getting along. 'You're more of a number today. You can work all day and see no one.'

But machinery is essential, Michael Hickson explains, and if one man with a tractor and chain-saw can build a fence, that's the way it must be done. Every planting is carefully planned so that it won't leave awkward corners which machines can't reach. Weedkillers are used, too, to control grass around the woodland beds and shrubs. Though he distrusts the manufacturers' assurances that they become inert in the soil, he believes they do less damage to shallow rooting plants than scraping off the topsoil along with the weeds. On the beds themselves, however, the rule is no hoeing, only hand weeding. A hoe destroys the self-seeding wild plants he would like to encourage.

The badgers, which the fence below the park is to be strong enough to resist, do no damage themselves, but rip ordinary wire netting, making holes which let in such other pests such as rabbits. More serious than rabbits are roe deer. 'Last year they made a meal of most of our mahonias.' Still more destructive are grey squirrels, which can kill a full-size tree by ring-barking.

Nature, in the forms of drought and storm, has also done damage recently at Knightshayes. The drought of 1976 killed many beeches and birches. 'We had never imagined,' says Lady Amory, 'that full-size trees could just disappear in this way, and had not prepared.' New plantings have now been made for the future. In the winter of 1981–82 a freak storm of heavy wet snow from the north-west brought down a whole plantation of beech, oak and chestnut. But Michael Hickson accepts such natural setbacks more philosophically than pest damage. 'A garden is the result of working with, not against nature. No lopping or pruning could have made that Lebanon cedar the lovely shape it is.'

Twenty years at Knightshayes have not exhausted his plans for it. In 1973, the first year it opened, it had 9000 visitors, in 1981, 49,000. 'Slowly we're getting known,' he says modestly. 'And we're adding new features all the time. Twelve years ago we made the new Willow Garden.' This is outside the main gardens, in a shallow valley to the west of the house. The whole area was cleared except for some old Ghent azaleas, and planted with quick-growing willows. There is no spring water at Knightshayes, but enough rainwater drains from the surrounding slopes to form a decent sized reservoir behind a dam. This small valley, framed on one side by a fine copper beech, on the other by a tall old Cornish red rhododendron, makes a pleasant contrast to the park and the Garden in the Wood.

For the future, Michael Hickson would like to develop a walk through the stand of Douglas firs which were planted 100 years ago by the late Sir John's grandfather, and which by 1979 were some of them 150 feet high. He would like to bring visitors in through the old stable block designed, like the house, by the eccentric architect, William Burges.

He is also keen to extend the work of propagation at Knightshayes, which occupies one of his four gardeners full time, and is carried out in the old walled vegetable garden. 'We make a bit of money for the National Trust. And when our plants need replacing we can do it. That's why some gardens look tatty. There's often nowhere they can go for replacements, now that nurseries have cut down the varieties they stock by three quarters. So we can help them too.'

Whatever new features are added or changes made, the Garden in the Wood must remain Knightshayes' most delightful feature, where the love and care which Sir John and Lady Amory brought to their gardening is still so apparent in the plantings they made, and where they can still be pictured in their first enthusiasm, she on her knees by the peat-edged beds, he, back from a day at the lace factory, attending her with his barrow.

EAST LAMBROOK

In the 15th-century, stone-floored sitting-room of East Lambrook Manor in Somerset, Francis Boyd-Carpenter explains why he and his wife moved here 14 years ago from their suburban home at Gerrards Cross. They came to save the garden. 'There was outline planning permission on it for 36 bungalows.' It had been the garden of his sister-in-law, Margery Fish, who, by the time she died in 1969, had been accepted by British gardeners as the leading lady of their craft. 'Though *we* didn't know it,' he says.

'We'd never taken her gardening seriously. I suppose she didn't tell us much because she was afraid of boring us. When we heard her obituaries on the wireless we were amazed.

'She left the house and garden to our son Henry, but Henry didn't want to live here, so eventually he let us become his tenants. Quite unsuitable. We didn't know a daisy from a dahlia. If Margery heard we were here she'd have a fit.'

Margery Fish had not started gardening herself until she was middle-aged. For many years she worked in Fleet Street, first as one of Northcliffe's secretaries, then as secretary to successive editors of the Daily Mail. She was 49 before she married Walter Fish, her current boss. Together in 1938 they left London and bought East Lambrook Manor. With its large malt-house and $2\frac{3}{4}$ acres of garden, it cost £1000.

This was about all it was worth, Francis Boyd-Carpenter says. 'It was a wreck, corrugated iron on the roof, the garden full of rock and chicken wire. We told them they were crazy. Almost the only plant was the variegated maple which we've still got on the lawn. And the Monthly Rose, *Rosa chinensis*, on the wall by the back door. There's an old woman in the village who says her grandmother remembers that rose. If she's right it could be 100 years old. It's done what it's meant to do all the time we've been here. Never a month in the year when it hasn't got a bloom of some sort. Margery's first sight of that maple through the back door may explain why she came to love all variegated plants. Her original plan was just to make a garden round the tree. Now look at it.'

Short, stoutly built, 79 years old and walking with something of a sea-man's sway, Francis Boyd-Carpenter points across Margery Fish's rocky terraces to her closely interwoven, densely planted beds. Today her garden remains not so much the cottage garden she originally meant it to be, but more like seven or eight cottage gardens set side by side with an extensive

Back lawn at East Lambrook Manor, with the original variegated maple.

Map legend:

1 House
2 Front Garden
3 Cottage Garden
4 Silver Garden
5 White Garden
6 Terrace Garden
7 Back Gate
8 Herb Garden
9 Lawn
10 Top Lawn
11 Malt House
12 Barton
13 Green Gate
14 Green Garden
15 Green Garden
16 Orchard
17 Hellebore Garden
18 Stream bed
19 Strip
20 Stock Beds
21 Sundial Garden

nursery at the far end.

'Two thousand species, we calculate,' he says. 'And fresh ones are still turning up.' He bends to show a small plant half hidden by neighbouring euphorbias, with chive-like foliage and five-petalled blue flowers, a green streak on the reverse of every other petal. 'Could be an allium, could be an ipheion, but I don't think so. I've asked the Royal Horticultural Society, but they can't help.'

Francis Boyd-Carpenter may have been a beginner when, at the age of 65, he took to gardening but he now names plants as fluently as if he has known them all his life. 'Listen to him,' Mrs Boyd-Carpenter says, as he identifies *Stachys olympica*. 'You've no idea if he's right, and nor have I, but I bet he is.'

For two years Francis Boyd-Carpenter wandered around saying, 'I haven't a clue.' Eventually he invited down Chris Brickell, Director of the Royal Horticultural Society's gardens at Wisley. 'He was a good friend of Margery's; in fact she helped him get his job. We went up and down the beds with a bagful of labels sticking them in. There wasn't a single one at that time. Margery said she wouldn't have her garden looking like a cemetery. Now we've taken them all up again. We try to keep things more or less as she made them.'

This is not always possible. Some plants flourish and others disappear. 'Margery had a wonderful collection of primroses till she lost them all in the 1968 drought. We're gradually getting them back. There's a green one.' He points to a bed beside the backdoor. 'You can't regiment primroses. They like to nestle up to things. And they like to be moved every two years.' Close to the primrose is the first of the garden's many variegated species: strawberries with green and golden leaves. They don't, unfortunately, fruit.

'She liked to grow plants which are indigenous to the district. Wild flowers too.' The border around the oval lawn below that original variegated maple provides evidence. Bluebells, forget-me-nots, dead nettle and four

Avenue of Chamaecyparis lawsoniana *'Fletcheri' in East Lambrook's terrace garden.*

sorts of comfrey, the tall pink and white *Symphytum officinale*, the shorter lilac and pink variety *lilacina*, the white or yellowish white *officinale ochroleucum* and the blue *caucasicum*, are intermingled with more usual garden perennials. Hardy perennials were the plants she preferred and she grew few annuals, believing that these today make too much work.

Because the soil in this low lying district is a limey clay, certain plants won't grow – rhododendrons, azaleas, ericas – apart from winter-flowering ones. 'Some people try to grow them on peat but you have to use Scottish or Irish – Somerset peat contains lime. Margery was always being given camellias but they hardly ever flowered.'

Left from the lawn, steps – or alternatively a narrow winding path – climb a series of stone terraces which Margery Fish created. The planting here is at its densest. Roses come at the centre – 'Elsa Polson,' 'the Fairy' – and around them a multitude of shrubs and plants of all sizes and many dozen varieties. Typically a *Mahonia japonica*, obliged to be prostrate, appears from below a spreading cupressus. It was these terrace beds which Margery Fish found such a problem, only realising when she had made them that they had to look right from four sides. The terrace walls are still hung with the aubrietas, arabis and saxifrages which she set to drape them.

The steps level off in a small avenue of *chamaecyparis lawsoniana* 'Fletcheri' – 'pudding bushes' to the Boyd-Carpenters. 'We shave them with a kitchen knife.' He demonstrates the sort of upward swipe required. 'But they still get too big. You have to be ruthless in a garden, so in the end we take them out and start again with small ones.'

Below the avenue of pudding bushes, beside the road on the driest and least fertile slope, is Margery Fish's Silver Garden. Here a large variety of silver foliage plants cover the ground, from the pale lavender, *Lavandula spica* 'Vera' to Margery Fish's wormwood, *Artemisia absinthium* 'Lambrook Silver'. Many silver plants are only half hardy and need replanting in spring, but by late May this small square garden is already thickly carpeted in silver and white, a contrast in its uniform colouring to the cottagey complexity elsewhere.

The way now leads past a small orchard with a well-grown pink-flowering judas tree, along the back of the malthouse to a dry stream bed with pollarded willows. Below these, on either bank the abundance continues: variegated hostas, red and green fennel, Solomon's seal, *Peltiphyllum peltatum*, *Phormium tenax*. The emphasis is again on foliage plants. At the bottom, from which the water drained away as soon as Margery Fish cleared it, a few of her Asiatic primulas survive, though they too suffered in the 1968 drought.

Facing the willows across the dry stream bed are old apple trees up which she trained roses, turning them in summer into tall pink and white pillars: *longicuspis*, 'Ash Wednesday,' 'Dorothy Perkins,' 'Garland,' 'Gardeners Pink.' The last she discovered in the ruins of the old garden, and when she couldn't identify it gave it this name. Today it is widely grown.

Beyond a hedge of roses and clematis is the nursery department. Margery Fish began this herself when she realized that she must propagate plants to replace those she was always giving away. She was also persuaded that by selling plants she could afford more help. Today the nursery still

Francis Boyd Carpenter, who preserves his sister-in-law's garden in the style she would have wished.

Margery Fish, creator of East Lambrook Manor's gardens and a prolific gardening author.

contributes to the upkeep of the garden, although during their 14 years here the Boyd-Carpenters have never made a profit. The very modest prices they charge for plants and entrance make this hardly surprising.

Now that Mrs Boyd-Carpenter's sight is poor she does the potting, and her husband keeps a record: 982 so far this year, 11,831 in total last year. 'I'm so lucky to have something I enjoy doing when I'm old,' she says. Sales are steady, 50 or 60 plants on an average day at a week-end; 168 the record for a day.

Here in the greenhouses, Mark Stainer is at work – the one full-time gardener at East Lambrook, where there used to be 13. He came straight from school eight years ago and lives only a field away. His only garden training has been at a day release course. His father is a milk roundsman, and fish-tank gardening is the closest anyone in his family has ever before come to plant gardening. His other passion is Wagner. When he listens, in the special extension to their house which his parents have built for him, it can be heard all over the village. He worked first in the Silver Garden and it remains his favourite, but he is enthusiastic about any part he mentions, and considers East Lambrook Manor a second home.

Returning from the nursery, parallel to the dry stream, a path leads between the hellebore beds. These have increased since Margery Fish's time and are believed to be the finest collection in the country, perhaps in the world. Lately a north country hellebore authority spent a day with them. 'He was ecstatic. He found 41 different colour variations.'

A path between the hellebores leads back to one end of the malthouse where a silver, and a rare gold variegated jasmine both survived the 1981 frost. So – just – did a *Pittosporum tenuifolium* in Margery Fish's last creation. Close to the drive gate, once her vegetable garden, this is now the Green Garden. Here too is a white judas tree, and other rarities, including a yellow-flowering honeysuckle, *Lonicera chaetocarpa*, which a party of horticultural students recently gathered round in delight; a plant they had never seen outside Kew Gardens.

On the other side of the drive comes the 'barton' a Somerset word meaning something like 'midden', where the horse which worked the cider press used to walk in circles. Now it is a round lawn with a mulberry tree at the centre, saved by the Boyd-Carpenters during the 1976 drought by a daily bucketful of bath water. Behind the barton is the entrance to the malthouse. On this side too the malthouse is clothed in climbing shrubs: a wisteria, several clematis, *Ceanothus* 'Cascade', and a fig.

Twenty-five years ago, when Margery Fish was staying with the Boyd-Carpenters at Gerrards Cross she was telephoned at 3 a.m. to be told that her malthouse was on fire. Instantly she set out for Somerset but the building was gutted, losing floor and roof. One local fireman remembers his chief's instructions that night: 'Don't you worry about the fire, you just water the walls. If she loses them creepers we'll never be forgiven.' They survived.

The malthouse, rebuilt, is a workshop for garden frames upstairs, an office and plant shop downstairs. Mrs Burgess runs the office. She is the longest serving of East Lambrook's eight part-timers and started working for Margery Fish 25 years ago. 'She was very direct and very tenacious,' Mrs Burgess says. 'A firm person with a soft heart, I'd call her.' Mrs Burgess keeps the records, and these keep her too busy to work in the garden. The closest she gets to plants is the despatching of them by mail. They are still wrapped in Margery Fish's manner, no plastic, just wet newspaper surrounded by dry newspaper.

With Mrs Burgess is East Lambrook's oldest part-timer, Mrs Skeggs, who claims to be between 81 and 84, according to her mood. Mrs Skeggs didn't think much of the garden when she first saw it. 'All that angelica!' Now she loves to work here. 'None of us have special jobs, we just see something which needs doing and do it.'

On sale too are Margery Fish's books. 'We Made a Garden,' is the most popular. It was to have been called 'Gardening with Walter', but the first publisher to see it commented, 'Too much Walter and too little gardening,' so book and title were revised. In it she nevertheless gives her husband credit for much help, especially with the underlying structure of the garden. 'But frankly,' Francis Boyd-Carpenter says, 'Walter's idea of gardening was paths and lawns with straight edges, and that was hardly Margery's.' Hers was the luxuriance and bountifulness which the Boyd-Carpenters are preserving. Today East Lambrook remains a cottage garden in concept but a plantsman's in its detail. In an age when cottage garden concepts have invaded so many stately gardens, it is right that East Lambrook should stand alongside Hidcote and Sissinghurst.

Flag irises in the dry stream bed.

Typical cottage-garden style of planting at East Lambrook Manor.

181

FALKLAND PALACE

In 1947, soon after the late Major Michael Crichton Stuart, M.C., hereditary Constable, Captain and Keeper of the Royal Palace of Falkland in Fife, came with his wife to live at the palace, they advertised for a head gardener. They needed one. Much had been done by the previous two generations of his family to restore the palace itself (in particular by his grandfather the third Marquess of Bute who had acquired it in 1871) but little was done to the garden, and during the war it had been turned into a potato field.

'We had 97 replies,' Mrs Crichton Stuart says. 'We were daunted by the prospect of showing 20 a day our potato patch. The first one we saw was Jenkin, and we took him. I couldn't resist his Cheshire-cat smile.'

Between them, the Crichton Stuarts and W. J. Jenkin (a Cornishman who had been trained in the gardens at Tresco on the Isles of Scilly) created the garden at Falkland as it exists today. But they found that they required professional advice – for example about the ultimate size and rate of growth of the trees they were planning to plant – and consulted Percy Cane, designer of the Emperor of Ethiopia's palace gardens at Addis Ababa. 'He had vision, that little man,' says Mrs Crichton Stuart of Percy Cane.

They asked him to create a garden which could not all be seen at a glance. 'We wanted to get some mystery into it.' They were also able to show him a print of the gardens in 1693. This print and their desire for mystery were the basis from which Percy Cane worked.

The brief was not an easy one for the area was small, consisting essentially of a two-acre rectangle. This was looked down on from one side by the ruins of the east range of the palace and the raised ground where an earlier 12th-century castle had stood. On the other side it was enclosed by a long 12-foot high brick wall.

His design turned this long rectangle (the East Garden) into what can best be described as a formal woodland glade. Down each side he placed mixed borders – part shrub, part herbaceous – then, swelling out from these borders towards the centre, a succession of half-moon shaped beds. Here and there about the lawn he planted trees, but it is the beds which create the impression of a restrained woodland glade. They achieve this by each of them rising like pyramids from herbaceous plants around their edges, first to shrubs, then to trees at their centres (chiefly prunus) which will always remain of modest height.

Percy Cane returned seven years later to make at the far end of this East Garden a formal yew-hedged garden with raised rectangular pools and pillars of fastigiate juniper. And on the higher ground to the west, where the

Above: Andrew McCarron, Falkland Palace's head gardener. Right: foundations of the twelfth-century well tower transformed by Percy Cane into a rockery.

182

old castle once stood, he planted a rockery and surrounded this whole area with 22 well-spaced cupressus. But the East Garden remains his principal contribution, effectively seeming to magnify its modest area and create hidden places, just as the Crichton Stuarts hoped.

Though Percy Cane must be given credit, Major Crichton Stuart was certainly in part responsible for a design which is essentially architectural. 'He always wanted to be an architect,' Mrs Crichton Stuart says. 'At Eton he won all the drawing prizes.' In fact her husband went into the family regiment, the Scots Guards, was severely wounded in the desert war, and in his later years could only look down on the garden from the windows of the palace.

From the garden entrance you arrive first at a small paved corner where a game of draughts is laid out on a board of coloured paving stones, with draughtsmen a foot in diameter and boat hooks to move them. Nearby is a herb bed with most of the usual herbs (lovage, mint, fennel, chives, thyme, lemon balm, hyssop, tarragon, horse-radish, wormwood) and a few less usual ones (curry plant, self-heal). All is observed by a three-foot stone owl presented by a Perth antique dealer.

Beyond comes the East Garden with its long lawn, individual sycamores and swelling half-moon beds. Most impressive is the vast border which reaches the full length of the outer wall, 165 paces long, 18 feet deep. It was not meant to be so unbroken, Mrs Crichton Stuart explains. There should have been a recess. Jenkin was the problem. 'Dear Jenkin, he was marvellous, a tremendous worker, but very opinionated. The first time Percy Cane called out "Gardener!" you could see Jenkin squirm. If you told him to do something he was inclined to do the opposite.'

Vitis coignetiae *against the grey stonework of Falkland's part-ruined palace.*

The long border is separated from the half-moon beds by grass paths so that you can walk its full length without interruption. First come shrubs: deutzias, weigelas, lilacs and philadelphuses, which all do well here. A long herbaceous section follows, the colours mostly subdued – nepeta, shrubby potentillas, echinops, with silver foliage plants along the edge, but also brighter poppies, peonies and the small *Potentilla* 'Gibson's Scarlet'. Wide mesh hessian nets stretched horizontally 18 inches from the ground support the taller species which grow up through them. The long border ends with more shrubs, predominantly viburnums. Against its wall are roses and purple clematis.

Each half-moon bed is planted differently. At their centres, as well as green and purple prunuses, are maples, crab apples and a number of weeping pears which are small now but will grow up to join them. So will magnolias and eucryphias. The shrubs include forsythia, philadelphus, kalmia, hydrangea, berberis and the dogwood *Cornus alba* 'Elegantissima' with its white-edged leaves. Also small rhododendrons. 'They grow like weeds here,' Mrs Crichton Stuart says. For plants around the edges there are hostas, *Alchemilla mollis*, grasses, tobacco of many colours, violas and numerous erigerons.

The inner bed, below the ruined East Range of the palace and the old castle site, is planted in larger blocks, one of bearded irises for June, another of massed lupins for July. Again there are roses along the wall, which for much of its length is topped with cat mint.

The yew-hedged garden (Percy Cane's later addition) which lies at the end of the East Garden is entirely different in character, and strictly formal, with its eight Irish junipers, two prostrate ones (*Juniperus* x *media* 'Pfit-zerana') and two raised rectangular pools. The pools have lilies and should have goldfish, 'but this ruddy heron comes and scoops them all up,' says Mrs Crichton Stuart. 'They're a danger for children too. With 60,000 visitors a year we have to think of these things.' Recently, a child who was peering down onto the East Garden from the palace got its head stuck in the railings and the local blacksmith had to be called to free it.

A royal tennis court, oldest of its kind in Scotland, stands to the north of the formal garden. Here visitors can watch this ancient game, the court walls marked with ornate crowns, from a gallery where they are protected by a net. The court was built in 1539 by James V. Here the Stuart kings and their courtiers would play, at first using their hands to hit the ball instead of rackets.

Standing at the entrance of the formal garden and looking back up the East Garden you have the best of Falkland's views. Beyond Percy Cane's glade the palace rises formidably to the right, but is dwarfed by the great bulk of East Lomond Hill which stands beyond, above palace and village.

Nearby is one surviving greenhouse from those built in the 1890s by the third Marquess of Bute. It is the pride of Andrew McCarron, today's successor to Jenkin. Despite terrible losses in recent hard winters, it is now more spectacular than ever – a red, pink and white pyramid of pelargoniums, fuchsias, begonias and arbutuses, with two daturas at its summit. Against the back wall are two outstanding *Pelargonium* 'Mrs Morris', planted by Jenkin in 1948, now 14 feet high, which carry scarlet flowers every month of the year.

Beyond the tennis court, a vegetable garden (worth a visit for its sweet-scented purple bush roses) and some specimen trees including a young blue cedar (*Cedrus atlantica* 'Glauca') – a remarkable sight for its thousands of little upright cones – complete the gardens on this level. Climb next to the area once occupied by the old castle, now defined by Percy Cane's tall pillars of *Chamaecyparis* 'Fletcheri'. From here you can look down on the East Garden, or look in the opposite direction, over an orchard. 'We gave that to the National Trust as well,' Mrs Crichton Stuart says, 'to stop anyone building bungalows there if we all went under a bus.'

The foundations of the old well tower are the basis for Percy Cane's rockery, planted mainly with heathers, and with *Cotoneaster horizontalis*, which climbs down over its stones. The rest of this higher ground has been left as lawn. At its summit six old oaks form a ring. 'They're a problem,' Mrs Crichton Stuart says. 'We ought to plant new ones outside them because they're "going back", as people round here say. I love that. That's what I'm doing, going back.'

Closer to the palace a small *Acer pseudoplatanus* 'Worlei', planted by the Queen Mother in 1981 to celebrate the golden jubilee of the Scottish National Trust, struggles for life in the garden's most exposed position. 'There used to be a beautiful magnolia here,' Mrs Crichton Stuart says. 'The one with those rude little red fruits and lovely creamy white flowers. God knows how it ever survived.'

Clematis in Falkland's long border, which runs the full length of the East Garden.

Close above come the foundations of the old North Range of the palace, accidentally burned down in 1654 by Cromwell's occupying troops. Yellow and red large-flowered hybrid tea roses were planted here before Percy Cane's time. The open courtyard beyond, where the Scots Guards were first given their name by Charles II, is closed to the public, though some wander in. 'Especially the French,' Mrs Crichton Stuart says. 'They like to get into our cellar where we hang up our washing and see if we use Marks and Spencers undies, like they do.'

Steps return from here down to the East Garden, passing on the way a group of old Scottish rose bushes (*Rosa pimpinellifolia*) with their white button roses and strange black hips. Opposite, the fire which destroyed the North Range, blackened the end wall of the East Range. To hide this Mrs Crichton Stuart suggested the planting of a Russian vine, *Polygonum baldschuanicum*. It has grown enormous and today is the garden's most sen-

sational plant, all summer an avalanche of pale cream flowers. 'I keep telling the National Trust it's going to pull the wall down,' Mrs Crichton Stuart says. 'But they're so pleased to have Andrew McCarron they hardly ever come.'

Mrs Crichton Stuart is equally pleased. To replace Jenkin, who died nine days before Major Crichton Stuart, cannot have been easy. McCarron has only one assistant gardener (Jenkin's son) but, with the exception of a small area of bindweed, he considers the garden has few problems. Saturdays and Sundays too, he visits it from his cottage across the orchard, to water his cornucopial greenhouse and make sure all else is well. During the great frost he sat up all night with his dying greenhouse plants, unable to do anything for them because the diesel oil for the furnace had frozen. If he has not had Jenkin's task of making a garden out of a potato field he worthily sustains the result, which again gives Falkland the setting a royal palace deserves.

The centre, herbaceous section of Falkland's long border, where horizontal netting is used to support the taller plants.

GARDEN VISITORS GUIDE

Gardens featured in the book

Arley Hall, Near Northwich, Cheshire
Open from Easter to mid October, 2pm–6pm, every day except Monday. (Tel: Arley 284 for information). Best visiting times: early April for bulbs, May for flowering shrubs, June–August for herbaceous colour. Plants for sale.

Barrington Court, Nr Ilminster, Somerset
Open Easter to end September, Sunday to Wednesday inclusive, 2pm–5.30pm. Best visiting times: end of May to end July. Plants for sale.

Bodnant Gardens, Tal-Y-Cafn, Colwyn Bay, Gwynedd
Open every day 13th March to end of October, 10am–5pm. Best visiting times: March/April for spring bulbs and magnolia; May/June for shrubs and Laburnum Arch. Chilean Firebush flowers beginning of June. Garden Centre.

Chatsworth, Bakewell, Derbyshire
Open 1st April to end October, every day, 11.30am–5pm. Best visiting times: March/April for spring bulbs and camellias; May/June for flowering shrubs. Garden Centre.

Great Dixter, Northiam, East Sussex
Open 1st April (or earlier for Easter) to mid October, every day except Monday, 2pm–5.30pm. (Tel: 07974 3160 for further information). Best visiting time: July. Plants for sale.

Hidcote Manor Garden, Hidcote Bartrim, Nr Chipping Campden, Gloucestershire
Open April to end October, every day except Tuesday and Friday, 11am–7pm (or one hour before sunset). Best visiting time: late June/July. Plants for sale.

Howick Hall, Alnwick, Northumberland
Open 1st April to 30th September, 2pm–7pm, every day. Best visiting time: early spring for daffodils, May for flowering shrubs.

Kiftsgate Court, Nr Chipping Campden, Gloucestershire
Open April to end September, Wednesday, Thursday and Sunday, 2pm–6pm. Best visiting times: May and June. Plants for sale.

Knightshayes, Nr Tiverton, Devon
Open daily from 1st April to 31st October, 11am–5.30pm. All year round garden. Plants for sale.

Cranborne Manor, Dorset
Open April to October, first Saturday and Sunday of each month, 9am–5pm, and on other days as advertised locally. Open 2pm–5pm on Sundays. (Tel: Cranborne 248 for information). Best visiting times: spring for bulbs, June/July for roses, October for autumn colours. Garden Centre, open every day except Sunday mornings.

Drummond Castle, Nr Crieff, Perthshire
Open 1st April to end October, Wednesday and Sunday, 2pm–6pm. Best visiting times:

July, August and September for the roses. Plants for sale first Sunday in August.

East Lambrook Manor, South Petherton, Somerset
Open all year round, every day including Christmas Day, 9am–5pm. Best visiting times: mid February to mid March (for hellebores), June/July for climbing roses.

Falkland Palace Gardens, Fife, Scotland
Open 1st April to end October, Monday to Saturday, 10am–6pm, Sunday, 2pm–6pm. All year round garden.

Leonardslee, Horsham, West Sussex
Open last week in April to second week in June, Wednesday, Thursday, Saturday and Sunday, 10am–6pm. Also open May Bank Holiday Monday and a weekend in October. (Tel: Lower Beeding 212 for information). Extensive spring-flowering shrub garden, aboreta, magnificent autumn tints. Plants for sale.

Packwood, Nr Hockley Heath, Warwickshire
Open: April – every day except Monday and Tuesday (and Easter Bank Holiday Monday), 2pm–5pm. May to September (and all Bank Holiday Mondays), 2pm–6pm. October – Saturday and Sunday only, 2pm–5pm. Best visiting times: mid-June to early August.

Powis Castle, Welshpool, Powys
Open 1st May to end of September, every day except Monday and Tuesday, 1pm–6pm. Also open around Easter for approximately 10 days. (Tel: Welshpool 2952 for information). Best visiting time: throughout season. Plants for sale.

Pusey House, Nr Faringdon, Oxfordshire
Open Easter to mid June, Tuesday, Thursday and Sunday, 2pm–6pm. After mid June, open every day except Monday and Friday. Closes nearest Sunday to 18th October. (Tel: Buckland 222 for opening information). Best visiting time: July for roses and herbaceous plants. Brilliant autumn colours. Plants for sale.

Rockingham Castle, Nr Corby, Northants
Open Easter Sunday to 30th September, Thursday and Sunday, 2pm–6pm. Also open Bank Holiday Mondays and the Tuesdays following. Best visiting times: late June/early July for roses; mid July for lime blossom. Lovely autumn tints.

Rodmarton Manor, Nr Tetbury, Gloucestershire
Open every Thursday in June, July and August, 2pm–6pm. Also one Sunday in each of those months. (See NGS guidebook or telephone: 028 584 219). Herbaceous borders (best in July), topiary, avenue of hornbeam. Plants for sale.

Rousham, Steeple Aston, Oxfordshire
Rousham Park is William Kent's only surviving landscape design. The gardens are open all year, every day, 10am–5pm. Best visiting times: early spring for daffodils; June/July for roses and herbaceous plants; October for autumn tints.

Sezincote, Moreton-in-Marsh, Gloucestershire
Open throughout year except December, Thursday, Friday and Bank Holiday Mondays, 2pm–6pm. An all year round garden.

Sheffield Park Garden, Nr Uckfield, East Sussex
Open Easter to mid November, Tuesday to Saturday, 11am–6pm, and Sunday, 2pm–6pm. Closed Monday. Open Bank Holiday Mondays but closed the subsequent Tuesday. (Tel: Danehill 790655 for further information on opening times). House privately owned but open to the public: separate ticket required. Best visiting times: May for spring bulbs, July/August for waterlilies and October for autumn tints.

Stourhead, Stourton, Nr Mere, Wiltshire
Open every day throughout year, 8am–7pm (or dusk if earlier). Best visiting times: February/April for spring bulbs; May/June for flowering shrubs; October/early November for autumn tints.

Tyninghame, Dunbar, East Lothian, Scotland
Open 1st June to end September, Monday to Friday, 10.30am–4.30pm. Best visiting time: June and July for roses. Few plants for sale.

Publications advertising gardens open in the United Kingdom

Historic Houses, Castles & Gardens in Great Britain and Ireland (published every year)
Gardens Open to the Public in England and Wales under the National Gardens Scheme (published every year)
Gardens to Visit (published every year)
The National Trust: Properties Open (published every year)
Scotland's Gardens (published by Scotland's Gardens Scheme)
Illustrated London News (published monthly)

A selection of gardens open to the public

AVON

Clevedon Court, Nr Clevedon April to end September – Weds, Thurs & Suns, also Bank Hol Mons, 2.30–5.30

Vine House, Henbury Open by appointment throughout year. Tel: Bristol 503573

BEDFORDSHIRE

The Swiss Garden, Old Warden, Nr Biggleswade Open end March to end October – Weds, Sats, Suns, Bank Hol Mons & Good Friday (check first with Bedfordshire County Council as opening times vary)

Wrest Park, Silsoe April to September – Sats, Suns & Bank Hol Mons (except Spring Bank Hol Mon), 9.30–6.30

BERKSHIRE

Frogmore Gardens, Windsor For information on opening times enquire National Gardens' Scheme. Tel: 01-730 0359

The Old Rectory, Burghfield (as above)

Savill Garden, Windsor Great Park March 1 to December 24 – daily, 10–6

Valley Gardens, Windsor Great Park Open daily, sunrise to sunset

BUCKINGHAMSHIRE

Ascott, Wing April to end September – Weds & Thurs, and last Sun of each month. Also Sats August and September only and Bank Hol Mon in August, 2–6. (Enquiries Tel: Wing 242)

Cliveden, Maidenhead Open all year – daily, 11–6.30

Memorial Gardens, Stoke Poges All year – daily (except Sats), 9–dusk

West Wycombe Park, West Wycombe June – Mons to Fris; July to end August – daily (except Sats) 2.15–6. Also Easter Sun & Mon; Spring Bank Hol Sun & Mon

CAMBRIDGESHIRE

Anglesey Abbey, Nr Cambridge Opening times variable. Tel: Cambridge 811200 for information

Docwra's Manor, Shepreth Opening times variable. Tel: Royston 60235 for information or appointment

Peckover House, Wisbech April 1 to end of October – Tues, Weds, Thurs, Sats, Suns & Bank Hol Mons, 2–6

University Botanic Garden, Cambridge Open all year – daily, 8–7.30 (or dusk)

CHESHIRE

Arley Hall Gardens, Northwich (see Special List of Featured Gardens)

Lyme Park, Disley Open all year – daily, 8 to sunset

Ness Gardens, Wirral Open all year – daily, 9 to sunset

Tatton Park, Knutsford Open throughout year, variable times. Tel: Knutsford 3155 for information

CORNWALL

Trelissick Garden, Nr Truro Open April to October – weekdays, 11–6 (or dusk); Suns, 1–6 (or dusk)

Trengwainton Garden, Penzance March to October – Weds to Sats, and Bank Hol Mons, 11–6

Trerice, St Newlyn East April to end October – daily, 11–6

Trewithen, Probus, Nr Truro March to September – weekdays (inc. Bank Hol Mons), 2–4.30

CUMBRIA

Acorn Bank, Temple Sowerby April to end October – daily, 10–5.30

Graythwaite Hall, Ulverston April to June – daily, 10–6

Levens Hall, Kendal Easter Sunday to September 30 – daily, 11–5

Lingholme, Keswick April to October – weekdays, 10–5

Muncaster Castle, Ravenglass April 19 to October 3 – daily (except Fris, open Good Friday), 12–5

Rydal Mount, Ambleside March to end October – daily, 10–5.30. November to mid January – daily, 10–12.30, 2–4. Tel: Ambleside 3002 for further information.

Stagshaw, Ambleside March 20 to June 27 – daily, 10–6.30 (or dusk)

DERBYSHIRE

Chatsworth, Bakewell (see Special List of Featured Gardens)

Elvaston Castle, Nr Derby Open all year

Haddon Hall, Bakewell April to end September – daily (except Suns & Mons), 11–6. Also Easter, Spring & Summer Bank Hol Suns & Mons (Suns, 2–6)

Hardwick Hall, Nr Chesterfield Open April to end October – daily, 12–5.30 (closed Good Friday)

Lea Rhododendron Gardens, Lea March 20 to July 31 – daily, 10–7

Melbourne Hall, Melbourne Beginning June to beginning October – Suns only, 2–5.30. Or by appointment. Tel: Melbourne 2502 or 2163

DEVON

Arlington Court, Barnstaple November to end March – daily, during daylight hours

Bickham House, Roborough For information telephone National Gardens' Scheme: 01-730 0359

Castle Hill, Filleigh, Barnstaple April to October. Tel: Filleigh 336 for appointment

Combe Head, Bampton Open throughout year. Tel: Bampton 31583 for appointment

Fernwood, Ottery St Mary April to end September – daily, all day

The Garden House, Buckland Monachorum, Yelverton April to mid September – Mons, Weds & Fris, 2.30–7. Or Tel: Yelverton 4769 for appointment

Knightshayes Court, Nr Tiverton (see Special List of Featured Gardens)

Marwood Hill, Nr Barnstaple All year – daily (except Christmas Day), dawn to dusk

Overbecks Museum Garden, Sharpitor, Salcombe All year – daily

Rosemoor Garden, Great Torrington April to end October – daily, dawn to dusk

Saltram House, Plymouth November to end March – daily, dawn to dusk. April to end October – daily (except Mons, but open Bank Hol Mons)

Tapeley Park, Instow Tel: Instow 860528 for information

DORSET

Abbotsbury Sub-Tropical Gardens Mid March to mid October – daily, 10–5.30. Tel: Abbotsbury 387 for information

Athelhampton Tel: Puddletown 363 for information

Compton Acres Gardens April to end October – daily, 10.30–6.30

Cranborne Manor Gardens (see Special List of Featured Gardens)

Forde Abbey, Nr Chard Easter Sun & Mon, March, April & October – Suns only, 2–4.30. May to September – Suns, Weds & Bank Hol Mons, 2–6

Highbury, West Moors April to beginning September – Suns & Bank Hol Mons, 2–6

Mapperton, Beaminster March to beginning October – Mons to Fris, 2–6

Melbury House, Nr Yeovil Enquire through National Gardens' Scheme

Minterne, Dorchester April to June – Suns & Bank Hols, 2–7. Tel: Cerne Abbas 370 for information

Parnham House, Nr Beaminster April to end October – Weds, Suns & Bank Hols, 10–5

Smedmore, Kimmeridge June to beginning September – Weds, 2.15–5.30. Tel: Corfe Castle 480717 for other opening times

EAST SUSSEX

Beeches Farm, Uckfield All year – daily, 10–5

Charleston Manor, Westdean, Seaford Mons to Fris only – weather permitting

Cobblers Garden, Crowborough For opening times enquire National Gardens' Scheme. Tel: 01-730 0359

Great Dixter, Northiam (see Special List of Featured Gardens)

Horstead Place Gardens, Nr Uckfield Easter to end September – Weds, Thurs, Suns and Bank Hol Mons, 2–6

Sheffield Park Garden, Nr Uckfield (see Special List of Featured Gardens)

ESSEX

Beth Chatto Gardens, Elmstead Market All year – daily (except Suns & Bank Hols), Mons to Sats, 9–1, 1.30–5. Closed Sats November to end January

Hyde Hall, Rettenden Enquire National Gardens' Scheme. Tel: 01-730 0359

Saling Hall, Great Saling, Nr Braintree Enquire National Gardens' Scheme. Tel: 01-730 0359

GLOUCESTERSHIRE

Ampney Park Gardens, Nr Cirencester April to September – Tues & Suns and Bank Hols, 2–6

Barnsley House Garden, Barnsley, Nr Cirencester All year – Weds, 10–6 (or dusk); also first Suns in May, June & July. Other days by appointment. Tel: Bibury 406

Batsford Park Arboretum, Moreton-in-Marsh April to October – daily, 10–5

Hidcote Manor Garden, Nr Chipping Campden (see Special List of Featured Gardens)

Kiftsgate Court, Nr Chipping Campden (see Special List of Featured Gardens)

Sezincote, Moreton-in-Marsh (see Special List of Featured Gardens)

Upper Slaughter Manor, Cheltenham May to end September – Fris, 2–5.30

Westbury Court Garden, Westbury-on-Severn April & October – Sats, Suns & Easter Mon, 11–6. May to end September – daily (except Mons & Tues, but open Bank Hol Mons), 11–6

HAMPSHIRE

Exbury Gardens, Nr Southampton March to beginning July – daily, 1–6.30

Furzey Gardens, Minstead, Nr Lyndhurst All year – daily, 10–5

Houghton Lodge, Stockbridge March to July – Weds, 2–5. Open Easter Mon

Hurst Mill, Petersfield Enquiries through National Gardens' Scheme. Tel: 01-730 0359

Jenkyn Place, Bentley Enquiries through National Gardens' Scheme. Tel: 01-730 0359

MacPenny's Bransgore, Nr Christchurch All year – daily, Mons to Sats, 9–12.30, 1.30–5; Suns 2–5

Mottisfont Abbey April to September – Tues to Sats, 2.30–6

Spinners, Boldre Mid April to beginning September – daily (except Mons), 2–6. Other times by appointment. Tel: Lymington 73347

West Green House, Hartley Wintney April to end September – Weds, Thurs & Suns, 2–6

HEREFORD AND WORCESTER

Abbey Dore Court Garden March to end October – daily, 10.30–6.30

Bredon Springs, Ashton under Hill, Nr Evesham April to end October – Weds, Sats & Suns. Also Bank Hol Mons & Tues, 10 to dusk

Brobury House Garden, Nr Hereford May to September – Mons to Sats, 9–5; Suns, 2–5

Clent Hall, Nr Stourbridge Enquiries through National Gardens' Scheme. Tel: 01-730 0359

Hergest Croft Gardens, Kington Open for Easter, May to mid September – daily. October – Suns, 1.30–6.30

The Priory, Kemerton Enquiries through National Gardens' Scheme. Tel: 01-730 0359

Spetchley Park, Worcester April to end October – daily (except Sats), 11–5; Suns, 2–6; Bank Hol Mons, 11–6

Stone House Cottage, Kidderminster Tel: Kidderminster 69902 for information

HERTFORDSHIRE

Ashridge, Berkhamstead April to October – Sats & Suns, 2–6

Benington Lordship Gardens, Nr Stevenage Easter Monday. Then May to July – Weds & Suns, 2–5; also Bank Hols in May. Tel: Benington 668 for appointment, May to July

Knebworth House April to end September – daily (except Mons). October, Suns only, 11–6. (Open Bank Hol Mons)

Mackerye End, Nr Harpenden Enquiries through National Gardens' Scheme. Tel: 01-730 0359

St Paul's Walden Bury, Whitwell, Nr Hitchin Enquiries through National Gardens' Scheme. Tel: 01-730 0359

HUMBERSIDE

Sewerby Hall, Bridlington Open all year – daily, 9 to dusk

KENT

Crittenden House, Matfield Enquiries through National Gardens' Scheme. Tel: 01-730 0359

Emmetts Garden, Nr Brasted April & July to end October – Suns & Weds. May & June – Suns, Tues, Weds & Thurs, 2–6 (closed Bank Hols)

Great Comp, Nr Borough Green April to end October – Weds to Suns & Bank Hols, 11–6

Hall Place Gardens, Leigh May to mid June – Suns, 2.30–6.30

Hever Castle, Nr Edenbridge Tel: Edenbridge 862205 for further information. April to end October – Tues, Weds, Fris, Sats, Suns & Bank Hol Mons, 11.30–6

Hole Park, Rolvendon Enquiries through National Gardens' Scheme. Tel: 01-730 0359

Ladham House, Goudhurst Enquiries through National Gardens' Scheme. Tel: 01-730 0359

The Owl House, Lamberhurst All year – Mons, Weds, Fris & Bank Hol weekends, 11–6; Suns, 11–6 (August to March), 3–6 (April to July)

Riverhill House, Sevenoaks April to end August – Suns and Bank Hol Mons, 12–6 or view by appointment. Tel: Sevenoaks 452557

Sandling Park, Nr Hythe Enquiries through National Gardens' Scheme. Tel: 01-730 0359

Scotrey Castle, Lamberhurst April to October – Weds to Suns & Bank Hols 2–6

Sissinghurst Castle April to mid October – Tues to Fris, 1–6.30; Sats & Suns, 10–6.30. Closed Mondays inc. Bank Hols. Open Good Friday, 10–6.30

Sprivers Garden, Horsmonden April to end September – Weds only, 2–5.30

LANCASHIRE
Cranford, Aughton April to mid October – daily, 10 to dusk. Enquiries through National Gardens' Scheme. Tel: 01-730 0359

Windle Hall, St Helens Enquiries through National Gardens' Scheme. Tel: 01-730 0359

LINCOLNSHIRE
Gunby Hall, Burgh-le-Marsh April to end September – Thurs, 2–5, or by appointment. Tel: Scremby 212

Springfield Gardens, Spalding April to October – daily, 10–6

LONDON
Arkley Manor, Nr Barnet Enquiries through National Gardens' Scheme. Tel: 01-730 0359

Hall Place, Bexley All year – daily, dawn to dusk

Hampton Court Palace April to September – weekdays, 9.30–6; Suns, 11–6. October to March – weekdays, 9.30–6; Suns, 2–5. (Closed Christmas, New Year's Day, Good Friday & Spring Bank Hol)

Kew Gardens All year – daily (except Christmas & New Year's Day), open at 10.

Syon Park Gardens, Brentford All year – daily, 10–6 (or dusk)

NORFOLK
Blickling Hall, Aylsham April to end October – daily (except Mons & Fris). End of May to beginning October – daily, 2–6. Open Bank Hol Mons

Fritton Gardens, Nr Great Yarmouth April to beginning October – daily, 11–6

Holkham Hall, Wells June & September – Mons & Thurs, 2–5. July & August – Mons, Weds, Thurs & Bank Hol Mons

Oxburgh Hall, Swaffham April to October – Mons, Tues, Weds, Sats & Suns, 2–6. Tel: Gooderstone 258 for confirmation

NORTHAMPTONSHIRE
Deene Park, Nr Corby June, July & August – every Sun, 2–5.30. Also Easter, Spring & Summer Bank Hol Suns & Mons

Holdenby House Gardens, Northampton April to September – Suns & Bank Hol Mons, 2–6. June to August – also Thurs, 2–6

Rockingham Castle, Nr Corby (see Special List of Featured Gardens)

NORTHUMBERLAND
Cragside Country Park, Rothbury April to September – daily, 10.30–6. October – daily, 10.30–5. November to March – Sats & Suns. 10.30–4

Howick Gardens, Alnwick (see Special List of Featured Gardens)

Meldon Park, Morpeth End May to end June – daily, 2–5. Also Summer Bank Hol weekend

Wallington, Cambo All year – daily

NORTH YORKSHIRE
Broughton Hall, Skipton June – weekdays, 2–5. Also Spring and Summer Bank Hols, or by appointment. Tel: Skipton 2267

Constable Burton Hall, Leyburn May to beginning August – daily, 9–6

Duncombe Park, Helmsley May to August – Weds, 10–4

Fountains Abbey, Ripon All year – daily. Closed Christmas, New Year and Spring Bank Hol Mon

Newburgh Priory, Coxwold Mid May to end August – Weds only, 2–6

Ripley Castle Easter weekend to end May – Sats & Suns. June to September – Tues, Weds, Thurs, Sats & Suns, 2–6. Open Good Friday & Bank Hol Mons

Thorp Perrow Arboretum, Nr Snape End of March to end October – daily

OXFORDSHIRE
Botanic Gardens, Oxford All year – weekdays, 8.30–5; Suns, 10–12, 2–6. Closed Good Friday and Christmas Day

Brook Cottage, Alkerton Enquiries through National Gardens' Scheme. Tel: 01-730 0359

Kingston House, Kingston Bagpuize Easter to end June – Sats, Suns & Bank Hol Mons, 2–5.30. Also August Bank Hol weekend

Kingston Lisle Park, Nr Wantage August – Tues, Thurs & Suns. October – Thurs & Suns, 2–5.30. Also spring and summer Bank Hol weekends

Pusey House Gardens, Nr Faringdon (see Special List of Featured Gardens)

Rousham House, Steeple Aston (see Special List of Featured Gardens)

Waterperry Horticultural Centre, Nr Wheatley All year – daily, 10–6 (winter, 10–4) (closed at certain periods. Tel: Ickford 226 for information)

Wroxton Abbey, Nr Banbury Spring and summer Bank Hol Mons. Other days by appointment. Tel: Wroxton St Mary 551

SHROPSHIRE
Benthall Hall, Much Wenlock Easter Sat to September – Tues, Weds & Sats, 2–6. Also Bank Hol Mons

Hodnet Hall Gardens, Nr Market Drayton April to September – weekdays, 2–5; Suns & Bank Hols, 12–6

Weston Park, Nr Shifnal April to end September. April, May & September – weekends only; June, July & August – Tues, Weds, Thurs, Sats & Suns. Open Bank Hols during season

SOMERSET
Barford Park, Enmore May to September – Weds, Thurs & Bank Hol weekends, 2–6. Other times by appointment. Tel: Spaxton 269

Barrington Court, Ilminster (see Special List of Featured Gardens)

Clapton Court, Crewkerne All year – Mons to Fris, 10–5; Suns, 2–5. Closed Sats

East Lambrook Manor, South Petherton (see Special List of Featured Gardens)

Gaulden Manor, Tolland, Nr Taunton May to beginning September – Thurs & Suns, 2–6. Also Easter Sun & Mon and all Bank Hol Mons

Hadspen House, Castle Cary All year – Tues, Weds & Thurs, 10–5. April to October – Suns also, 2–5. Other times by appointment

Montacute House, Yeovil April to end October – daily (except Tues), 12.30–6

Stowell Hill, Templecombe Enquiries through National Gardens' Scheme. Tel: 01-730 0359

Tintinhull House, Yeovil April to end September – Weds, Thurs, Sats & Bank Hol Mons, 2–6

STAFFORDSHIRE
Clive Memorial Garden, Elds Wood, Willoughbridge March to October

Shugborough, Stafford Mid March to October – Tues to Fris & Bank Hol Mons, 10.30–5.30; Sats and Suns, 2–5.30

SUFFOLK
Euston Hall, Thetford June to end September – Thurs only, 2.30–5.30

Ickworth, Nr Bury St Edmunds April to end October – Tues, Weds, Thurs, Sats, Suns & Bank Hol Mons, 2–6

Kentwell Hall, Long Melford Mid April to July 1 – Weds, Thurs & Suns; Mid July to end September – Weds to Suns; also Easter & Bank Hol weekends, 2–6

Melford Hall, Nr Sudbury April to end September – Weds, Thurs, Sats & Bank Hol Mons, 2–6

SURREY
Chilworth Manor, Nr Guildford Enquiries through National Gardens' Scheme. Tel: 01-730 0359

Claremont, Esher All year – daily, 9–7 (winter, 9–4). Closed Christmas & New Year's Day

Detillens, Limpsfield May to June – Sats; July to September – Weds & Sats, 2–5. Also Bank Hols during season

Dunsborough Park, Ripley Enquiries through National Gardens' Scheme. Tel: 01-730 0359

Feathercombe Gardens, Hambledon Spring Bank Hol Suns & Mons, 2–6

Gorse Hill Manor, Virginia Water Enquiries through National Gardens' Scheme. Tel: 01-730 0359

Pinewood House, Worplesdon Hill Enquiries through National Gardens' Scheme. Tel: 01-730 0359

Polesdon Lacey, Nr Dorking All year – daily, 11 to dusk

Ramster, Chiddingfold Enquiries through National Gardens' Scheme. Tel: 01-730 0359

Vann, Hambledon Enquiries through National Gardens Scheme. Tel: 01-730 0359

Wisley Garden, Ripley All year – daily, 10–7; Suns, 2–7. Closed Christmas Day

WARWICKSHIRE
Packwood House, Hockley Heath (see Special List of Featured Gardens)

Upton House, Edge Hill April to September – Mons to Thurs, 2–6. Also open some weekends. Tel: Edge Hill 266 for details

WEST MIDLANDS
Wightwick Manor, Wolverhampton All year (except February) – Thurs, Sats, Bank Hol Suns & Mons, 2.30–5.30. May to end September – Weds also

WEST SUSSEX
Borde Hill Garden, Haywards Heath Mid March to end September – Weds, Thurs, Sats, Suns & Bank Hols, 10–6

Coates Manor, Nr Fittleworth Enquiries through National Gardens' Scheme. Tel: 01-730 0359

Denmans, Fontwell Enquiries through National Gardens' Scheme. Tel: 01-730 0359

Heaselands, Haywards Heath Enquiries through National Gardens' Scheme. Tel: 01-730 0359

The High Beeches, Handcross Spring Bank Hol Mons, 10–5. Also open one Sunday in October

Leonardslee, Horsham (see Special List of Featured Gardens)

Nymans Garden, Handcross April to end October – Tues, Weds, Thurs & Sats, 2–7; Suns & Bank Hols, 11–7 (or dusk)

Uppark, South Harting, Nr Petersfield April to September – Weds, Thurs, Suns & Bank Hol Mons, 2–6

Wakehurst Place Garden, Nr Ardingly All year – daily, 10–7 (winter, 10–5). Closed Christmas Day and New Year's Day

West Dean Gardens, Nr Chichester April to end September – Mons to Fris, 1–6; Suns & Bank Hol Mons, 1–7. Closed Sats

WEST YORKSHIRE
Bramham Park, Wetherby Easter to end September – Tues, Weds, Thurs, Suns & Bank Hol Mons, 1.15–5.30

Harewood House, Leeds April to end October – daily. Limited opening during winter. Tel: Harewood 886225 for details

WILTSHIRE
Bowood Gardens, Calne Good Friday to end September – daily (except Mons), 11–6. October – Suns only. Open Bank Hol Mons

Broadleas, Devizes April to October – Weds and every second Sun each month, 2–6

Heale House, Woodford, Salisbury Good Friday to end September – daily, 10–5

Luckington Court All year – Weds, 2–6

Sheldon Manor, Chippenham April to beginning October – Thurs, Suns & Bank Hols, 12.30–6

Stourhead, Stourton, Nr Mere (see Special List of Featured Gardens)

SCOTLAND

BORDERS REGION
Dawyck Arboretum, Nr Peebles April to September – daily, 10–5

Kailzie Gardens, By Peebles March to October – daily, 10–6

DUMFRIES & GALLOWAY
Arbigland Gardens, Kirkbean May to September – Tues, Thurs & Suns, 2–6

Castle Kennedy Gardens, Stranraer April to September – daily (except Sats), 10–5

Logan Botanic Garden, Port Logan April to September – daily, 10–5

Threave House, Nr Castle Douglas All year – daily, 9 to sunset

FIFE REGION
Falkland Palace Garden, Fife (see Special List of Featured Gardens)

GRAMPIAN REGION
Pitmedden, Udny All year – daily, 9.30 to sunset

HIGHLAND REGION
Inverewe, Poolewe, Wester Ross All year – daily, 9–9 (or dusk if earlier)

LOTHIAN REGION
Malleny Garden, Balerno May to end September – daily, 10 to dusk

Royal Botanic Garden, Edinburgh All year – daily (except New Year's Day), 9 to sunset. (Suns opens 11am)

Suntrap, Gogarbank, Nr Edinburgh All year – daily, 9 to dusk

Tyninghame Gardens, Nr East Linton (see Special List of Featured Gardens)

STRATHCLYDE REGION
Benmore April to October – daily, 10–6
Botanic Gardens, Glasgow All year – daily, 7 to dusk

Brodick Castle Garden, Isle of Arran All year – daily, 10–5

Greenbank Garden, Glasgow All year – daily, 10 to dusk

Pollok House, Glasgow All year – weekdays, 10–5, Suns 2–5

Torosay Castle, Craignure, Isle of Mull All year – during daylight hours

TAYSIDE REGION
Branklyn Garden, Perth March to end October – daily, 10 to dusk

Drummond Castle Gardens, Nr Crieff (see Special List of Featured Gardens)

Edzell Castle Garden, Edzell All year – weekdays, 9.30–7, Suns, 2–7. (Closes 4pm during winter months)

WALES
Erddig, Nr Wrexham April to end October – daily (except Fris but open Good Friday), 12–5.30. (Closes 4.30 during October)

DYFED
Colby Lodge Garden, Amroth May to end September – Tues & Thurs, 2–4. Or Weds by appointment only. Tel: Llandeilo 823476

GWYNEDD
Bodnant, Tal-y-Cafn, Colwyn Bay (see Special List of Featured Gardens)

Penrhyn Castle, Bangor April to end October – daily, 2–5. End May to end September and all Bank Hols, opens 11am

POWYS
Powis Castle, Welshpool (see Special List of Featured Gardens)

INDEX